New Horizons in Computational Linguistics for Religious Texts (Coling-Rel 2025)

Abu Dhabi, United Arab Emirates
19 January 2025

ISBN: 979-8-3313-1363-0

Printed from e-media with permission by:

Curran Associates, Inc.
57 Morehouse Lane
Red Hook, NY 12571

CURRAN ASSOCIATES INC. proceedings.com

Some format issues inherent in the e-media version may also appear in this print version.

Printed with permission by Curran Associates, Inc. (2026)

For permission requests, please contact the Association for Computational Linguistics at the address below.

Association for Computational Linguistics
209 N. Eighth Street
Stroudsburg, Pennsylvania 18360

Phone: 1-570-476-8006
Fax: 1-570-476-0860

acl@aclweb.org

Additional copies of this publication are available from:

Curran Associates, Inc.
57 Morehouse Lane
Red Hook, NY 12571 USA
Phone: 845-758-0400
Fax: 845-758-2633
Email: curran@proceedings.com
Web: www.proceedings.com

COLING 2025

The 31st International Conference on Computational Linguistics

Proceedings of the New Horizons in Computational Linguistics for Religious Texts (Coling-Rel)

Workshop chairs:

Majdi Sawalha, Sane Yagi, Faisal Alshargi,
Abdallah T. AlShdaifat, Ashraf Elnagar, Bayan Abu Shawar,
Norhan Abbas

19 January 2025

Order copies of this and other ACL proceedings from:

Association for Computational Linguistics (ACL)
209 N. Eighth Street
Stroudsburg, PA 18360
USA
Tel: +1-570-476-8006
Fax: +1-570-476-0860
acl@aclweb.org

Message from the Organizers

This workshop is focused on the intersection of language technology and religious texts. It encourages dialogue on cutting-edge Natural Language Processing applications within this domain. Traditionally, scholars have focused on analyzing faith-defining canons, authoritative interpretations, and extracting insights from sermons, liturgies, prayers, and religious poetry.

The emergence of Large Language Models (LLMs) has revolutionized many NLP disciplines. Leveraging these powerful models for novel research avenues in religious texts promises to significantly advance this field.

This workshop explores the potential of NLP to unlock profound new understandings of religious traditions and to chart the future of this exciting research area. It brings together researchers from computational linguistics, digital humanities, and related fields to engage in insightful discussions and to explore innovative approaches.

Organizing Committee

Majdi Sawalha, The University of Jordan, Jordan and Al-Ain University, UAE

Sane Yagi, University of Sharjah, UAE

Faisal Alshargi, Amazon Robotics, USA

Abdallah T. AlShdaifat, Mohamed Bin Zayed University for Humanities, UAE

Ashraf Elnagar, University of Sharjah, UAE

Bayan Abu Shawar, Al-Ain University, UAE

Norhan Abbas, The University of Leeds, UK

Program Committee

Majdi Sawalha, The University of Jordan, Jordan and Al-Ain University, UAE (Chair)

Sane Yagi, University of Sharjah, UAE (Chair)

Abdallah T. AlShdaifat, Mohamed Bin Zayed University for Humanities, UAE

Ahmad Ruby, Uppsala University, Sweden

Akram M. Zeki, International Islamic University Malaysia, Malaysia

Ashraf Elnagar, University of Sharjah, UAE

Azzedin Mazroui, University Mohammed First, Morocco

Bassam Hammo, Princess Sumaya University for Technology, Jordan

Bayan Abu Shawar, Al-Ain University, UAE

Faisal Alshargi, Amazon Robotics, USA

Khubaib Alam, Al-Ain University, UAE

Mohammad Khair, International Computing Institute for Quran and Islamic Sciences, USA

Nizar Habash, NYU Abu Dhabi, UAE

Norhan Abbas, The University of Leeds, UK

Table of Contents

Workshop Program

Sunday, January 19, 2025

09:30–09:45 **Opening remarks by the Organizing Committee**
Chair: Sane Yagi

09:45–10:30 **Plenary Speaker: Professor Ashraf Alnagar, College of Computing and Informatics, University of Sharjah**
Chair: Sane Yagi

11:00–12:30 **Session 1: Papers**
Chair: Majdi Sawalha

11:00–11:30 *Comparative Analysis of Religious Texts: NLP Approaches to the Bible, Quran, and Bhagavad Gita*
Mahit Nandan A D, Ishan Godbole, Pranav M Kapparad and Shrutilipi Bhattacharjee

11:30–12:00 *Messages from the Quran and the Bible in Mandarin through Factor Analysis with Syntactic and Semantic Tags*
Kuanlin Liu

12:00–12:30 *Semantic Analysis of Jurisprudential Zoroastrian Texts in Pahlavi: A Word Embedding Approach for an Extremely Under-Resourced, Extinct Language*
Rashin Rahnamoun and Ramin Rahnamoun

12:30–14:00 **Lunch Break**

14:00–15:30 **Session 2: Papers**
Chair: Bayan Abu Shawar

14:00–14:30 *Multi-stage Training of Bilingual Islamic LLM for Neural Passage Retrieval*
Vera Pavlova

14:30–15:00 *Automated Translation of Islamic Literature Using Large Language Models: Al-Shamela Library Application*
Mohammad Mohammad Khair and Majdi Sawalha

15:00–15:30 *Automated Authentication of Quranic Verses Using BERT (Bidirectional Encoder Representations from Transformers) based Language Models*
Khubaib Amjad Alam, Maryam Khalid, Syed Ahmed Ali, Haroon Mahmood, Qaisar Shafi, Muhammad Haroon and Zulqarnain Haider

Sunday, January 19, 2025 (continued)

16:00–17:30	**Session 3: Papers** Chair: Abdallah T. AlShdaifat
16:00–16:30	*MASAQ Parser: A Fine-grained MorphoSyntactic Analyzer for the Quran* Majdi Sawalha, Faisal Alshargi, Sane Yagi, Abdallah T. AlShdaifat and Bassam Hammo
16:30–17:00	*Leveraging AI to Bridge Classical Arabic and Modern Standard Arabic for Text Simplification* Shatha Altammami
17:00–17:30	*Word boundaries and the morphology-syntax trade-off* Pablo Mosteiro and Damián Blasi
17:30–18:15	**Session 4: Posters** Chair: Norhan Abbas
	18:15–close Panel Discussion Chair: Organizers

Comparative Analysis of Religious Texts: NLP Approaches to the Bible, Quran, and Bhagavad Gita

A D Mahit Nandan, Ishan Godbole, Pranav Kapparad, Dr. Shrutilipi Bhattacharjee
Department of Information Technology
National Institute of Technology Karnataka
Surathkal, India
mahitnandanad.211ai001@nitk.edu.in, ishangodbole.211ai020@nitk.edu.in,
pranavkapparad.211ai026@nitk.edu.in, shrutilipi@nitk.edu.in

Abstract

Religious texts have long influenced cultural, moral, and ethical systems, and have shaped societies for generations. Scriptures like the Bible, the Quran, and the Bhagavad Gita offer insights into fundamental human values and societal norms. Analyzing these texts with advanced methods can help improve our understanding of their significance and the similarities or differences between them. This study uses Natural Language Processing (NLP) techniques to examine these religious texts. Latent Dirichlet allocation (LDA) is used for topic modeling to explore key themes, while GloVe embeddings and Sentence transformers are used to comapre topics between the texts. Sentiment analysis using Valence Aware Dictionary and sEntiment Reasoner (VADER) assesses the emotional tone of the verses, and corpus distance measurement is done to analyze semantic similarities and differences. The findings reveal unique and shared themes and sentiment patterns across the Bible, the Quran, and the Bhagavad Gita, offering new perspectives in computational religious studies.

***Keywords*—** Religious texts, Natural Language Processing, topic modeling, sentiment analysis, corpus distance, Bible, Quran, Bhagavad Gita.

1 Introduction

Religious texts played a very crucial role in forming the moral and ethical frames of society and have, therefore, influenced the way societies changed with time. Such texts as the Bible, the Quran, and the Bhagavad Gita have been indispensable in providing core human conceptions of justice, morality, and common social values. These aspects have historical importance since they are in a position to shape the ethics of humans, introduce social norms, and provide philosophical and spiritual guidance that can be seen across various cultures and eras.

Despite their ancient origins, religious texts continue to adapt to modern interpretations, showing the shifting priorities and evolving ethics of societies. The need for analysis of these texts arises from the desire to further understand their long-lasting relevance, uncover hidden connections, and find how their teachings have influenced and been influenced by different historical and cultural contexts. Modern computational tools provide new ways to examine these texts, offering insights that go beyond traditional interpretations.

Natural Language Processing (NLP) techniques provide a systematic and data-driven approach to the analysis of religious literature. They further aid in exploring themes, patterns of sentiment, and semantic relationships that may not emerge from analyses conducted through conventional means. This is possible through advanced NLP tools that can draw cross-textual comparisons to trace the evolution of ideas across different religious traditions. This research applies NLP techniques, such as topic modeling, sentiment analysis, and corpus distance measurement, to investigate the Bible, the Quran, and the Bhagavad Gita. Topic modeling is used to identify key themes in texts; the distribution of sentiment within texts is explored; and semantic similarities and differences are analyzed through corpus distance analysis. This seeks to highlight the commonalities and unique aspects of these revered writings, providing a fuller understanding of their cultural and moral impacts.

In the subsequent sections, this paper studies the content of these scriptures and compares them to further establish their linguistic relationships. Such an approach aims to contribute to the wider field of computational religious studies by demonstrating how NLP techniques may help unveil new perspectives about religious thought and its cultural applicability.

Proceedings of the New Horizons in Computational Linguistics for Religious Texts (Coling-Rel), pages 1–10
January 19, 2025.

2 Literature Survey

Applying Natural Language Processing (NLP) to religious texts is now an important area of research, given the depth of context in these texts. Joulin et al. (Joulin et al., 2017) investigated the FastText model for text classification-a core method for representing words in continuous space. This technique has been found to be very effective in analyzing large religious corpora, such as the Bible and Quran, and is crucial in understanding word-level representations in sacred texts. In addition, Hutchinson et al. (Hutchinson, 2024) discusses the broader ethical considerations of applying NLP to religious corpora, such as the Bible and Quran, particularly focusing on tasks like machine translation and sentiment analysis. This therefore calls for sensitivity while handling the sacred writings in NLP.

Chandra et al. (Chandra and Ranjan, 2022) (Chandra and Kulkarni, 2022a) focused on the semantic and sentiment analysis of the Bhagwad Gita, and finding out its similarity with other texts in Hindu philosophy, like the Upanishads. Alhawarat et al (Alhawarat, 2015) used generative models to perform topic modeling on the Holy Quran, but failed to capture meaningful results. The research (Abbasi et al., 2022) on toxic language identification has explored the use of machine learning models to classify harmful comments in online communication. However, some models have shown bias by assigning high toxicity ratings to non-toxic comments containing identity-related descriptors. Studies have compared various word embeddings, such as GloVe, Word2Vec, and FastText, for multilabel toxic comment classification. These studies found that different embeddings influenced the classification results, highlighting their role in improving the accuracy of detecting toxic language while addressing potential biases. In (Chandra and Kulkarni, 2022b) explores the comparison of English translations of the Bhagavad Gita using deep learning-based semantic and sentiment analysis. Motivated by the limitations of traditional translations, the authors employ BERT, a state-of-the-art language model, to analyze sentiment and semantic similarity across different translations. By utilizing a hand-labelled sentiment dataset for tuning, the study demonstrates that despite variations in style and vocabulary, the core message conveyed in the translations remains largely consistent.

In recent times, advanced techniques like the Fréchet Inception Distance (FID), initially developed for image generation models, have been adapted to text corpora to quantify distribution differences between embeddings (Heusel et al., 2018). Similarly, the IBM CompCor framework has gained attention for its ability to compute corpus-level distances, offering a robust methodology for evaluating the overall divergence in linguistic features (Kour et al., 2022). State-of-the-art metrics, such as those based on contextual embeddings from transformer models like BERT, provide richer semantic comparisons by capturing nuanced meanings, enabling more accurate measurements of semantic mismatch (Reimers and Gurevych, 2019). These modern metrics show improved sensitivity in detecting distribution mismatches, while classical methods tend to be more sensitive to surface-level perturbations. The integration of both classical and modern approaches is still an open challenge; there is no standardized framework for interpreting and comparing the effectiveness of these measures. Thereby, this creates an incentive for evaluation measures that are interpretable for ranking semantic similarity and its underlying characteristics, an ongoing theme recently discussed in various works.

VADER (Valence Aware Dictionary and sEntiment Reasoner) (Hutto and Gilbert, 2014) was introduced as a robust, rule-based model for sentiment analysis, specifically designed for handling microblog like contexts. The foundational study demonstrated its effectiveness by combining a validated lexicon with syntactical rules, achieving high F1 classification accuracy that surpass human raters. While VADER's origin lies in social media analysis, its adaptability makes it suitable for examining complex texts, including religious scriptures. Subsequent studies have applied sentiment analysis techniques to religious texts to uncover patterns in sentiment and thematic frameworks. One study (Peuriekeu et al., 2021) employed NLP and machine learning techniques to classify nine sacred texts and found that methods like Multinomial Naive Bayes achieved significant accuracy. Another comparative analysis of the Bible, Quran, and Bhagavad Gita (Goel and Arsiwala, 2024), utilized NLP tools to perform sentiment analysis and topic modeling, shedding light on emotional distributions and similarities between these texts. These works illustrate how VADER and related sentiment analysis approaches can offer deeper insights into the emotional and philosophical nuances of religious literature.

3 Methodology

The following sections explain the series of analyses that, using different approaches, investigate linguistic, thematic, and semantic aspects of the Bhagavad Gita, Bible, and Quran and examine relationships and connections between them.

3.1 Word Count Analysis

To gain insights into the linguistic and thematic focus of the Bhagavad Gita, Bible, and Quran, a word frequency analysis was conducted. The texts were first preprocessed to ensure uniformity by converting all text to lowercase, removing punctuation, and filtering out common stop words. This preprocessing step was essential for eliminating noise and ensuring that the analysis concentrated on meaningful terms. Following this, tokenization was performed to break the text into individual words, which were then analyzed to compute their frequency. The top 20 most frequently occurring words in each text were determined, which highlights the recurring concepts and thematic emphasis. Visualizations, such as bar plots as shown in figures 6, 8 and 7, were created to show these findings, which provided a comparative view of word distribution across the three texts.

3.2 Topic Modeling Using Latent Dirichlet Allocation (LDA)

To uncover the thematic structure within the Bhagavad Gita, Bible, and Quran, Latent Dirichlet Allocation (LDA) was used for topic modeling. Each text underwent preprocessing to standardize the format, including steps like text normalization, converting to lowercase, and removing stop words. The LDA model was then applied for each text separately, set to extract 10 unique topics for each text. Each topic was represented by 10 prominent keywords that provided insight into the main themes as shown in figure 4. This approach aimed to reveal hidden structures and thematic patterns in the texts.

3.3 Topic Comparison Across Texts with GloVe Embeddings and Sentence Transformers

To explore the thematic similarities and differences between the Bhagavad Gita, Bible, and Quran, embeddings were used to quantify the semantic relationships among the topics generated through Latent Dirichlet Allocation (LDA). Each text was analyzed to extract 10 topics, represented by sets of 10 significant keywords. These keywords were then transformed into vector representations using two methods: GloVe embeddings and SentenceTransformer embeddings (paraphrase-MiniLM-L6-v2). The keywords for each topic were concatenated into a string and encoded into a single topic embedding. The semantic similarity between topics was assessed using cosine similarity, providing a measure of how closely related the topics were across the texts. Heatmaps were created to visualize these similarities, offering an intuitive representation of thematic overlap and divergence.

3.4 Sentiment Analysis of Verses Using VADER

Sentiment analysis is applied to the corpus using Valence Aware Dictionary and sEntiment Reasoner (VADER), which is an unsupervised model that classifies text into positive, negative, and neutral sentiments. VADER first breaks down the text into individual words, and assigns a score to each word based on its polarity, with -4 being the most negative and +4 being the most positive. It also considers the intensity of the sentiment, which can be indicated by capitalization and punctuation. For example, an exclamation point can make a positive word even more positive. The overall sentiment score of the text is calculated based on the scores assigned to each word. The score ranges from -1 to 1, with -1 being very negative and 1 being very positive.

3.5 Corpus Distance Measurement

The following types of corpus distance analyses were conducted:

3.5.1 Corpus Distance Analysis Using IBM CompCor

The corpus distance between the religious texts was measured using IBM CompCor, with the Fréchet Inception Distance (FID) applied through the corpus_metrics.fid_distance function. This metric was used to quantify the distribution differences between the embeddings of the corpora, effectively capturing semantic and linguistic variations. The embeddings were generated using STTokenizerEmbedder, ensuring that the representations of the texts retained essential semantic features. Pairwise comparisons were conducted between the Bible, Gita, and Quran to assess the relative distances, with higher FID values indicating greater divergence in thematic and linguistic content. This approach provided a robust quantitative basis for analyzing how these influential texts differ in their language and semantics.

3.5.2 Semantic Similarity Analysis Using Cosine Similarity

To assess the semantic similarity between the religious texts, the STTokenizerEmbedder with the model all-MiniLM-L12-v2 was utilized to generate embeddings for each corpus. The embeddings were averaged to create a representative vector for each text set: the Bible, Gita, and Quran. Using these averaged embeddings, pairwise cosine similarities were computed with cosine_similarity from the sklearn.metrics.pairwise module. This method measured how closely aligned the corpora were in terms of semantic content, with values ranging from -1 (completely dissimilar) to 1 (identical). The results provided a direct comparison of the similarity between the religious texts, revealing the degrees of linguistic and thematic alignment between them.

3.5.3 Structural Relationship Analysis Using KMeans Clustering

To further investigate the structural relationships between the religious texts, KMeans clustering was applied to the embeddings generated using STTokenizerEmbedder with the all-MiniLM-L12-v2 model. The embeddings for the Bible, Gita, and Quran were clustered into 5 groups, which allowed the identification of central semantic themes within each corpus. The methodology is as below:

1. Clustering: Each corpus was clustered separately using KMeans with 5 clusters (modifiable based on corpus characteristics). The cluster centroids represented the core semantic centers of the texts.
2. Centroid Similarity: Cosine similarity and Euclidean distance metrics were calculated between the centroids of different corpora to quantify their relative alignment and semantic differences.
3. Comparison Function: A function iterated over each centroid pair between two corpora to compute their similarity or distance, providing an average measure for each pairwise corpus comparison.

4 Experimental Results

The above mentioned mehthodology were applied to the English translations of three religious texts - the Bible, the Quran, and the Bhagavad Gita. The results for the various experiments are mentioned in the following sections.

4.1 Word Count Analysis

The analysis revealed distinct linguistic focuses for each of the religious texts, highlighting their unique thematic elements:

1. Bhagavad Gita: The analysis showed that terms like arjuna (119 occurrences), action (80), and krishna (68) were predominant, emphasizing the philosophical dialogues between Arjuna and Krishna centered around ethical dilemmas, self-realization, and duty. Words such as mind (63), desire (53), and supreme (54) further underscored the text's spiritual and psychological dimensions.

2. Bible: High-frequency terms included give (8847), lord (7887), and god (4558), highlighting themes of divine instruction, moral teachings, and covenant relationships. Other frequently appearing words such as king (3079), man (3055), and people (2779) reflected the narrative and historical aspects of the text, illustrating societal and human interactions.

3. Quran: The word allah appeared most frequently (2833 occurrences), followed by lord (1014) and believe (525), emphasizing the text's focus on faith and divine will. Additional terms such as day (551), messenger (361), and people (256) indicated eschatological themes and the role of the prophetic tradition.

These results were visualized using bar plots in figures 6, 7 and 8, enabling a clear comparison of the top 20 words from each text. The visual representations provided a comprehensive perspective on both shared and distinctive linguistic emphases among the texts, enhancing the understanding of their thematic structures.

4.2 Topic Modeling Using Latent Dirichlet Allocation (LDA)

The application of LDA to the three religious texts yielded informative which can be seen in figure 4:

1. Bhagavad Gita: The topics derived included keywords such as duty, soul, wisdom, battle, and divine, which highlighted the philosophical and spiritual discourse central to

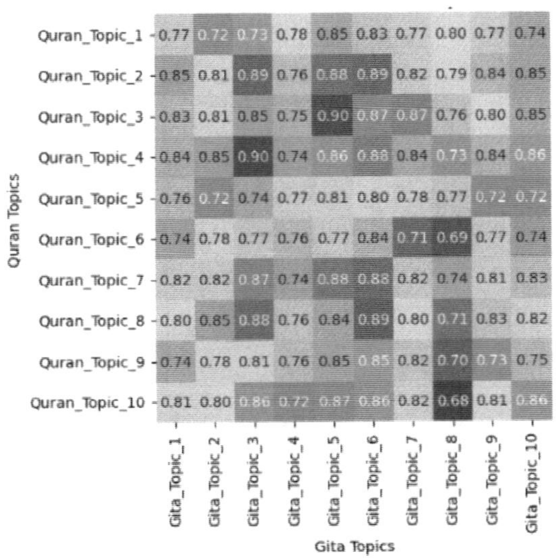

Figure 1: Topic Similarity between Quran and Gita using GLOVE

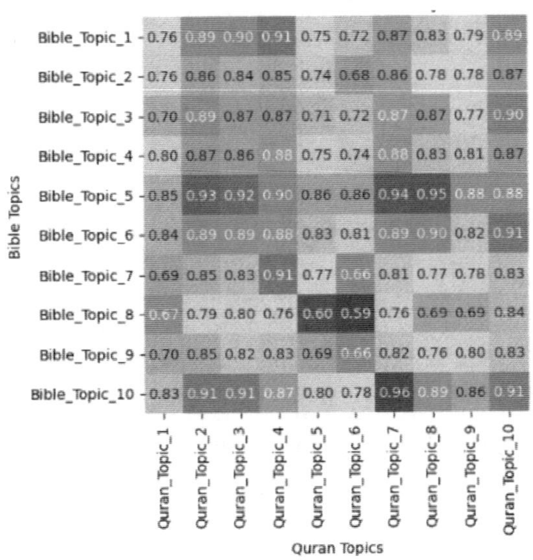

Figure 2: Topic Similarity between Bible and Quran using GLOVE

the dialogue between Krishna and Arjuna. The themes focused on moral duties, self-realization, and ethical dilemmas.

2. Bible: The identified topics featured words like covenant, kingdom, prophets, faith, and law, emphasizing its broad narrative of divine instructions, historical accounts, and religious teachings. This reflected the Bible's multi-faceted nature, combining guidance, historical context, and spiritual lessons.

3. Quran: Topics contained terms such as mercy,

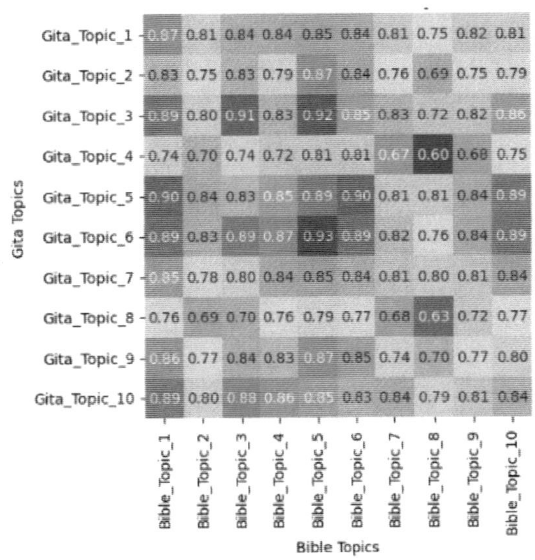

Figure 3: Topic Similarity between Gita and Bible using GLOVE

believers, guidance, prophet, and judgment, showcasing its focus on the divine message, moral conduct, and eschatological themes. The recurring emphasis was on faith, righteous living, and the role of prophets in guiding believers.

4.3 Topic Comparison Across Texts with GloVe Embeddings and Sentence Transformers

In this section, we discuss the results obtained form the pairwise comparison of the texts using Glove Embeddings and Sentence Transformers.

4.3.1 GLOVE

We can draw the following inference from the heatmaps show in figures 1, 2 and 3.

1. Quran vs. Gita: The Quran and the Gita both emphasize themes of spiritual guidance and moral conduct. Topics in the Quran like Quran Topic 2 and Quran Topic 7 align with Gita Topic 4 and Gita Topic 3, where terms such as "lord," "believe," and "path" reflect a shared focus on enlightenment and ethical living. The strongest overlap occurs between Quran Topic 4 and Gita Topic 4, where keywords like "evil," "heaven," and "path" suggest common views on cosmic order and morality. Differences emerge in Quran Topic 5 and Gita Topic 5, with the Quran addressing themes of earth and doom, while the Gita centers on

Topic Number	Gita Topics	Bible Topics	Quran Topics
1	arjuna, mind, world, krishna, great, attain, self, work, thus, body	death, man, without, power, dead, right, take, life, world, evil	allah, lord, seek, ever, upon, forgive, mercy, merciful, wherein, near
2	action, worship, among, path, self, know, attachment, yoga, wisdom, desire	go, land, come, glory, town, great, jerusalem, waste, king, take	lord, turn, good, save, away, none, hath, believe, work, favour
3	sense, mind, without, free, even, good, meditation, offer, action, evil	take, food, give, true, good, man, need, wealth, much, fruit	lord, verily, say, among, another, folk, believe, man, destroy, see
4	arjuna, attain, brahman, desire, path, knowledge, krishna, time, remember, pleasure	make, holy, take, body, priest, part, lord, place, unclean, every	evil, create, heaven, ward, light, like, use, whose, path, hear
5	arjuna, among, krishna, path, time, death, seek, god, know, life	give, god, lord, thing, faith, say, word, make, spirit, keep	earth, allah, doom, lord, heavens, fire, convey, good, disbelieve, owner
6	life, arjuna, spiritual, even, wisdom, free, offer, every, action, god	father, give, love, make, brother, desire, god, name, clear, christ	allah, messenger, religion, whoso, keep, duty, hath, disbeliever, well, promise
7	arjuna, world, among, creature, three, krishna, describe, listen, divine, every	like, fire, make, foot, earth, though, heaven, water, beast, round	say, worship, know, would, ease, lord, surely, moses, send, hand
8	arjuna, supreme, creature, krishna, goal, attain, lord, self, wise, action	child, number, israel, son, thousand, hundred, four, little, family, twelve	allah, hath, give, heart, reveal, concern, believe, scripture, good, make
9	supreme, self, within, lord, without, desire, free, selfish, attachment, knowledge	day, time, righteousness, first, come, year, light, till, rule, seven	day, allah, bring, night, people, disbelieve, scripture, naught, hell, forth
10	every, selfless, body, give, service, other, bear, without, creature, arjuna	say, lord, come, give, jesus, king, word, go, take, send	say, give, orphan, wife, find, make, garden, day, thereof, father

Figure 4: Comparison of topics from the Gita, Bible, and Quran by topic number

personal spiritual pursuits involving Arjuna and Krishna.

2. Bible vs. Quran: The Bible and the Quran share strong themes of faith and devotion. Bible Topic 5 and Quran Topic 5 both highlight "god," "faith," and "lord," reflecting a mutual emphasis on submission and belief. Bible Topic 10 and Quran Topic 7 also align, with figures like "jesus" and "moses" underscoring themes of divine communication through prominent religious figures. However, Bible Topic 8, focused on lineage (e.g., "child," "israel"), differs from Quran Topic 8, which emphasizes universal faith themes, highlighting the Bible's specific cultural focus.

3. Gita vs. Bible: The Gita and the Bible similarly stress mental discipline, faith, and virtue. Gita Topic 3 and Bible Topic 5 share themes of mental control and faith, with terms like "mind," "free," and "spirit." The strongest overlap is between Gita Topic 6 and Bible Topic 6, which emphasize spirituality and love through terms such as "life," "wisdom," and "brother." Some topics differ, such as Gita Topic 4 and Bible Topic 8: the Gita focuses on

self-realization, while the Bible emphasizes lineage, showcasing different cultural narratives.

4.3.2 Sentence Transformer

We can draw the following inference from the heatmaps show in figures 9, 10 and 11, as presented in the appendix.

1. Quran vs. Gita: The Quran and Gita intersect on themes of divine guidance and spiritual reflection. Quran Topic 1 and Gita Topic 4 focus on seeking and attaining divine wisdom. Quran Topic 6 and Gita Topic 6 both mention duty and spiritual practices. Differences arise with Quran Topic 8's focus on scripture compared to Gita Topic 5's take on life and spiritual transformation.

2. Bible vs. Quran: The Bible and the Quran share thematic overlaps, particularly in themes of divine principles and moral guidance. Bible Topic 5 and Quran Topic 6 highlight "lord," "faith," and "god," reflecting devotion to a higher power. Bible Topic 10 and Quran Topic 1 align on divine will and revelations through prophets. However, Bible Topic 8's focus on lineage contrasts with the Quran's universal themes, as seen in Quran Topic 3, centering on communal beliefs.

3. Gita vs. Bible: The Gita and Bible align on spiritual conduct and duty. Gita Topic 1 and Bible Topic 5 share themes of moral responsibility and divine wisdom. Gita Topic 3 and Bible Topic 3 both touch on "mind" and "action," highlighting the pursuit of righteousness. Distinctions include Bible Topic 8's lineage emphasis versus Gita Topic 7's philosophical discussions on divine duties.

4.4 Sentiment Analysis of Verses Using VADER

Using the VADER sentiment analysis, we obtain the sentiment scores for each verse of each book. Figure 5 shows the distribution of sentiment scores for the three religious texts. Here, we should note that the sentiment scores do not represent the moral positive or negative sentiment, but rather the use of positive or negative words, regardless of the context they are used in. From the figure, we see that the Bible and the Quran have a higher percentage of neutral verses, while the Gita has a higher percentage of positively classified verses. This can be interpreted the Gita uses a higher percentage of words that have positive sentiments, regardless of the context they are used in.

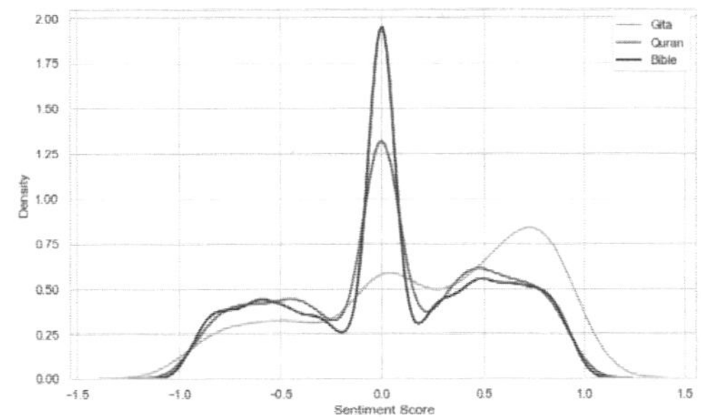

Figure 5: Distribution of sentiment scores of religious texts

4.5 Corpus Distance Measurement

The analysis of corpus distances and similarities between the religious texts revealed several key insights. The FID distance (Table 1), indicated that the Bible vs Quran pair had the closest distribution similarity (0.1664), while the Bible vs Gita and Gita vs Quran comparisons showed higher values, suggesting more divergence. In terms of semantic similarity, cosine similarity of averaged embeddings (Table 2) showed the Bible vs Quran pair had the highest similarity (0.8980), with the Bible vs Gita and Gita vs Quran pairs demonstrating lower similarities. KMeans clustering further reinforced these findings, with centroid based cosine similarity (Table 3, 4) being highest for Bible vs Quran (0.7035) and the lowest Euclidean distance (0.4170), indicating closer semantic structures, while the Bible vs Gita comparison showed greater dissimilarity.

Table 1: FID distance (no embeddings)

Comparison	FID Distance
Bible vs Gita	0.3868
Bible vs Quran	0.1664
Gita vs Quran	0.3801

Table 2: Cosine similarity (embeddings averaged)

Comparison	Cosine Similarity
Bible vs Gita	0.7278
Bible vs Quran	0.8980
Gita vs Quran	0.7757

Table 3: Average cosine similarity between Centroids

Comparison	Avg. Cosine Sim.
Bible vs Gita	0.5423
Bible vs Quran	0.7035
Gita vs Quran	0.6226

Table 4: Average euclidean distance between Centroids

Comparison	Avg. Euclidean Dist.
Bible vs Gita	0.5284
Bible vs Quran	0.4170
Gita vs Quran	0.4911

5 Conclusion and Future Work

Natural Language Processing (NLP) techniques have proven to be highly effective in analyzing and comparing the thematic and emotional dimensions of the Bible, Quran, and Bhagavad Gita. By utilizing methods such as Latent Dirichlet Allocation (LDA) for topic modeling, VADER for sentiment analysis, and semantic comparison through embeddings, distinct linguistic focuses and shared themes have been uncovered across these sacred texts. The analysis highlights unique philosophical dialogues and moral imperatives in each text while also revealing common ethical frameworks and human values that connect them. This research offers valuable insights into how religious texts continue to influence and shape cultural, ethical, and moral systems in contemporary society.

For further understanding of religious texts, future research could expand the scope by including additional texts from diverse religious traditions. Advanced NLP techniques, such as transformer-based models for sentiment analysis and topic modeling, could offer more nuanced insights into the complex language and meanings within these scriptures. Additionally, alternative text comparison metrics like BLEU and METEOR could be explored to enhance analysis. Furthermore, longitudinal studies examining the evolving interpretations of these texts over time, particularly in response to societal changes, could provide a broader view of their continued relevance. Interdisciplinary collaborations combining theology, linguistics, and cultural studies would also enhance the depth and scope of computational religious studies, offering richer perspectives on the texts' ongoing influence.

6 Limitations and Ethical Considerations

This study relies on the English translations of the three religious texts, which may introduce inherent biases due to potential variations in translation. Additionally, the use of pre-trained models (such as VADER, GloVe, Sentence Transformer, etc.) may further contribute to biases in the obtained results. The sentiment values obtained using VADER are also not representative of the moral sentiment of the verses in the text, but only based on the polarity of the words in them. Hence, while the findings provide meaningful insights, they should be interpreted with caution, considering these limitations.

In conducting research on religious texts using NLP techniques, it is imperative to approach the work with cultural sensitivity and respect for the diverse beliefs and values these texts embody. Efforts have been made to ensure that the analyses, including topic modeling and sentiment analysis, are presented objectively, without bias or misrepresentation of the texts' meanings or contexts. The results are intended solely for academic exploration and understanding, not for promoting ideological agendas or controversial interpretations. Researchers acknowledge the profound significance of these texts to their adherents and have prioritized ethical use and dissemination of findings to avoid any misuse or miscommunication.

References

Ahmed Abbasi, Abdul Rehman Javed, Farkhund Iqbal, Natalia Kryvinska, and Zunera Jalil. 2022. Deep learning for religious and continent-based toxic content detection and classification. *Scientific Reports*, 12(1):17478.

Mohammad Alhawarat. 2015. Extracting topics from the holy quran using generative models. *International Journal of Advanced Computer Science and Applications*, 6(12):288–294.

Rohitash Chandra and Venkatesh Kulkarni. 2022a. Semantic and sentiment analysis of selected bhagavad gita translations using bert-based language framework. *IEEE Access*, 10:21291–21315.

Rohitash Chandra and Venkatesh Kulkarni. 2022b. Semantic and sentiment analysis of selected bhagavad gita translations using bert-based language framework. *IEEE Access*, 10:21291–21315.

Rohitash Chandra and Mukul Ranjan. 2022. Artificial intelligence for topic modelling in hindu philosophy: Mapping themes between the upanishads and the bhagavad gita. *Plos one*, 17(9):e0273476.

Pramit Goel and Rashida Arsiwala. 2024. A comparative study of religious scriptures using natural language processing. *Journal of Student Research*, 13(2).

Martin Heusel, Hubert Ramsauer, Thomas Unterthiner, Bernhard Nessler, and Sepp Hochreiter. 2018. Gans trained by a two time-scale update rule converge to a local nash equilibrium. *Preprint*, arXiv:1706.08500.

Ben Hutchinson. 2024. Modeling the sacred: Considerations when using religious texts in natural language processing. In *Findings of the Association for Computational Linguistics: NAACL 2024*, pages 1029–1043.

Clayton Hutto and Eric Gilbert. 2014. Vader: A parsimonious rule-based model for sentiment analysis of social media text. In *Proceedings of the international AAAI conference on web and social media*, volume 8, pages 216–225.

Armand Joulin, Edouard Grave, Piotr Bojanowski, and Tomas Mikolov. 2017. Bag of tricks for efficient text classification. *arXiv preprint arXiv:1607.01759*.

George Kour, Samuel Ackerman, Eitan Farchi, Orna Raz, Boaz Carmeli, and Ateret Anaby-Tavor. 2022. Measuring the measuring tools: An automatic evaluation of semantic metrics for text corpora. In *Proceedings of the 2nd Workshop on Natural Language Generation, Evaluation, and Metrics (GEM 2022)*. Association for Computational Linguistics.

Younous Mofenjou Peuriekeu, Victoire Djimna Noyum, Cyrille Feudjio, Alkan Goktug, and Ernest Fokoue. 2021. A text mining discovery of similarities and dissimilarities among sacred scriptures. *arXiv preprint arXiv:2102.04421*.

Nils Reimers and Iryna Gurevych. 2019. Sentence-BERT: Sentence embeddings using Siamese BERT-networks. In *Proceedings of the 2019 Conference on Empirical Methods in Natural Language Processing and the 9th International Joint Conference on Natural Language Processing (EMNLP-IJCNLP)*, pages 3982–3992, Hong Kong, China. Association for Computational Linguistics.

A Appendix

Figures 6, 7, 8 show the word counts of the three religious texts.

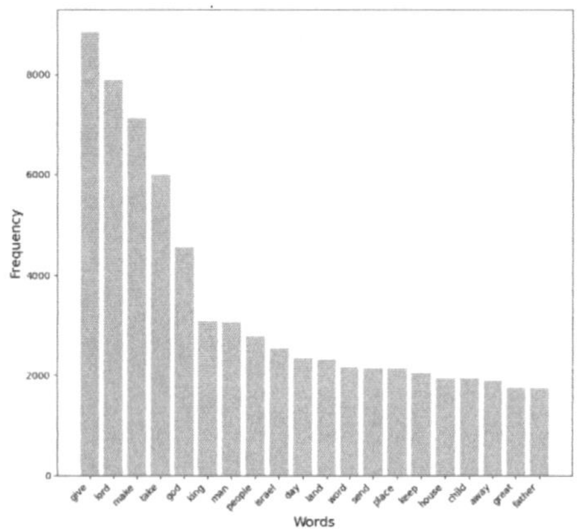

Figure 6: Word count for Bible

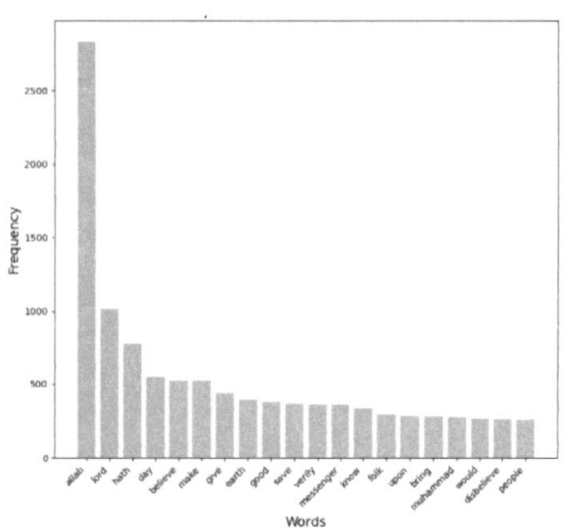

Figure 7: Word count for Quran

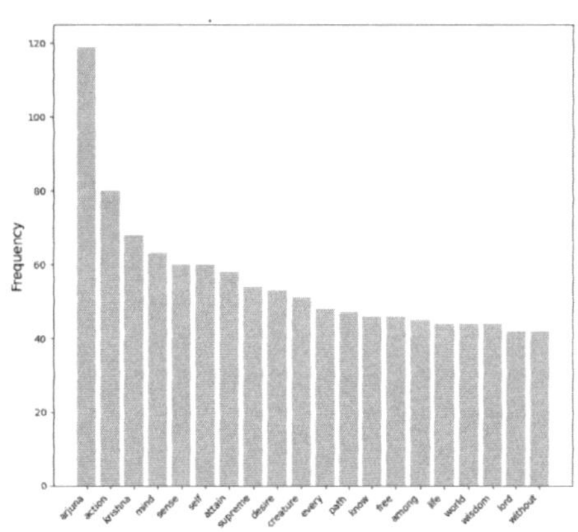

Figure 8: Word count for Bhagavad Gita

Figures 9, 10, 11 show the topic similarity between religious texts using Sentence Transformer

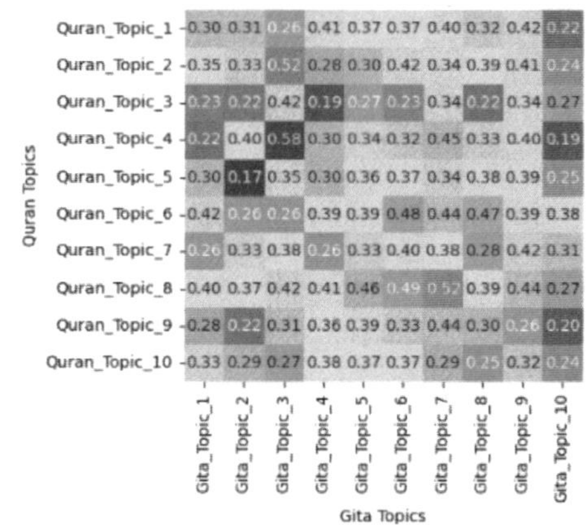

Figure 9: Topic similarity between Quran and Gita using Sentence Transformer

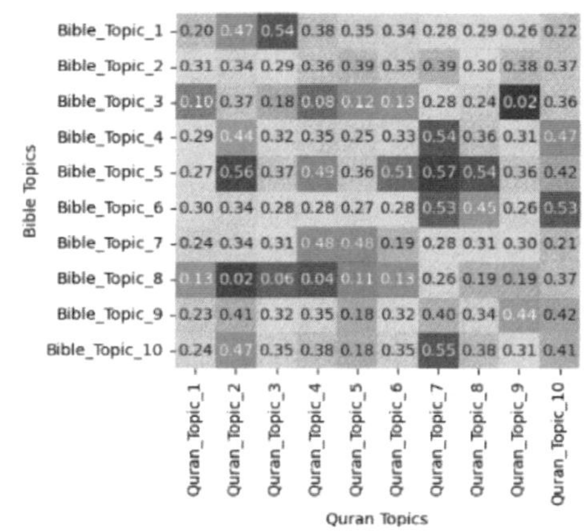

Figure 10: Topic similarity between Bible and Quran using Sentence Transformer

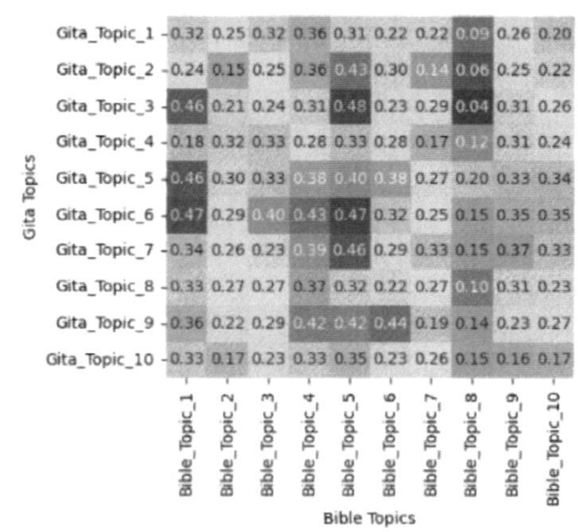

Figure 11: Topic similarity between Gita and Bible using Sentence Transformer

Messages from the Quran and the Bible in Mandarin through Factor Analysis with Syntactic and Semantic Tags

Kuanlin Liu
National Taipei University of Business
No. 100, Fulong Rd., Pingzhen Dist., Taoyuan City, Taiwan
kennyliu@ntub.edu.tw

Abstract

This paper tries to decipher messages from the Quran and the Bible's Mandarin translation using the multidimensional factor analysis (MDA) approach. Part-of-speech and word-meaning annotations were employed for data tagging. Seven syntactic and six semantic factors derived from the tagging systems demonstrated how the two scriptures are interpreted on the factor score scales. The analyses indicated that both holy books uphold a "persuade" and "preach" style with higher frequencies of *imperative, advocative, and explanatory* expressions. In addition, both favor the "interpersonal, non-numeric, and indicative" strategies to *impress* followers and practitioners alike with more *elaborative* wordings. The factor analysis approach also revealed that the Bible differs from the Quran by adopting more "motion, direction, and transportation" information, reflecting the deviation in their historical and religious backgrounds.

1 Introduction

Rendering messages of the Gods[1] from scriptures might be the most intriguing yet challenging task for the faithful and spiritual shareholders. Religious texts are passed down from long ago, and practitioners are believed to rely conventionally on a literal interpretation of the scriptures. The messages rendered from the scriptures come through the endeavors of reverends or believers. However, the divine messages might have been altered or diverted along with the time or varied interpretations. Are there other ways to hear from the Gods based on a deeper examination of the words of doctrine?

As one of the most adopted techniques for investigating linguistic data, Factor Analysis can identify clustered language features in a dataset comprised of various texts. If the factor score schemes (see 3.1) are applied, individual texts (presumably including the Quran and the Bible) will show particular preferences regarding their *linguistic factor* tendencies.

Factor Analysis relies on language tags to annotate each token used in the texts. Traditionally, multidimensional investigations were adopted to conduct genre analysis or stylistic categorization. Most tagging projects employ syntactic Part-of-speech (POS) annotations, and Stylometry has become one of the most prominent fields in linguistic studies. However, the Mandarin versions of the Quran and the Bible did not seem to have been viewed from a multidimensional perspective yet.

This paper aims to hear from the holy books using two factor-score systems: syntactic POS tagging and semantic word-meaning annotation. Some hidden messages are expected to emerge from the syntax-semantic approach to interpreting the religious scriptures, as holy texts like the Quran and the Bible can be distinctively regarded as a specific genre type. Some renderings or interpretations not brought up by early reverends or practitioners might be found from a multidimensional perspective. This paper tries to answer one fundamental question: how would the

[1] This paper withholds the polytheism/monotheism dichotomy; please see the author's disclaimer in 5.3.

Proceedings of the New Horizons in Computational Linguistics for Religious Texts (Coling-Rel), pages 11–22
January 19, 2025.

Quran and the Bible be measured by the Mandarin version of the factor score scales? Moreover, how would these scores reveal the untold/unknown messages from the scriptures?

2 Features of religious texts and linguistic multidimensional analysis

This section first reports on some common features found in the literature on religious texts, followed by the two sets of tagging systems: the syntactic POS tags and the semantic annotations.

2.1 Previous linguistic investigations of religious texts

Religious texts have always been an esteemed research direction for many linguists. Islamic and Christian scriptures received significant attention regarding their formality, word choice, or stylistics. The review in this section focuses on the commonly shared features found in religious texts.

Razzaq (2023) identified some linguistic features in Islamic holy scripture, which tend to maintain spirituality, morality, and religious practices using parallelism, repetition, and antithesis expressions. One essential character is the "persuasive strategies" of the Islamic scripture. Emotional, logical, authoritative, story-telling, and analogical expressions are used to achieve the goals.

Otabek et al. (2023) reported that Islamic scriptures are perceived as having a higher status. Religious expressions are not ordinary daily conversations with comparatively more prestigious wordings and lexicons involved. Religious texts adopt more figurative words to describe and more metaphorical expressions to "denote and preach".

The "persuade" and "preach" purposes are also found in the Bible. Adetuyi (2020) stated that religious texts use graphological elements to *persuade* and win trust and belief. Religious texts achieve this goal by using word choices especially to inform, convince, persuade, or impress. The religious style was distinguished as an individual type of itself according to Crystal's (1987) classification.

Kapranov et al. (2024) classified religious texts into informative and agitational types by analyzing the core parameters of objectives, fundamental concepts, genre diversity, communicative purpose, and linguistic features. These core parameters are presumably related to the purpose of *preaching*.

Other functions and features of religious texts were also mentioned. Al-Ebadi (2012), studying specifically the Epistle of James with the system-functional approach, concluded that MP (material phrases), RP (relational phrases), and MnP (mental phrases) constitute more than 96% of religious words. The MPs were used to activate believers, the RPs to describe and identify religious relationships, and MnPs arose desire and belief as a warning to unfaithful people.

Uhunmwangho and Oghiator (2022) studied the syntactic structures in Chapter 9 of the Book of Proverbs and found that substantial repetitions achieve aesthetic, rhythmic, and cohesive values. The religious style is similar to the "contemporary living" one in Crystal and Davy (1969).

Acheoah and Abdulraheem (2015) compared the Gospel of Matthew in the Bible with the Evergreen Islamic Sermon. They found that the former uses more acceptable fragments and the latter more causal (e.g., *so, therefore*) and conditional (e.g., *if*) words. The fragments were meant to *impress* followers, while the causal/condition words were to *persuade*.

Several common factors emerged based on the short review of the selected literature reported above. Religious texts tend to *persuade* and *preach* with several distinctive functions, such as repetition, figurative words, and fragments to *impress* or *agitate* believers.

However, it is believed that some other factors also play a part in religious texts, which could be found by the multidimensional technique designed to identify distinctive factors in selected texts. It is assumed that the MDA approach can single out the hidden, untold, or unknown factors and the constituting features contributing to the linguistic factors.

2.2 MDA and stylistic studies

The MDA of languages has a time-honored tradition (Biber, 1986a,1986b, 1988, 1992), and it has contributed significantly to genre and stylistic investigations in several languages, including

English, Nukulaelae Tuvaluan, Korean, and Somali (Biber, 1995). In Sardinha and Pinto (2014), linguistic features in Brazilian Portuguese and Spanish were identified by conducting MDA. Some specialized genres have also been further identified and discussed, such as language uses on the Internet and pre-Internet eras (Sardinha, 2014), languages in movies (Pinto, 2014) and pop songs (Bertoli-Dutra, 2014), and linguistic feature differences in *Time* magazine (de Souza, 2014). This paper follows the perspective of Crystal (1987) and Crystal and Davy (1969) that religious texts should also be classified as a specific genre.

The MDA approach has been applied to investigate languages used in function-specific scenarios. For example, Xiao (2009) studied the linguistic types and English dialects in multiple geographic distributions. With MDA, register-diversified corpora (Biber, 1993) became an effective tool for language studies. Using semantic tags, MDA has also been applied to business fields (e.g., Piao et al., 2015). Moreover, Cao and Xiao (2013) used the MDA in English to examine the contrast between native and non-native speakers. Huang and Ren (2019) compared different editorial styles used in *China Daily* and *The New York Times*. Ren and Lu (2021) compared the discussions in Chinese and American corporate annual reports.

Nevertheless, religious texts in Mandarin remain a genre seldom examined by the MDA approach. The analysis of linguistic tags appears to bear promising potential when paired with the appropriate interpretation. Applying the MDA to religious texts might lead to more fruitful results. This paper holds that Factor Analysis is a plausible approach to a deeper understanding of the two holy scriptures.

2.3 The factor components

Multidimensional analysis has been used to investigate stylistic differences or genre-type variation based on linguistic features reflected by co-occurring POS tags (as factors). The constituting features (the annotating tags) are crucial in conducting multidimensional analysis and linguistic stylometric studies. Factor analysis relied on the identified factors to compare how genre types differ in each factor.

This section reports on the factor distributions across languages. In Biber (1988, 1995), English can be analyzed with six factors: (1) involved vs. *informational*; (2) *narrative* vs. non-narrative; (3) situation-dependent vs. elaborated; (4) overtly *argumentative* vs. not overtly argumentative; (5) non-abstract vs. abstract; (6) online informational vs. edited or not informational. (The 7th factor, academic hedging, was not included in the factor score scheme).

On a dialect in Chinese, Tiu (2000) identified the five factors for Taiwan Southern Min (TSM): (1) interpersonal vs. informational; (2) the personal expression of emotion; (3) *persuasion*: *logical* vs. temporal linking; (4) *narrative*; (5) involved exposition vs. precise reportage.

In Mandarin Chinese, seven factors were identified: (1) interpersonal vs. *informational*; (2) descriptive vs. vocal; (3) *elaborative* vs. non-elaborative; (4) explanatory vs. *narrative*; (5) locative vs. non-locative; (6) numeric vs. non-numeric; (7) indicative vs. casual.

The three sets of factor components in different languages share certain common factors. For example, delivering *information* is crucial in all three languages mentioned above. How one *narrates* is also a common concern. The factor components show that these three languages try to impress/persuade people from slightly different perspectives: "argumentative" in English, "logical" in TSM, and "elaborative" in Mandarin.

The three sets of factor components indicated that some factors are highly related to the religious texts' word choices, especially the "persuade" and "preach" expressions (through elaborative, explanatory, or indicative factors), as they are found in both the literature and the factor listings. The typical "narrative" factor would be a vital indicator for analyzing religious texts, as it is reported in all three languages' factor sets. These initial findings should be examined with prudence. This paper adopted a methodology based on the factor score schemes to see how religious texts are mapped on the scoring systems. The focus is on whether these factors in religious texts stand out when compared to the model/other text types.

3 Methodology

This section presents the two adopted analytical schemes and how to arrive at the factor scores. The factor scores are calculated based on a model corpus with 20 genre types of 28 million tokens (see Appendix (1)). Through MDA, 33 out of 71 POS tags and 24 out of 129 semantic tags were included. Appendices (4) and (5) listed

Code	Features	Factor loadings
Factor 1: Interpersonal vs. informational		
FPP3	Third-person pronoun	0.811
VE	Active verb with a sentential object	0.745
VK	Stative verb with a sentential object	0.558
Nh	Pronoun	0.525
Caa	Conjunctive conjunction	-0.374
A	Non-predicative adjective	-0.479
Na	Common noun	-0.549
VHC	Stative causative verb	-0.594
Factor 2: Descriptive vs. vocal		
VF	Active verb with a verbal object	0.765
Nc	Place noun	0.514
Nd	Time noun	0.470
EMPH	Emphatics	-0.395
DWNT	Downtoners	-0.514
AMP	Amplifier	-0.553
SHI	*SHI* "copula"	-0.554
Factor 3: Elaborative (vs. non-elaborative)		
Cbb	Correlative conjunction	0.768
CONC	Concessive adverbial	0.709
V_2	*you* "have/possess"	0.497
VJ	Stative transitive verb	0.478
Ng	Postposition	0.407
Factor 4: Explanatory vs. narrative		
CAUS	"because"	0.641
PRMD	Predictive modal	0.500
PERF	Perfect tense	0.418
DE2	*DE* "attribute/possessive marker"	-0.606
Factor 5: Locative (vs. non-locative)		
Ncd	Localizer	0.845
VCL	Active verb with a locative object	0.740
Factor 6: Numeric (vs. non-numeric)		
Neu	Numeral determinatives	0.894
Neqb	Post-quantitative determinatives	0.640
Factor 7: Indicative vs. casual		
P	Preposition	0.790
Dfb	Post-verbal adverb of degree	-0.472
I	Interjection	-0.673

Table 1: 7 POS factors and components

the exemplary tokens of the included tags. The factors listed in Tables 1 and 2 are based on the tokens and genre types as the *model*. The figures in Appendices (2) and (3) are the sum of standardized tag frequencies of the identified factor components (grouped sets of tags). The scores in each scale are used as indexes to indicate genre-type differences between the religious texts and the model texts.

Factors Tags Loadings	1 Exposition	2 Events	3 Affection
demonstrative (M)	0.972		
number (M)	0.937		
factual (static v.)	0.713		
degree (M)	0.612		
evaluation (M)	0.533		
certainty (M)	0.395		
time (M)	-0.368		
sequence (M)	0.325		
animal (N)	0.438		
event (N)		0.745	
activity (N)		0.390	
idea (N)		0.353	
joy (N)			0.534
alive (M)			0.499
psych (static v.)			0.366
Factors Tags Loadings	**4 Motion**	**5 Places**	**6 Items**
moving (acts/v.)	0.687		
direction (M)	0.493		
transportation (N)	0.453		
place (N)		0.578	
organization (N)		0.543	
fear (N)		0.315	
item (N)			0.542
academics (N)			0.377
sensation(static v.)			0.331

Table 2: 6 semantic factors and components (M=modifiers, N=nominals, v.=verbs)

3.1 Seven POS factors in Mandarin and calculating factor scores

As reported in 2.3, Mandarin corpus data are represented by seven factors based on POS tags. Table 1 lists the components (clustered features) for each factor. Each feature might have positive or negative factor loadings (ranging from 1 to minus 1). Features with more significant loadings have higher frequencies, whereas features with negative or lesser loadings have lower frequencies. For example, a text high on Factor 1 is interpreted as more "interpersonal", for having higher "third-person pronouns, active/stative verbs with sentential objects, and pronouns" but fewer "conjunctives, non-predicate adjectives, common nouns, and stative causative verbs" tags. A text with an opposite formation of these tags is regarded as "informational".

The feature components can be used to calculate factor scores with their normalized and standardized frequencies compared with the averaged frequencies and SDs (standard deviation) of the original model that reported the factor loadings. To illustrate, if one would like to calculate the factor score of a newly collected text. The factor scores are arrived at by first normalizing the text's tag frequencies to per 1000 tokens. The normalization allows the intended text to be placed on the same frequency scale as the model texts. The normalized tag frequencies are then standardized using each tag's model frequency averages and SDs. For example, a text's Factor 1 score is the sum of the standardized frequencies of the FPP3, VE, VK, and Nh (positive loading features) tags, subtracted by that of Caa, A, Na, and VHC (negative loading features). The POS tag features of Factor 1 to Factor 7 are listed in Table 1. Appendix (2) contains the factor score scales for Factors 1 to 7, in which the score distributions of the four representative genres from the model and the two religious texts are illustrated. In section 4, the POS tag analysis compares the 7-factor scores of the Quran and the Bible.

In addition to the POS tagset, another factor analysis of Mandarin used semantic tags. The semantic multidimensional explorations identified six semantic factors in Mandarin. They are: (1) Exposition; (2) Events; (3) Affection; (4) Motion; (5) Places; and (6) Items. The semantic factor components are listed in Table 2. With the feature components based on semantic tagging, the semantic factor scores can also be calculated using the normalized and standardized semantic tag frequencies. The arithmetic procedures are the same as those reported in 3.1, with only the difference in semantic tag component features and their frequencies. Appendix (3) reports on the semantic factor scores of the representative text types on each factor.

4 Messages rendered by the factor scores

This section discusses the inferring from the religious texts through the POS and semantic factor scores. The two systems reported some common factors the Quran and the Bible shared. A few scripture-specific factors are also identified.

4.1 Hearing from the Gods with POS factor scores

How the two scriptures differ from the original model genre types can be illustrated by the score scales in Appendix (2). Each factor scale lists six representative type scores (two from each of the highest, middle-ranging, and lowest ones, sorted by scores and chosen from the 20 original model genre types). The relative scale positionings of the religious texts illuminate their characteristics.

For Factor 1, the Quran and the Bible are highly "interpersonal" by the definition of Factor 1 features. However, the literature indicates that religious texts are supposed to contain substantial *information* (e.g., Razzaq, 2023, to "persuade" with story-telling, and Otabek, 2023, to "preach" with prestigious lexicons). These factor-score results do not seem to comply with the findings in the literature by having a high "interpersonal" score. Nevertheless, it is argued that there arises no contradiction here. It should be noted that the content of the two religious texts is *informative*, and their delivery style remains *interpersonal*. To account for this dual-directional division, the purpose of the scriptures should be considered when communicating with the believers and followers, and a friendly preaching approach helps to achieve the goal of offering information in an interpersonal style. The higher frequencies of the interpersonal features are believed to achieve the *imperative* and *advocative* purposes in persuading and preaching.

For Factor 2, both the Quran and the Bible are moderately "descriptive" compared to model text types. This again differs slightly from the literature that religious texts should be of "higher status" (Otabek et al., 2023). The analysis shows that neither holy scripture stood out in *descriptiveness* based on the POS tags. Their Factor 2 scores rank in the middle, similar to W4-newspaper reports and S2-documentary narratives, and maintain a moderately descriptive style. This tendency is believed to be a result of translating the holy books. When Islam and Christianity were introduced to Mandarin-speaking areas, the general public was the target of the religious missions. The Mandarin translations of the classic scriptures were made fairly descriptive (and colloquialized) to be understood by the masses of the society, and the descriptive features were used to *advocate* for certain causes.

For Factor 3, both religious texts are moderately "elaborative". However, the Quran is slightly more "elaborative" than the Bible. Compared to the model genre types, the Quran has a factor score similar to that of W1-fictional works regarding elaborateness. It is not as detailed as

W6-commentaries (newspaper editorials), yet it maintains a touch of seriousness. The Bible, on the other hand, has a score similar to that of S8-TV variety shows. It adopts a more conversational approach when conveying messages. Again, the endeavor of the religious texts to *preach* in a tone similar to a daily-life conversation was made explicit from the factor score perspective. The *elaborative* tendency indicated the explanatory purpose of the religious texts.

For Factor 4, both scriptures are powerfully "explanatory" with relatively high factor scores. It is assumed that religious texts need to explain things in more detail. Both scriptures adopt a style similar to that of S3-TV news magazines. In this way, the religious texts can report and explain issues in a fashion that is as detailed as possible.

For Factor 5, the Bible is significantly more "locative" than the Quran. This situation might result from the comparatively higher frequencies of *instructions* and *calls for action* in the Bible. This does not mean the Quran did not use directional or action words at all. The contrast only indicated that the Quran uses *localizers* and *location-related verbs* more conservatively.

For Factor 6, both holy books are comparatively "non-numeric". This lower use of numerical information can be expected as number terms are not the main subject of religious texts. Numbers are relatively refrained in the religious texts as more focus would be placed on the spiritual mentality.

For Factor 7, both scriptures are highly indicative, which reflects their "preaching" purpose. The *indicativeness* is realized by using the "interjection" and "degree adverbs". It is assumed that the purpose of *impressing* followers also resulted in the higher use of these features.

The analysis based on POS tags demonstrated several features of the two religious scriptures under discussion. The common ones reflect that the religious texts are more interpersonal (F1), descriptive (F2), explanatory (F4), non-numeric (F6), and indicative (F7). The reasons behind these same features are believed to be that the religious texts must communicate with believers, explain ideas, give guidance, or convince/impress followers without relying on numbers. A couple of text-specific features are also identified. The Quran is comparatively more non-elaborative (F3) and non-locative (F5) than the Bible. The Quran might resort to a style that uses fewer colloquial explanations to communicate with believers. As mentioned, both scriptures use fewer direction/action words, and the Quran cuts down even more on location information.

4.2 Interpreting the religious texts with semantic factor scores

The semantic factor score scheme for the Quran and the Bible also tells something exceptional that had not been revealed before. The score scales in Appendix (3) list the six sets of semantic factor scores of the model text types and that of the two holy scriptures. Some common factors are found among them; a few scripture-specific factors also emerged.

According to Factor 1 scores, both holy texts are low on the "exposition" factor, in which the exposition refers to a public-talking and spoken style. That is to say, both scriptures utilized comparatively *fewer* "factual, degree, evaluation, and certainty" features used in expressions. This strategy is believed to be due to the need for the holy texts to keep a *reserved, diplomatic,* and relatively *formal* style, to win the trust of followers and practitioners alike. Therefore, the *frank* and *direct* "exposition" factor is restrained for the religious texts, and a style similar to W10-captions (in a fashion analogous to story-telling) and W02-announcements (for raising awareness) was detected. It could be summarized that the way the religious texts convey to followers is *interpersonal* and *tactful*, using a "story-telling" style to *persuade* and "agitational" words to *preach*. This echoes and explains the perceivable POS contradiction of the bidirectional use of both informational and interpersonal features simultaneously, as discussed for the syntactic POS Factor 1.

For Factor 2, neither of the holy texts is high on the "events" factor. The expressions of "event and activity (see Table 2 for factor components)" seem cut down in the religious texts. This situation is probably because the expressions of *ideology, mentality,* and *spirituality* are more stressed in the holy texts.

For Factor 3, both are low on the "affection" factor. The "joy, alive, and psych (Table 2)" expressions constitute the affection factor. Re-examining the original texts with annotation tags, the "joy" tag is mainly tagged to *love* words, the "alive" to *life* words, and the "psych" to *willing/intend* verbs. This could prove that the Quran and the Bible do not employ a pretentious approach to communicating with followers. The holy texts involve more expressions to showcase *care, commitment, guidance for life, precaution,* or *advice* (partly illustrated by the excerpt in Appendix (6), in which a focus on "psych" words was used).

For Factor 4, the Bible is higher, while the Quran is moderate on the "motion" scale. Both Factor Analyses with POS and semantic tags identified the "localizer/moving" related factor as one of the key components in Mandarin. The Bible is believed to contain more descriptions of "moving, direction, and transportation (Table 2)" expressions. The POS Factor 5 discussed in 4.1 has already pointed out this unique characteristic of the Bible. As Appendix (7) demonstrates, wordings such as those in the Book of Exodus reported higher frequencies of semantic "motion" tags (e.g., "direction" and "moving" tags).

However, if the scope is limited to "place names" only (Factor 5), the Quran and the Bible are relatively low on the scale, indicating that place names are relatively rarely used in both the religious texts.

Finally, both holy texts are low on Factor 6 "items", as sacred texts would abstain from materialistic expressions. The religious texts would focus more on the faithfulness and the spiritual aspects of human life.

The semantic factor score scheme identified five common factors shared by the Quran and the Bible (both are low on "exposition (F1), events (F2), affection (F3), places (F5), and items (F6)" factors). The semantic scales managed to notice the non-materialism in the holy texts. One distinctive factor of the Bible has been noted: there are comparatively more "motion (F4)" expressions (with the "moving, direction, and transportation" tags) than that in the Quran, and this is the only factor in the Quran that differs drastically from the Bible.

5 Conclusion

This paper investigated the two holy scriptures from a multidimensional perspective. The perceived features in the sacred texts were first reviewed in the literature. These features were then re-examined using two factor-score systems: the POS and the semantic tagging schemes. Some common factors and certain distinctive/scripture-specific characteristics were identified and discussed (see 4.1 and 4.2). In essence, both of the holy books use *impressive* and *elaborative* strategies to *persuade* and *preach to* followers. The Bible differs from the Quran in being more elaborative, locative, and motion-oriented. The author assumes these differences reflect the deviation in their religious/historical backgrounds. This section ends the paper by reporting on this study's limitations, possible bias, and ethical concerns.

5.1 Limitations in building tagsets

This study adopted the POS and semantic tagsets in Mandarin. Compared to the available full POS tagset (all tokens can be POS tagged), the semantic one is still under development. The semantic factor score system has managed to semantically tag 67% of the tokens in the collected scriptures. Therefore, some might wonder why both of the religious texts tend to score low on the five semantic factors. It is contended that both religious texts performed the way reflected by the semantic factor scores, and tests using other genre types supported the accuracy of the semantic factor scales. The relatively insensitive prediction or identification power, if any as shown in 4.2, is probably due to the gap between an entirely constructed semantic tagset and the ongoing semi-completed one used in this study. A more complete semantic tagset will improve its categorizing and identifying abilities.

The annotating and tagging project required a substantial amount of manual work. It awaits further efforts to improve the effectiveness of the semantic Factor Analysis scheme. Future works can alleviate this limitation by perfecting the semantic tagging project. With a more complete semantic tagset, the analysis could be more precise, and the referencing results could be more persuasive.

5.2 Possible bias in the translated religious texts

This study focuses on the Mandarin versions of the Quran and the Bible because the author did not possess the necessary command of Arabic, Greek, or Hebrew (the original languages of the scriptures being written). The author resorted to their first-language translated versions. For the Quran, the included corpus was the traditional Chinese version of Muhammad Ma Jia (1906-1978), who studied in Egypt. The included corpus of the Bible was that of the Chinese Union Version (made by the Union Bible Societies). Therefore, the perspectives reflected Sunni Islam (not Shia Muslims) and Protestantism (not Catholicism or Orthodoxism). The findings through the factor analysis in this paper only partly reflect these two sects.

5.3 Ethical considerations and disclaimer

This study is simply an academic exploration based on the multidimensional approach with POS and semantic tags. The statements made by the author are of no intentional disrespect. On investigating the two holy books of Islam and Christianity, it is of no blasphemy intended to assume polytheism. The author himself is neither an Islamic nor a Christian, and the discussions were made with reasonings as objective as possible. Hopefully, this paper's findings, results, and claims could answer the research questions, including what untold messages could be rendered from the multidimensional perspective.

References

John Emikr Acheoah and Hamzah Abdulraheem. 2015. Style in Christian and Islamic Sermons: A Linguistic Analysis. *American Research Journal of English and Literature*. 1(2), P23-31.

Chris Adetuyi and Charles Patrick Alex. 2020. A stylistic analysis of selected Christian religion print advertisement in Ibadan metropolis, Oyo state. *Romanian Journal of English Studies*. (17), P81-90.

Hani Al-Ebadi. 2012. A Systemic-Functional Analysis of Religious Texts concerning the Epistle of 'James'. *Journal of Thi Qar Arts*. 2. P1-20.

Patrica Bertoli-Dutra. 2014. Chapter 2.2 Multidimensional analysis of pop songs. In Tony Berber Sardinha and Marcia Veirano Pinto. (Eds.) Multidimensional Analysis, 25 years on, P149-176.

Douglas Biber. 1986a. On the investigation of spoken/written differences. *Studia Linguistica,* 40(1), 1-21.

Douglas Biber. 1986b. Spoken and Written Textual Dimensions in English: Resolving the Contradictory Findings. *Language,* 62(2), 384-414.

Douglas Biber. 1988. *Variation across Speech and Writing*. Cambridge: Cambridge University Press.

Douglas Biber. 1992. The Multidimensional Approach to Linguistic Analyses of Genre Variation: An Overview of Methodology and Findings. *Computers and the Humanities,* 26(5), 331-345.

Douglas Biber. 1993. Using Register-Diversified Corpora for General Language Studies. *Computational Linguistics*, 19(2), 219-241.

Douglas Biber. 1995. *Dimensions of Register Variation: A Cross-Linguistic Comparison*. Cambridge: Cambridge University Press

Yan Cao and Richard Xiao. 2013. A multidimensional contrastive study of English abstracts by native and non-native writers. *Corpora*. 8(2), 209-234.

David Crystal. 1987. *The Cambridge encyclopedia of language*. Cambridge University Press.

David Crystal and Derek Davy. 1969. *Investigating English Style*. London and New York, NY: Routledge.

Ying Huang and Wei Ren. 2019. A novel multidimensional analysis of writing styles of editorials from China Daily and The New York Times. *Lingua,* 235. Doi: 10.1016/j.lingua.2019.102781.

Yan Kapranov, Olesya Cherkhava, and Anna Wierzchowska. 2024. Parameters of religious popular discourse within theolinguistic frameworks. *Journal of Modern Science*. DOI: doi.org/10.13166/jms/187200. P239-262.

Bektoshev Otabek, Shodmonov Sherzod Hursanaliyevich, and Tirkashev Dilshod Sharobiddin ugli. 2023. The Specificity Of Religious Language In Modern Linguistics. *Journal of Positive School Psychology*. 7(1), P914-920.

Scott Piao, Xiaopeng Hu, and Paul Rayson. 2015. Towards a Semantic Tagger for Analyzing Contents of Chinese Corporate Reports. *Proceedings of ISCC 2015*.

Marcia Veirano Pinto. 2014. Dimensions of Variation in North American Movies. In Tony Berber Sardinha and Marcia Veirano

Pinto (Eds.) *Multidimensional Analysis, 25 years on-A tribute to Douglas Biber*. Amsterdam: John Benjamins Publishing.
Nasir Razzaq. 2023. Language and Religious Discourse: An Analysis of the Linguistic Features and Persuasive Strategies in Islamic Sermons. IQAN(10), 5(2), P17-34.
Chaowang Ren and Xiaofei Lu. 2021. A multidimensional analysis of the management's discussion and analysis narratives in Chinese and American corporate annual reports. *English for Specific Purposes*, 62, 84-99.
Tony Berber Sardinha and Marcia Veirano Pinto. (Eds.) 2014. *Multidimensional Analysis, 25 years on-A tribute to Douglas Biber*. Amsterdam: John Benjamins Publishing.
Tony Berber Sardinha. 2014. 25 years later: comparing Internet and pre-Internet registers. In Sardinha & Pinto (Eds.) *Multidimensional Analysis, 25 years on-A tribute to Douglas Biber*. Amsterdam: John Benjamins Publishing.
Renata Condi de Souza. 2014. Dimensions of variation in TIME magazine. In Sardinha & Pinto (Eds.) *Multidimensional Analysis, 25 years on-A tribute to Douglas Biber*. Amsterdam: John Benjamins Publishing.
Hak-khiam Tiu. 2000. A Multidimensional Analysis of Spoken and Written Taiwanese Register. *Language and Linguistics*, 1(1), 89-117.
Amen Uhunmwangho and Florence Etuwe Oghiator. 2022. The language of religion as discourse: analysis of the syntactic structures in Proverbs Chapter Nine. *International Journal of Culture and Religious Studies*. 3(1), P31-47.
Richard Xiao. 2009. Multidimensional analysis and the study of world Englishes. *World Englishes*, 28(4), 421-450.

Appendices:

(1) Number of tokens by genre texts

Genres	No. of tokens
S1. Lectures/speeches	2,862,521
S2. Documentary narratives	3,712,698
S3. TV News magazines	2,987,873
S4. Private conversations	125,154
S5. Interviews (public conversations)	4,269,528
S6. Drama series talks	467,073
S7. Group/panel discussions	4,152,415
S8. Talks in game/variety shows	379,204
S9. Meeting minutes	9,767
S10. Play scripts	2,825
W1. Works of fiction	1,994,370
W2. Announcements	37,822
W3. Letters	79,985
W4. Newspaper reports	5,467,737
W5. Prose works	881,290
W6. Commentaries	1,118,735
W7. Biographies and diaries	27,637
W8. Poems and lyrics	35,858
W9. Manuals and handbooks	101,812
W10. Advertisements/pic. captions	23,429
Total (S1~W10 model texts)	28,737,733
The Quran	180,091
The Bible	792,600

(2) Scores Comparison in Seven Factors

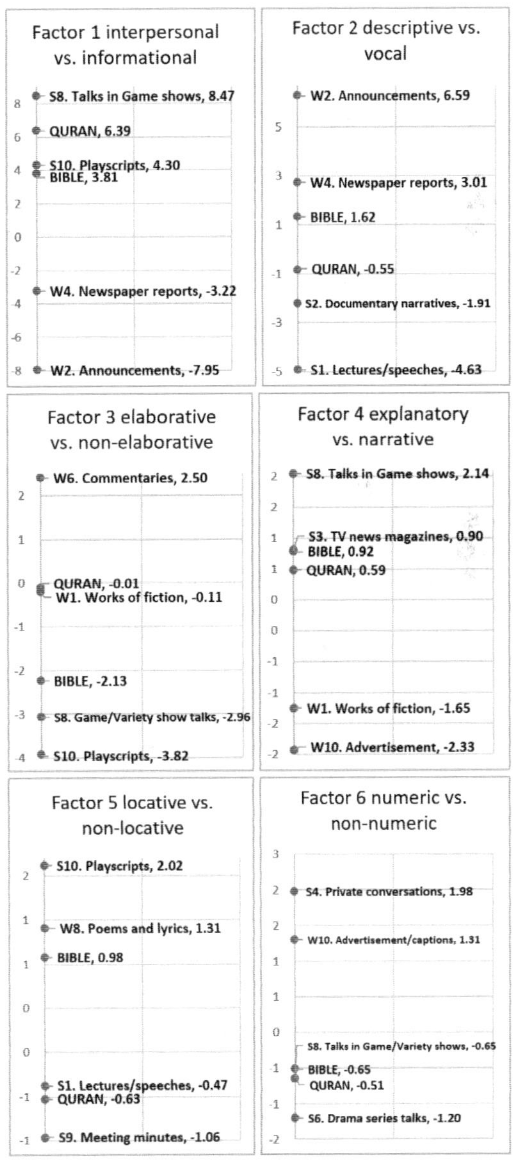

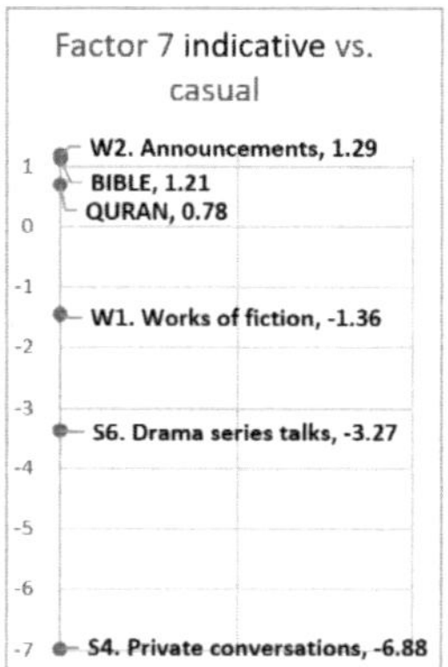

(3) Semantic Scores in Six Factors

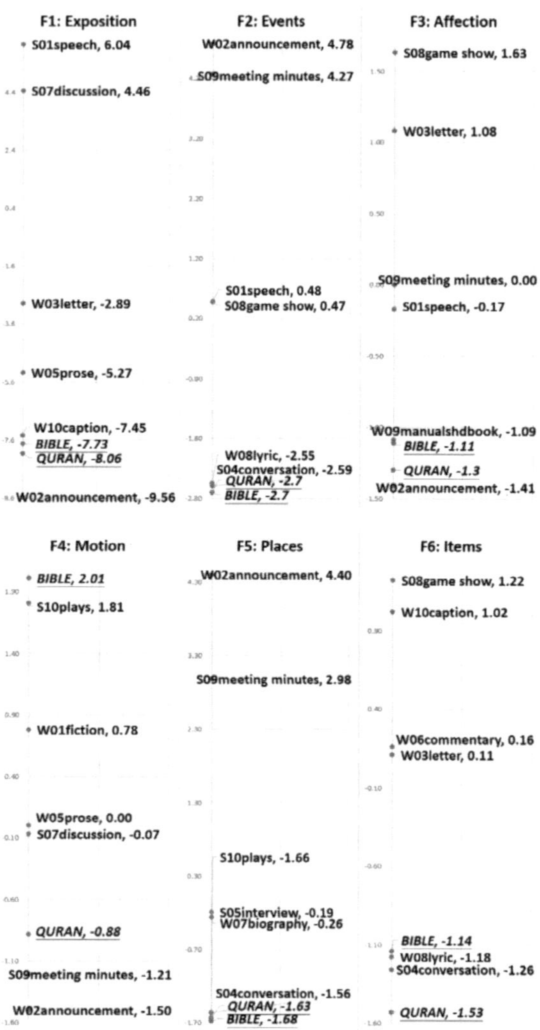

(4) The POS tagset (31 out of 77tags listed)

No	Tag	Full name	Exemplary tokens for each feature (tag)
A7	FPP3	Third person pronoun	*ta* 'he', *da-jia* 'everyone', *dui-fang* 'they'
B37	VE	Active verb with a sentential object	*suo* 'say', *gao-shu* 'tell'
B44	VK	Stative verb with a sentential object	*jiang-jiu* 'be strict about', *zhi-dao* 'know'
B27	Nh	Pronoun	*da-jia* 'everyone', *dui-fang* 'they'
B2	Caa	Conjunctive conjunction	*he* 'and'
B1	A	Non-predicative adjective	*ge-shi-ge-yang* 'various'
B15	Na	Common noun	*shou* 'hand', *guan-zhong* 'audience'
B41	VHC	Stative causative verb	*ping-heng* 'balance, *chang-sheng* 'produce'
B38	VF	Active verb with a verbal object	*ji-xu* 'continue'
B17	Nc	Place noun	*jia* 'home', *can-ting* 'restaurant'
B19	Nd	Time noun	*yi-qian* 'before', *zao-qi* 'early times'
A21	EMPH	Emphatics	*jiu-shi* 'exactly', *zhen-de* 'truly'
A18	DWNT	Downtoners	*ji-hu* 'almost', *hen-shao* 'rarely'
A20	AMP	Amplifiers	*jue-dui* 'absolutely', *que-shi* 'indeed'
B29	SHI	SHI	*shi* 'is' copula
B5	Cbb	Correlative conjunction	*ke-shi* 'but, *dan-shi* 'but'
A14	CONC	Concessive adverbial	*sui-ran* 'however'
B46	V_2	*You*	*you* 'have'
B43	VJ	Stative transitive verb	*shou-dao* 'affected by', *cheng-sian* 'show'
B26	Ng	Postposition	*shou(shang)* 'in hand'
A13	CAUS	"because"	*yin-wei* 'because'
A25	PRMD	Predictive modal	*yao* 'will', *ying* 'should', *xu* 'need to'
A2	PERF	Perfect tense	yi-jing 'already', ceng-jing 'ever'
B8	DE2	*De* (2)	*de* marker (*de* other than *de* (1))
B18	Ncd	Localizer	*shang-fang* 'on top', *di-bu* 'bottom'
B35	VCL	Active verb with a locative object	*lai (dao)* 'come to', *zhun-bei (shang)* 'prepare to'
B24	Neu	Numeral determinatives	*shi* 'ten', *si* 'four'
B22	Neqb	Post-quantitative determinatives	11 *dang (duo)* 'minutes past 11'
B28	P	Preposition	*zai* 'at', *dang* 'when'
B10	Dfb	Post-verbal adverb of degree	…*de duo* 'even more …'
B14	I	Interjection	*dui-le* 'oh yes', *oh* 'oh'

(5) The two-level semantic tags (24 out of 129 semantic tags listed)

Category	Sub-Category	Tag	Examples
Nominals (Nouns)	**(01) Substantiality**	(01) Animal	*shan-yang* 'goat', *da-xiang* elephant'
		(03) Organization	*xian-zheng-fu* 'council', *gong-si* 'company'
		(07) Transportation	*fei-ji* 'airplanes', *qi-che* 'cars', *zi-xing-che* 'bicycles'
		(09) Activity	*jiang-hua* 'talks', *hui-yi* 'meetings', *pai-dui* 'parties'
		(10) Place	*gong-che-zhan* 'bus station', *bo-wu-guan* 'museum'
		(11) Item	*sha-fa* 'sofa', *cha-zi* 'fork', *yao-shi* 'keys'
		(12) Academics	*shu-ji* 'books', *wen-zhang*, 'papers', *biao-ge* 'forms'
	(02) Positive-emotions	(20) Joy	*gao-xing* 'happiness', *yu-yue* 'amusement', *kuai-le* 'glee'
	(03) Negative - emotions	(25) Fear	*dan-you* 'concern', *dan-xin* 'worry'
	(04) Neutral-emotions	(31) Number	*yi-xiao-shi* 'one hour', *shi-nian* 'ten years'
		(32) Idea	*tui-li* 'reasoning', *luo-ji* 'logics'
		(34) Event	*ji-hui* 'convention', *shi-wu* 'affair(s)'
Acts (Verbs)	**(05) Acts**	(39) Moving	*yi-ju* 'migration'', chu-*kou* 'exportation'
	(06) Static	(44) Psych	*nan-shou* 'mourn', *nan-guo* 'lament', *hou-hui* 'regret', *shi-huai* 'be mean', *wu-ru* 'belittle'
		(46) Factual	*cheng-gong* 'succeed', *jing-jue* 'caution', *hui-yi* 'recall', *fan-bo* negate', *shi* copula
		(49) Sensation	*ting-dao* 'hear', *jian-dao* 'see', *wendao* 'smell'
Modifiers (adj/adv)	**(10) Status**	(73) Alive	*sheng* 'alive', *si* 'dead'
	(11) Spatial	(78) Direction	*qian-jin* 'forward', *hou-tui* 'backward'
		(86) Demonstrative	*na-xie* 'those', *na-ge* 'that', *zhe-ge* 'this'
	(12) Temporal	(87) Time	*zao* 'early', *chi* 'late'
		(90) Sequence	*zhi-hou* 'after', *zui-hou*, 'last'
	(17) Judgment	(120) Evaluation	*hao-de* 'good', *xie-er-de* 'evil'
		(122) Certainty	*que-ding* 'certain', *bu-queding* 'unclear/uncertain'
		(128) Degree	*quan-xin-quan-yi* 'full-hearted', *xie-wei* 'slightly'

(6) Example excerpt (Al-Hujurat: 49-15)

xin-shi 'believers', (Na),
，, (COMMACATEGORY),
zhi-shi 'only', (DWNT), judgment, effectiveness
que-xin 'believe', (PUBV),
zhen-zhu 'Allah', (Na),
he 'and', (Caa),
shi-zhe 'messengers', (Na),
，, (COMMACATEGORY),
ran-hou 'then', (OSUB),
mei-you 'not', (D), judgment, accuracy
huai-yi 'doubt', (PRIV), static, **psych**
，, (COMMACATEGORY),
neng 'able', (D), temporal, modal
yi 'by', (P),
zi-ji 'self', (Nh), substantiality, human
de 'possessive', (DE0),
cai-chan 'possessions', (Na),
he 'and', (Caa),
sheng-ming 'life', (Na), neutral-emo, **alive**
wei 'copula', (VG), static, factual
zhu-dao 'main road', (Na),
er 'then', (Cbb),
fen-dou 'fight', (VA),
de 'possessive', (DE0),
ren 'people', (Na), substantiality, human
；, (SEMICOLONCATEGORY),
zhe 'this', (Nep), spatial, demonstrative
deng 'these', (Cab),
ren 'people' , (Na), substantiality, human
que 'but' , (D),
shi 'copula' , (SHI), static, factual
cheng-shi 'honest', (VH),
de 'possessive', (DE0),

'The believers are only the ones who have believed in Allah and His Messenger and then doubt not but strive with their properties and their lives in the cause of Allah. It is those who are the truthful.'

(7) Example excerpt (Book of Exodus 19)

Token 'translation', (Syn Code), Sem code1, code2:
ta-men 'they', (FPP3), substantiality, human
li-kai 'leave', (VC)
le 'PAST-marker', (PAST)
li-fei-din 'Rephidim', (Nc)
lai-dao 'came to', (**VCL**), acts, **moving**
xi-nai 'Sinai', (Nc)
de 'possessive-marker', (DE0)
guang-ye 'wildness' , (Na)

、, (PAUSECATEGORY)
jiu 'then' , (D), temporal, sequence
cai 'at', (P)
na-li 'there' , (**Ncd**), spatial, **direction**
de 'possessive-marker', (DE0)
san 'mountain' , (Na), substantiality, place
xia 'under' , (PLA), spatial, location
an-ying 'camp' , (VA)
mo-xi 'mosses' , (Nb)
dao 'to' , (P)
shen 'god', (FW)
na-li 'there' , (**Ncd**), spatial, **direction**
、, (PAUSECATEGORY)
ye-he-hua 'Jehovah', (Nb)
cong 'from', (P)
san 'mountain' , (Na), substantiality, place
shang 'up' , (PLA), spatial, **direction**
hu-huan 'call' , (VC)
ta 'him' , (FPP3), substantiality, human
suo 'say' , (VE), acts, motion

'After they set out from Rephidim, they entered the Desert of Sinai, and Israel camped there in the desert in front of the mountain. Then Moses went up to God, and the Lord called to him from the mountain and said: … '

Semantic Analysis of Jurisprudential Zoroastrian Texts in Pahlavi: A Word Embedding Approach for an Extremely Under-Resourced, Extinct Language

Rashin Rahnamoun
Shahid Beheshti University, Tehran, Iran
rahnamounrashin@gmail.com

Ramin Rahnamoun
Central Tehran Branch, Islamic Azad University, Tehran, Iran
r.rahnamoun@iauctb.ac.ir

Abstract

Zoroastrianism, one of the earliest known religions, reached its height of influence during the Sassanian period, embedding itself within the governmental structure before the rise of Islam in the 7th century led to a significant shift. Subsequently, a substantial body of Zoroastrian literature in Middle Persian (Pahlavi) emerged, primarily addressing religious, ethical, and legal topics and reflecting Zoroastrian responses to evolving Islamic jurisprudence. The text *Šāyist nē šāyist* (Licit and Illicit), which is central to this study, provides guidance on purity and pollution, offering insights into Zoroastrian legal principles during the late Sassanian period. This study marks the first known application of machine processing to Book Pahlavi texts, focusing on a jurisprudential Zoroastrian text. A Pahlavi corpus was compiled, and word embedding techniques were applied to uncover semantic relationships within the selected text. Given the lack of digital resources and data standards for Pahlavi, a unique dataset of vocabulary pairs was created for evaluating embedding models, allowing for the selection of optimal methods and hyperparameter settings. By constructing a complex network using these embeddings, and leveraging the scarcity of texts in this field, we used complex network analysis to extract additional information about the features of the text. We applied this approach to the chapters of the *Šāyist nē šāyist* book, uncovering more insights from each chapter. This approach facilitated the initial semantic analysis of Pahlavi legal concepts, contributing to the computational exploration of Middle Persian religious literature.

1 Introduction

Zoroastrianism is one of the world's oldest religions, with origins dating back approximately three thousand years to the Avestan period. Historical texts suggest that King Goshtasp (Vishtaspa) Kiani was the first monarch to adopt Zoroastrianism; however, some scholars regard him as a mythical figure (Boyce, 2017). The Sassanian period, however, marked the height of Zoroastrian influence within governmental structures, establishing the religion as an integral component of the state (Tessmann, 2022). In the 7th century, the Sassanid Empire fell with the expansion of Muslim forces, marking a significant shift in Zoroastrianism's societal role. With the loss of governmental authority, Zoroastrian scholars placed greater emphasis on defending and preserving their beliefs. Consequently, a substantial portion of Zoroastrian religious literature was produced post-Sassanid Empire, during the Islamic Caliphate (Choksy, 1987).

The Persian language, a member of the Indo-Iranian subgroup of the Indo-European language family, has evolved through three main historical phases: Old, Middle, and Modern Persian (Windfuhr, 2013). Old Persian was the primary language during the Achaemenid Empire, originating in the Fars region of present-day Iran. Middle Persian, prevalent during the Sassanian period and early Islamic Caliphate, served as the primary language for religious and scholarly texts of that time.

Modern Persian emerged around the 10th and 11th centuries, spreading throughout the remnants of the Sassanian Empire's territory. Surviving Middle Persian texts primarily address Zoroastrian religious themes, covering topics such as philosophy, prophecy, ethics, exhortation, debate, jurisprudence, and law (Daryaee, 2018). As mentioned earlier, during the Sassanian era, religious debates between Zoroastrian jurists and their counterparts from other faiths became increasingly intense. Additionally, significant interpretative differences emerged within the Zoroastrian scholarly community itself. Following the fall of the Sassanian kingdom and the establishment of Islamic rule in former Zoroastrian territories, numerous questions arose concerning religious laws and practices. This trend began under the Sassanians, where various Zoroastrian legal scholars debated the correct

Proceedings of the New Horizons in Computational Linguistics for Religious Texts (Coling-Rel), pages 23–41
January 19, 2025.

interpretation of religious law (Janos, 2005).

One of the key works addressing these issues is *Šāyist nē šāyist* (Licit and Illicit), which provides religious rulings on topics such as purity and pollution, offering authoritative perspectives on common questions of the time. This book, along with other Middle Persian texts, reflects Zoroastrian scholars' inquiries into the relationship between Zoroastrian legal principles at the end of the Sassanian period and emerging Islamic jurisprudence (Janos, 2005).

In this study, to the authors' knowledge, machine processing of Book Pahlavi texts is explored for the first time. The selected text is a jurisprudential Zoroastrian text, with the goal of uncovering semantic relationships between words and phrases within the text. Word embedding methods were applied for this purpose. It is important to note that Pahlavi is an extinct and extremely under-resourced language[1], which poses unique challenges for machine processing.

To embed words in the text, a Book Pahlavi corpus was prepared, and word embeddings were generated from this corpus. To evaluate the embeddings, a dataset of vocabulary pairs was created, allowing for the comparison of different methods. Based on this comparative dataset, the optimal method and hyperparameter settings were selected. Using these models, semantic analysis of words in the Pahlavi legal text was performed, representing, to the authors' knowledge, the first time these processes have been conducted in this context.

We constructed a complex network of words from the *Šāyist nē šāyist* book by representing each word as a node, with edges created based on cosine similarity of their embeddings. Analyzing structural properties such as degree distribution, clustering coefficient, and degree centrality enabled us to explore word relationships and semantic patterns, offering deeper insights into this extremely under-resourced language.

2 Related Work

2.1 Middle Persian Language (Pahlavi)

Middle Persian, or Pahlavi, was the language used by Zoroastrian scholars for religious texts during the Sassanian period and the early Islamic Caliphate. At the same time, it was also employed for Christian and Manichaean writings, and Sassanian inscriptions (Boyce, 1990). However, since this article focuses specifically on Zoroastrian religious texts in the Pahlavi language, these other areas will not be discussed, despite their importance in the overall corpus of Pahlavi literature.

The Pahlavi language was written in various scripts, all derived from the Aramaic script, which served as the official court language during part of the Achaemenid period. One of these scripts is Manichaean, developed by the Prophet Mani, and several texts written in this script have survived (Goshtasb et al., 2021). Another is Pazand, written in the Avestan alphabet, introduced to make Zoroastrian texts in Pahlavi more accessible, as the original Pahlavi script posed challenges for readers of Avestan. The Pahlavi inscription script (MacKenzie, 2014), used for Sassanian inscriptions, consists of separate letters. Finally, the Pahlavi book script, used specifically for Zoroastrian religious writings, is the primary focus of this article (Cereti et al., 2005).

The Book Pahlavi language presents complexities at multiple levels. One challenge is that certain letters are connected through ligatures, making them difficult to read. Additionally, many letters in this script are ambiguous, allowing a single word to be interpreted in several different ways. This characteristic has led to multiple interpretations of Pahlavi Zoroastrian texts. Furthermore, adjacent letters often form shapes that can resemble various sequences of letters, adding further layers of interpretative difficulty. Another significant issue arises from the fact that Book Pahlavi is an extinct language that has not been spoken for centuries. Consequently, there are substantial disagreements over the meanings of certain words. Like many other languages, Book Pahlavi contains ambiguity in word meanings, with some words exhibiting homonymy or polysemy. At the sentence level, additional ambiguities make interpreting text meaning particularly challenging. Currently, three primary online sources provide access to Pahlavi texts. The first is the Thesaurus Indogermanischer Sprach- und Textmaterialien (TITUS) [2], which has made a substantial collection of Pahlavi texts publicly available for years (Gippert, 2002). The second source is the Parsig database, (Goshtasb et al.,

[1]The standard terminology refers to it as a low-resource language, though terms like "extinct" and "extremely under-resourced language" (Coto-Solano, 2022b) are also used, as these languages lack an active speaking community and are often ancient. Moreover, there is a shortage of datasets due to the scarcity of remaining resources available for these languages.

[2]https://titus.uni-frankfurt.de/

2021)[3]an open-access web-based resource that provides Pahlavi texts in their original script, along with transliterations, transcriptions, and translations into both Persian and English. Furthermore, since the Book Pahlavi character set has not yet been added to the Unicode standard [4], the texts in Pahlavi script use the site's own custom font.

The third source is the Zoroastrian Middle Persian Digital Corpus and Dictionary (MPCD) [5], which offers a substantial collection of Pahlavi texts that have been transliterated and transcribed (Neuefeind et al., 2022). It also includes English and German translations of these texts, as well as a Pahlavi-English dictionary. Notably, the MPCD provides a REST API on its website, allowing easy access to its data sources. Consequently, this research utilizes the MPCD database as a primary source of information.

2.2 Word Embedding Methods

Word embedding is a type of shallow neural network widely used in Natural Language Processing (NLP) tasks (Torregrossa et al., 2021). In this approach, words are represented as vectors and mapped to a lower-dimensional latent space that preserves semantic properties. Within this space, words with similar meanings are located close to one another, facilitating the capture of semantic relationships (Patil et al., 2023).

In this study, we use two popular static word embedding models: Word2Vec and FastText. Word2Vec (Mikolov et al., 2013) is a static word embedding algorithm that can be implemented with two different models: Continuous Bag of Words (CBOW) and Skip-Gram (SG). The core idea behind this algorithm is that words appearing in similar contexts are likely to have similar meanings. However, Word2Vec does not capture word order within a sentence, treating each word as an independent unit. In contrast, FastText (Bojanowski et al., 2017) incorporates subword information by representing each word as a set of character n-grams, making it sensitive to word morphology and capable of handling rare and misspelled words.

2.3 Word Embedding and Evaluations in Low-Resource Languages

Evaluations in word embeddings for low-resource languages is more challenging than for high-resource languages, as these models require large text corpora, which are often unavailable for low-resource languages (Arppe et al., 2023). However, studies have demonstrated promising results even with limited datasets for such languages (Coto-Solano, 2022a). While word embedding evaluation in high-resource languages is widely studied and supported by numerous evaluation benchmarks, it remains a challenging task in low-resource languages (Ngomane et al., 2023).

Two primary evaluation methods exist: intrinsic and extrinsic. Intrinsic evaluation includes techniques such as analogy and categorization tasks; in low-resource languages, OddOneOut and Top-k are particularly common (Stringham and Izbicki, 2020). Extrinsic methods involve using word embeddings within an NLP application (e.g., text classification) and evaluating performance based on the application's outcomes. However, since this study does not apply word embeddings in a specific extrinsic task, extrinsic evaluation is beyond our scope. Different evaluation methods have been successfully applied to a range of low-resource languages, yielding insightful results (Coto-Solano, 2022a; Ngomane et al., 2023; Lugli et al., 2022; Lakmal et al., 2020).

2.4 Texts and Complex Networks

Representing texts as graphs, such as knowledge graphs (Chen et al., 2020), is not a new concept. Previous works have also utilized complex network representations of text and applied statistical analyses, such as (Ferraz de Arruda et al., 2018), (Stanisz et al., 2024). One challenge with most complex network analysis algorithms is their high computational complexity, which makes them impractical for very large datasets. However, in our study, we focus on Pahlavi, an extinct and extremely under-resourced language, where available data is limited. This allows us to construct and perform complex network analyses, such as calculating clustering coefficients (Holland and Leinhardt, 1971), (Soffer and Vazquez, 2005) and degree centrality distributions (Zhang and Luo, 2017), to gain a deeper understanding of the language's features in written texts.

3 Methodology

In this paper, we first examine various word embedding methodologies applied to Pahlavi, an extinct and extremely under-resourced language in

[3]https://www.parsigdatabase.com/
[4]https://www.unicode.org/standard/unsupported.html
[5]https://www.mpcorpus.org/

Table 1: This table summarizes the key characteristics of the Pahlavi texts analyzed in this study, including the file names, total lines, total tokens, unique tokens, average sentence length, and the length of the longest sentence in each text. The data highlights the variability in text length and complexity, as well as differences in token diversity across the texts.

File Name	Total Lines	Total Tokens	Unique Tokens	Avg Sentence Length	Longest Sentence
Great Bundahišn	2,393	36,894	4,343	15.42	339
Dādestān ī dēnīg	1,144	18,278	3,325	15.98	138
Dādestān ī mēnōy ī xrad	737	10,887	1,672	14.77	98
Dēnkard 3	2,472	80,507	7,747	32.57	288
Dēnkard 6	2,382	27,612	2,329	11.59	45
Dēnkard 8	1,031	23,577	3,088	22.87	102
Dēnkard 9	1,019	35,627	3,811	34.96	318
Hazār dādestān	1,743	38,750	1,751	22.23	131
Nāmagīhā ī manuščihr	343	11,001	2,028	32.07	276
Nērangestān	2,525	30,114	3,739	11.93	100
Pahlavi Wīdēwdād	3,404	53,448	4,039	15.70	131
Pahlavi Yasna	2,832	58,649	3,663	20.71	228
Rivāyat of Ādurfarnbay	1,086	12,341	1,286	11.36	90
Šāyist nē šāyist	1,320	16,575	2,061	12.56	73
Wizīdagīhā ī zādspram	913	18,240	3,053	19.98	128
Zand ī pargard ī juddēwdād	3,015	35,600	2,641	11.81	52

which most surviving texts center around religious themes. Given that this is the first study of its kind on Pahlavi, there is no comparable prior research; therefore, we conducted our own evaluation tasks to determine the most effective embedding approach, as detailed in the following sections.

Additionally, we investigate the religious text *Šāyist nē šāyist*, a Zoroastrian Middle Persian compilation of diverse laws and customs concerning sin, ritual purity, and various ceremonial and religious practices (Müller, 1880). Using the most effective embeddings identified through our optimized hyperparameters, we construct a complex network of nodes and edges for this text, applying network analysis to illuminate its structural features. This process illustrates how computational methods can provide a more in-depth examination of this text.

3.1 Data Collection and Preparation

As previously noted, Book Pahlavi texts are written in a connected script that is challenging to read, and this alphabet is not yet supported by the Unicode standard. Consequently, the source[6] used in this study provides transcriptions of the texts rather than the original Book Pahlavi script. Thus, the input files of the analyzed texts contain transcriptions rather than the original Book Pahlavi characters. Table 1 presents key information and specifications of the texts used in this study.

The preliminary analysis of Table 1 indicates that the *Šāyist nē šāyist* text lacks sufficient volume to yield reliable results using various word embedding methods, a limitation confirmed during implementation. Consequently, other accessible Pahlavi texts with an adequate word count were utilized in this study. Tokenization of the texts was straightforward, as words were already separated by spaces. After preparing the text corpus, a method was needed to evaluate various word embedding techniques. This presented unique challenges in the context of the Pahlavi language, as no prior studies exist in this area. Using English benchmark datasets, such as *WordSim353*, was not effective. Pahlavi texts primarily focus on the Zoroastrian religion, and *Šāyist nē šāyist* specifically addresses religious rulings within Zoroastrianism. Although most words in these texts can be translated into English, their semantic similarity rarely aligns with the types of semantic relationships found in datasets like *WordSim353*. Following these considerations, this research employs a set of paired vocabulary items divided into two categories: related and unrelated words. The first category includes related words, encompassing several types: relational nouns and adjectives, such as *pašm* (wool) and *pašmēn* (woolen); singular and plural forms, like *yašt* (a type of prayer) and *yaštan* (praying); compound nouns and their root nouns, such as *dād* (justice) and *dādestān* (judgment); and synonyms, like *mōy* (hair) and *nāxun* (nail). The second category consists of unrelated words, for which it is expected that their generated vectors will not be similar. A total of 54 word pairs were selected

[6] https://www.mpcorpus.org/

and used to compare the performance of various methods and hyperparameter settings.

3.2 Word Embeddings

We conducted experiments on our corpus, as shown in Table 1, using two word embedding methodologies: Word2Vec (Mikolov et al., 2013) and FastText (Bojanowski et al., 2017). We tested various hyperparameters, including vector size, window size, and the Skip-Gram model. The results are presented in Section 4.

One common approach for word embedding in low-resource languages is Cross-lingual Word Embedding, where a high-resource language is used as the primary source to support a language with limited resources (Ngomane et al., 2023). This method has been successfully applied to many low-resource languages, yielding promising results. However, a key consideration for Zoroastrian texts in Pahlavi is that the word similarities between Zoroastrian religious concepts are vastly different from those in high-resource languages. Therefore, this approach is not pursued in this study.

3.3 From Text to Networks

Inspired by (Ferraz de Arruda et al., 2018), we developed our own text representation in a network format to enable more detailed analysis of the chapters of the *Šāyist nē šāyist* book, aiming to investigate its features more thoroughly. We define a graph $G = (V, E)$, where each node $v \in V$ represents a unique word in the corpus. The edges $e_{ij} \in E$ between words v_i and v_j are based on the similarity of their embeddings, as calculated with cosine similarity.

For each word v, its embedding $\mathbf{w}$ can be generated using either the Word2Vec or FastText model.

3.3.1 Cosine Similarity and Edge Creation

To determine whether an edge e_{ij} should exist between two words v_i and v_j, we calculate the cosine similarity between their embeddings $\mathbf{w_i}$ and $\mathbf{w_j}$:

$$cosine\_similarity(v_i, v_j) = \frac{\mathbf{w_i} \cdot \mathbf{w_j}}{\|\mathbf{w_i}\| \|\mathbf{w_j}\|}$$

An edge e_{ij} is created between v_i and v_j if their cosine similarity is greater than a threshold T_M. In our experiments, we set T_M to values of 0.5, 0.65 and 0.75, but any other threshold can also be used based on the specific analysis requirements.

3.3.2 Graph Preprocessing

Due to the fact that nodes v with no connecting edges, e_{ij}, which are isolated, were removed from the graph, as our focus was on analyzing words with similar meanings. Additionally, nodes v with a degree of $deg(v) \leq 2$ were also removed to focus the analysis on more significant nodes.

3.4 Analytic of Complex Networks

In the analysis of complex networks, several key metrics help us understand the structure and significance of nodes within the graph. In this section, we define and calculate the degree distribution, clustering coefficient, and degree centrality for the network we constructed from *Šāyist nē šāyist* book.

3.4.1 Degree Distribution

In the context of our text-based network for the book, the degree of a node v (representing a unique word) is defined as the number of edges incident to v, which corresponds to the number of similar-word connections it has within the network. The degree distribution, denoted by $P(k)$, represents the probability that a randomly chosen word node has exactly k connections (Barabási, 2013). Mathematically, it can be expressed as:

$$P(k) = \frac{V_k}{V}$$

where:

- V_k is the number of nodes in the graph with degree k,
- V is the total number of nodes in the graph.

3.4.2 Clustering Coefficient

The clustering coefficient is a measure of how closely nodes in a network tend to form clusters. It quantifies the probability that the neighbors of a given node are also connected to one another, which can help in identifying communities within the network (Holland and Leinhardt, 1971), (Soffer and Vazquez, 2005). The words v that are strongly connected within communities due to their similarity, as indicated by the edges, are expected to have meaningful connections with other words.

For a given node v (representing a word in the text), the local clustering coefficient $C(v)$ is defined as:

$$C(v) = \frac{2e_v}{k_v(k_v - 1)}$$

where:

- e_v is the number of edges between the neighbors of node v,
- k_v is the degree of node v, or the number of neighbors connected to v.

The global clustering coefficient C of the entire network is then calculated as the average of the local clustering coefficients for all nodes:

$$C = \frac{1}{N} \sum_{v \in V} C(v)$$

where N is the total number of nodes in the network and V is the set of all nodes.

3.4.3 Degree Centrality

Degree centrality (Zhang and Luo, 2017) reflects the importance and influence of a node in a network, which in our case is a word, based on its connections that indicate similarity in meaning to other words. It highlights how significant a word is within the text by analyzing its semantic relations to others. It can be defined as:

$$C_D(v) = \frac{k_v}{V - 1}$$

where:

- k_v is the degree of node v,
- V is the total number of nodes in the network.

4 Experiments

In this section, we first experiment with different word embeddings, then construct a complex network using these embeddings. We apply network-based metrics to extract features from the *Šāyist nē šāyist* book, and subsequently analyze and discuss the results.

4.1 Results

In Table 2, we experimented with various configurations, including window size, vector size, and the SG value, to compare the performance of different word embeddings for FastText and Word2Vec, evaluating their effectiveness for the first time in Pahlavi (Bojanowski et al., 2017)(Mikolov et al., 2013).

- **Window size**: By defining the range of words that are taken into account around a target word, this parameter enables the model to record contextual information.

Table 2: Accuracy Comparison between FastText and Word2Vec Embeddings in percentage. All Word2Vec accuracy results are bolded. The best accuracy values for FastText and Word2Vec underlined. SG represents the Skip-Gram model (where 1 indicates Skip-Gram and 0 indicates CBOW). The vector size denotes the dimensionality of word embeddings, and the window size determines the range of neighboring words used for context.

Vector	Window	SG	FastText	Word2Vec
25	2	0	57.96	**64.40**
25	2	1	59.13	**67.78**
25	5	0	65.33	**68.88**
25	5	1	63.70	**70.66**
25	10	0	<u>71.27</u>	**<u>74.36</u>**
25	10	1	66.12	**70.16**
50	2	0	57.52	**62.86**
50	2	1	59.19	**68.52**
50	5	0	63.77	**68.84**
50	5	1	63.10	**68.74**
50	10	0	70.57	**73.51**
50	10	1	67.02	**67.90**
100	2	0	57.14	**60.52**
100	2	1	59.01	**67.97**
100	5	0	63.58	**67.84**
100	5	1	63.64	**69.69**
100	10	0	68.50	**73.28**
100	10	1	66.92	**68.25**

- **Vector size**: This is a reference to the word embeddings' dimensionality, or number of features.
- **SG (Skip-Gram) value**: The model type is specified by this option. The Skip-Gram model, which forecasts the words that surround a target word, is indicated by a value of 1. The Continuous Bag of Words (CBOW) model, on the other hand, predicts a target word based on its surrounding words and has a value of 0.

In the *Šāyist nē šāyist* book, a religious text containing 23 chapters, we selected and analyzed three chapters. The examination of the remaining chapters is similar in nature. These three chapters were chosen because they are conceptually related while also distinct from the others. The selected chapters include: the first chapter, which discusses sins; the third chapter, which addresses the rulings on women; and the twenty chapter , which focuses on advice and admonitions. The analysis is presented in a segmented manner with corresponding graphs which explained in Section 3.3 , and the results for chapters 1 in Fig. 1 and 20 in Fig. 2 are shown using Word2Vec, which demonstrates the

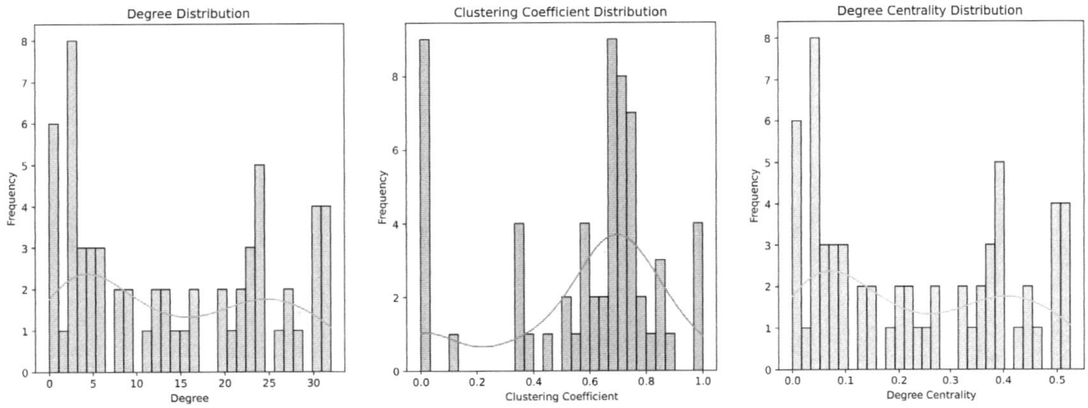

Figure 1: Degree distribution of the *Šāyist nē šāyist* book chapters (chapter 1), with $T_M = 0.75$, Word2Vec.

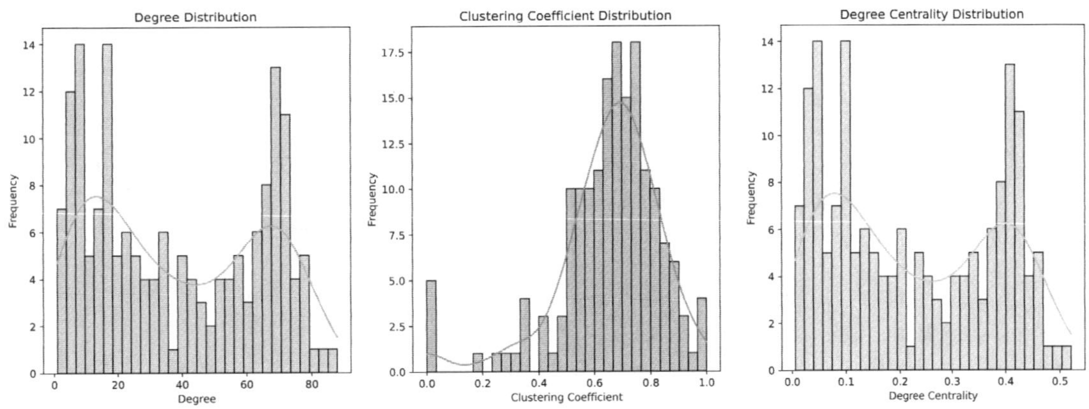

Figure 2: Clustering coefficient of the *Šāyist nē šāyist* book chapters (chapter 20), with $T_M = 0.75$, Word2Vec.

best performance with optimal hyperparameters in Table 2.

4.2 Discussion and Analysis

For the word embeddings presented in Table 2, we expected the best results when the vector size was minimized, the window size was maximized, and the Skip-Gram model was used. An interesting observation is that, for the Pahlavi language, the same hyperparameters in both Word2Vec and FastText produced the best results. Although Word2Vec slightly outperformed FastText in accuracy by approximately 3%, both models showed similar performance with these settings.

For a more detailed analysis, we examined the t-SNE visualization for both embeddings.The t-SNE visualization of FastText embeddings in two dimensions demonstrates this model's ability to capture the morphological structure of words in Pahlavi. In Fig. 3 in left side, a section of the t-SNE plot highlights words with the common suffix *ān*. For instance, *framān* (order) appears close to *mardōmān* (humans) in the embedding space, even though they are not semantically related. This outcome reflects FastText's sensitivity to the *ān* suffix, a common plural suffix in Pahlavi, which is frequently used in both singular and plural forms in our evaluation dataset. In another section of the t-SNE plot, shown in Fig. 3 in right side, words with the suffix *išn* are clustered near one another, forming a distinct group. While some words in this cluster have related meanings, others do not, reflecting the model's tendency to group words with similar morphological endings, regardless of semantic similarity.

The t-SNE visualization of Word2Vec embeddings in two dimensions demonstrates that this model can position semantically related words adjacently on the 2D map. In Fig. 4, *gētī* (the material world) and *mēnōy* (the spiritual world) appear close to each other, reflecting their related meanings. Another example is *yazadān* (god) and

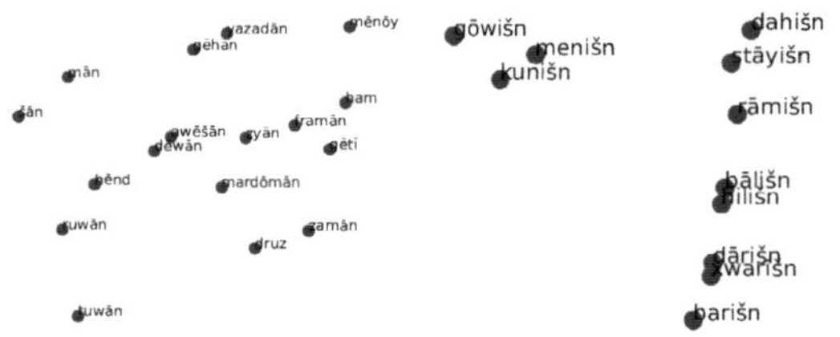

Figure 3: Parts of t-SNE visualization of FastText embeddings in two dimensions

zarduxšt ('Zarathustra'), which are also placed near one another due to their semantic association.

Figure 4: A part of t-SNE visualization of Word2Vec embeddings in two dimensions

The complete t-SNE visualization for both embeddings is provided in Appendix A.

By analyzing the book chapters, it is evident that Chapters 1 and 20 show significant differences in network structures and parameters. As shown in Figures 1 and 2, the clustering coefficient differs notably between these two chapters, indicating stronger, more meaningful connections and closer word associations in Chapter 20 compared to Chapter 1. Additionally, when we analyze degree centrality, we observe that words with stronger influence on contextual meaning appear more frequently in Chapter 20 than in Chapter 1. Moreover, for the degree distribution, high-degree words occur more frequently and in greater numbers in Chapter 20, suggesting that the words in Chapter 20 are more related and specific. In contrast, the words in Chapter 1 appear to be more general and less related to one another. All the graphs for these chapters can be found in the Appendix B.

5 Conclusions

In this paper, we present the first evaluation of word embeddings for Pahlavi, an extinct and extremely under-resourced Middle Persian language. After identifying suitable embedding parameters for this language, we constructed a complex network based on the chapters of the *Šāyist nē šāyist*, a religious book. The structure of this book, with its notably small chapters, facilitates easier analysis of its network. We extracted deeper features from each chapter, which could contribute to understanding this extinct language, particularly given the scarcity of remaining resources. While studies on high-resource languages often struggle with large graphs due to their high time complexity, our approach is different: the limited amount of available texts in Pahlavi allows us to leverage complex network analysis to gain a deeper understanding of the language, despite the typical challenges posed by big graphs in other contexts.

6 Limitations

In this study, an attempt was made, to the authors' knowledge, to embed words in the Pahlavi language for the first time, though significant limitations exist in this area. Zoroastrian text sources in Pahlavi face a lack of Unicode standardization, so Pahlavi texts are either unavailable in Pahlavi script across online sources or are presented in a custom font specific to the hosting site, complicating accessibility. This study employs transliteration, which places the challenges of word interpretation in the Pahlavi script onto the transliterator, potentially introducing inconsistencies. Like any language, Pahlavi has a unique morphological structure that requires stemming for each word. Although stemming has been extensively studied in modern Persian (a language closely related to Pahlavi), it remains complex, and thus this study does not address stemming.

Another major issue in the Pahlavi language is the lack of any dataset containing related or unrelated word groups with graded similarity or difference, as exists in English and modern Persian. Furthermore, other data types essential for evaluating word embedding methods, such as analogy datasets, are also absent in Pahlavi. This study presents a preliminary evaluation framework to compare different embedding models and adjust their hyperparameters; however, this dataset is basic and serves only for initial comparisons among methods. Consequently, it is evident that a more comprehensive dataset will be necessary for further progress in this field.

References

Antti Arppe, Andrew Neitsch, Daniel Dacanay, Jolene Poulin, Daniel Hieber, and Atticus Harrigan. 2023.

Finding words that aren't there: Using word embeddings to improve dictionary search for low-resource languages. In *Proceedings of the Workshop on Natural Language Processing for Indigenous Languages of the Americas (AmericasNLP)*, pages 144–155.

Albert-László Barabási. 2013. Network science. *Philosophical Transactions of the Royal Society A: Mathematical, Physical and Engineering Sciences*, 371(1987):20120375.

Piotr Bojanowski, Edouard Grave, Armand Joulin, and Tomas Mikolov. 2017. Enriching word vectors with subword information. *Transactions of the association for computational linguistics*, 5:135–146.

Mary Boyce. 1990. *Textual sources for the study of Zoroastrianism*. University of Chicago Press.

Mary Boyce. 2017. Zoroastrianism. *A new handbook of living religions*, pages 236–260.

Carlo Giovanni Cereti et al. 2005. A middle persian dictionary: Project proposal. In *Orientalia Romana VIII: Middle Iranian Lexicography*, pages 181–190. IsIAO.

Xiaojun Chen, Shengbin Jia, and Yang Xiang. 2020. A review: Knowledge reasoning over knowledge graph. *Expert systems with applications*, 141:112948.

Jamsheed K Choksy. 1987. Zoroastrians in muslim iran: selected problems of coexistence and interaction during the early medieval period. *Iranian Studies*, 20(1):17–30.

Rolando Coto-Solano. 2022a. Evaluating word embeddings in extremely under-resourced languages: A case study in bribri. In *Proceedings of the 29th International Conference on Computational Linguistics*, pages 4455–4467.

Rolando Coto-Solano. 2022b. Evaluating word embeddings in extremely under-resourced languages: A case study in bribri. In *Proceedings of the 29th International Conference on Computational Linguistics*, pages 4455–4467.

Touraj Daryaee. 2018. Middle persian (pahlavi). *A Companion to Late Antique Literature*, pages 103–121.

Henrique Ferraz de Arruda, Filipi Nascimento Silva, Vanessa Queiroz Marinho, Diego Raphael Amancio, and Luciano da Fontoura Costa. 2018. Representation of texts as complex networks: a mesoscopic approach. *Journal of Complex Networks*, 6(1):125–144.

Jost Gippert. 2002. Der titus-server: Grundlagen eines multilingualen online-retrieval-systems. *Historical Social Research/Historische Sozialforschung*, 27(1 (99):207–214.

Farzaneh Goshtasb, Masood Ghayoomi, and Nadia Hajipour Artarani. 2021. Corpus-based analysis of middle persian texts based on the pārsīg database. *Language Studies*, 12(1):255–280.

Paul W Holland and Samuel Leinhardt. 1971. Transitivity in structural models of small groups. *Comparative group studies*, 2(2):107–124.

Jany Janos. 2005. The four sources of law in zoroastrian and islamic jurisprudence. *Islamic Law and Society*, 12(3):291–332.

Dimuthu Lakmal, Surangika Ranathunga, Saman Peramuna, and Indu Herath. 2020. Word embedding evaluation for sinhala. In *Proceedings of the Twelfth Language Resources and Evaluation Conference*, pages 1874–1881.

Ligeia Lugli, Matej Martinc, Andraž Pelicon, and Senja Pollak. 2022. Embeddings models for buddhist sanskrit. In *Proceedings of the Thirteenth Language Resources and Evaluation Conference*, pages 3861–3871.

David Neil MacKenzie. 2014. *A concise Pahlavi dictionary*. Routledge.

Tomas Mikolov, Ilya Sutskever, Kai Chen, Greg S Corrado, and Jeff Dean. 2013. Distributed representations of words and phrases and their compositionality. *Advances in neural information processing systems*, 26.

Friedrich Max Müller. 1880. *The Sacred Books of the East: Pahlavi texts (pt. 1), translated by EW West*, volume 5. Clarendon Press, Oxford, UK.

Claes Neuefeind, Francisco Mondaca, Øyvind Eide, Iris Colditz, Thomas Jügel, Kianoosh Rezania, Arash Zeini, Alberto Cantera, Chagai Emanuel, and Shaul Shaked. 2022. Das zoroastrische mittelpersische digitales corpus und wörterbuch (mpcd). In *DHd*.

Derwin Ngomane, Rooweither Mabuya, Jade Abbott, and Vukosi Marivate. 2023. Unsupervised cross-lingual word embedding representation for english-isizulu. In *Proceedings of the Fourth workshop on Resources for African Indigenous Languages (RAIL 2023)*, pages 11–17.

Rajvardhan Patil, Sorio Boit, Venkat Gudivada, and Jagadeesh Nandigam. 2023. A survey of text representation and embedding techniques in nlp. *IEEE Access*, 11:36120–36146.

Sara Nadiv Soffer and Alexei Vazquez. 2005. Network clustering coefficient without degree-correlation biases. *Physical Review E—Statistical, Nonlinear, and Soft Matter Physics*, 71(5):057101.

Tomasz Stanisz, Stanisław Drożdż, and Jarosław Kwapień. 2024. Complex systems approach to natural language. *Physics Reports*, 1053:1–84.

Nathan Stringham and Mike Izbicki. 2020. Evaluating word embeddings on low-resource languages. In *Proceedings of the First Workshop on Evaluation and Comparison of NLP Systems*, pages 176–186.

Anna Tessmann. 2022. *The Wiley Blackwell Companion to Zoroastrianism*. John Wiley & Sons.

François Torregrossa, Robin Allesiardo, Vincent Claveau, Nihel Kooli, and Guillaume Gravier. 2021. A survey on training and evaluation of word embeddings. *International journal of data science and analytics*, 11(2):85–103.

Gernot Windfuhr. 2013. *The Iranian Languages*. Routledge.

Junlong Zhang and Yu Luo. 2017. Degree centrality, betweenness centrality, and closeness centrality in social network. In *2017 2nd international conference on modelling, simulation and applied mathematics (MSAM2017)*, pages 300–303. Atlantis press.

A t-SNE visualization

This section presents a complete t-SNE visualization of Word2Vec and FastText.

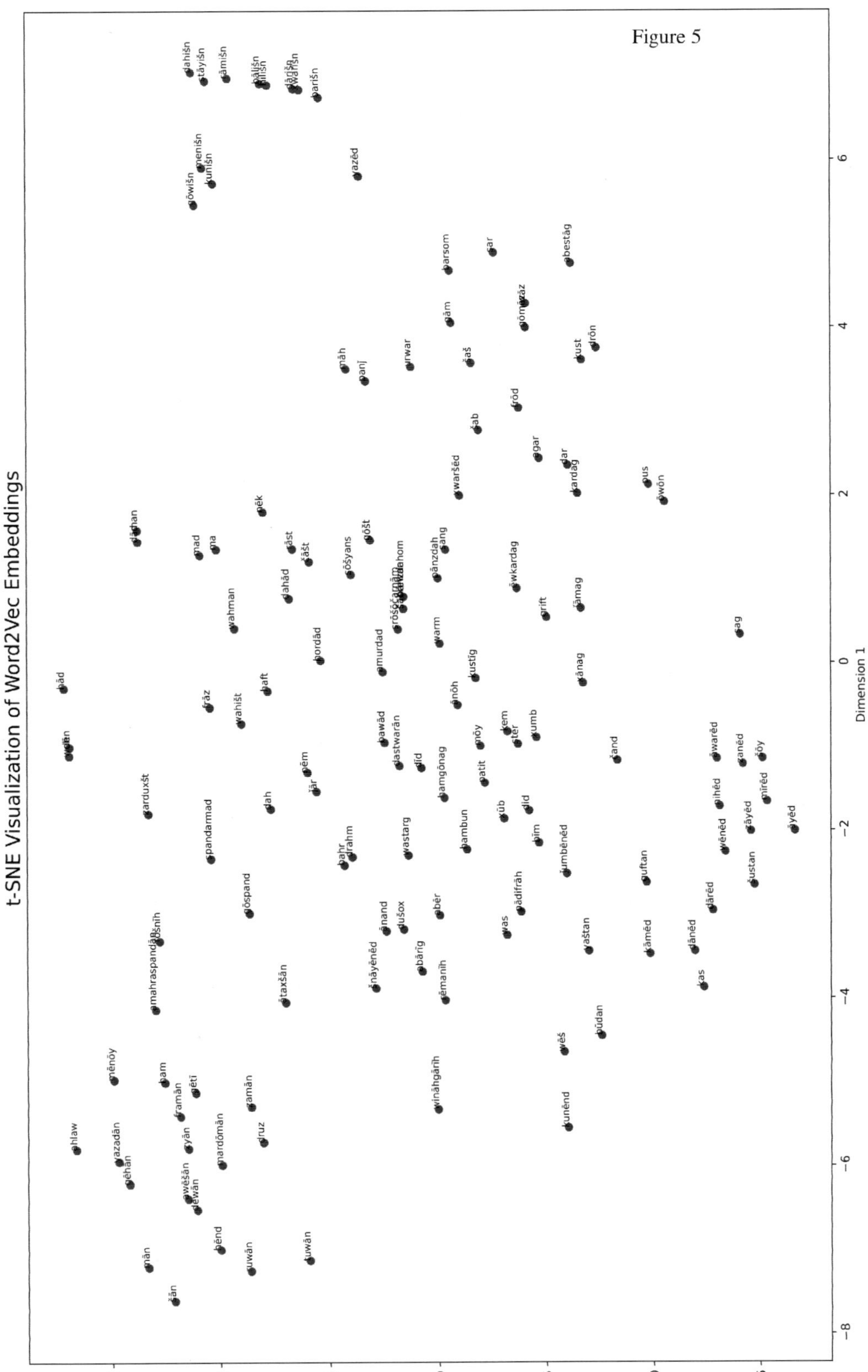
t-SNE Visualization of Word2Vec Embeddings
Dimension 1
Dimension 2

Figure 5

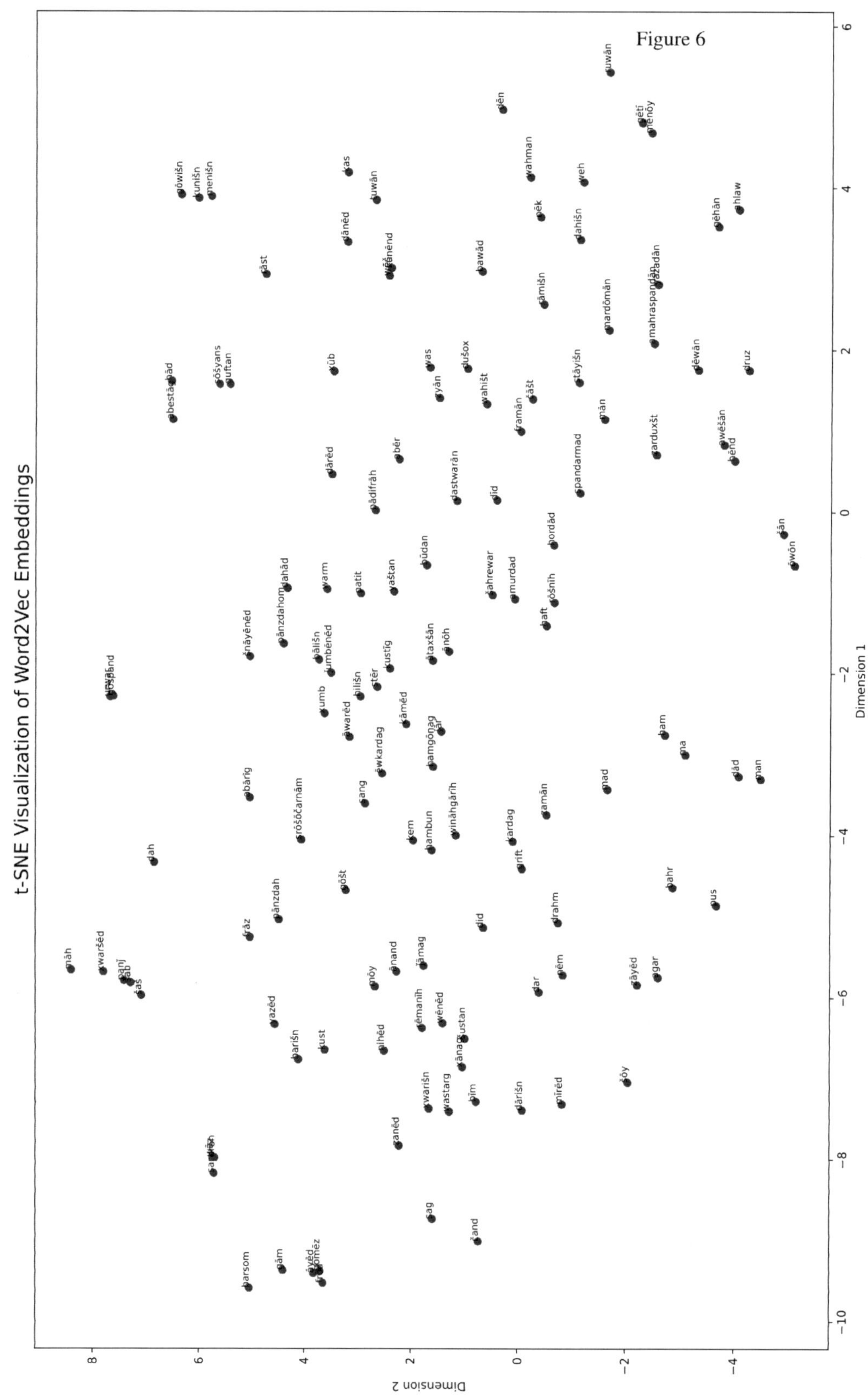
t-SNE Visualization of Word2Vec Embeddings
Dimension 1
Dimension 2
Figure 6

B Network Structures for Chapters 1, 3, and 20 of *Šāyist nē šāyist*

In this appendix, Chapters 1, 3, and 20 of the *Šāyist nē šāyist* book are presented, with similarity values of T_M set to 0.5, 0.65, and 0.75 for edge creation in the complex network. Both Word2Vec and FastText network structures are included.

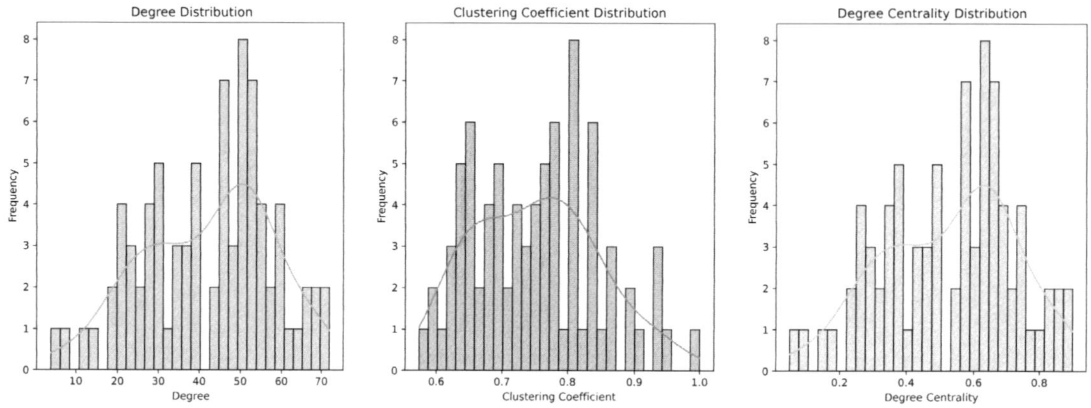

Figure 7: Degree distribution of the *Šāyist nē šāyist* book chapters (chapter 1), with $T_M = 0.5$, Word2Vec.

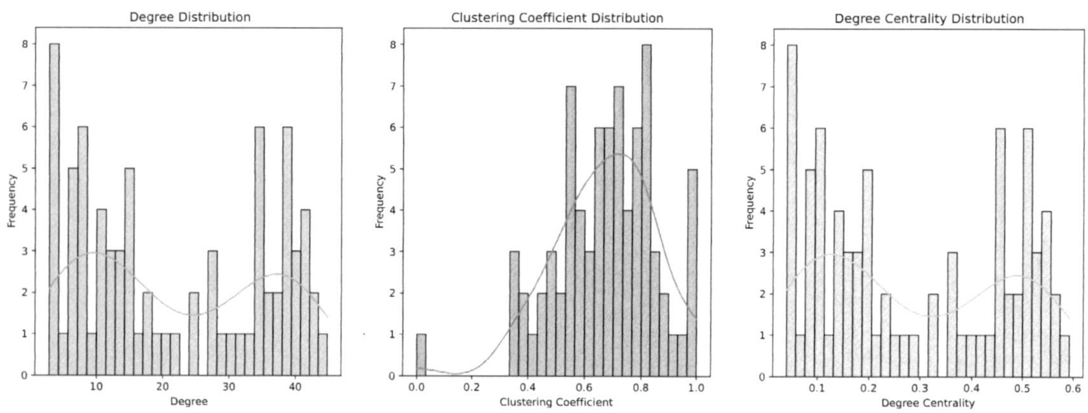

Figure 8: Degree distribution of the *Šāyist nē šāyist* book chapters (chapter 1), with $T_M = 0.65$, Word2Vec.

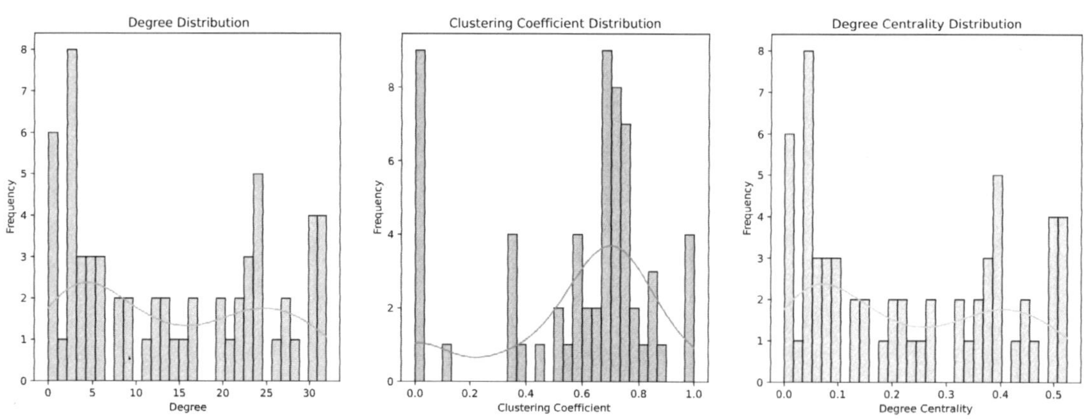

Figure 9: Degree distribution of the *Šāyist nē šāyist* book chapters (chapter 1), with $T_M = 0.75$, Word2Vec.

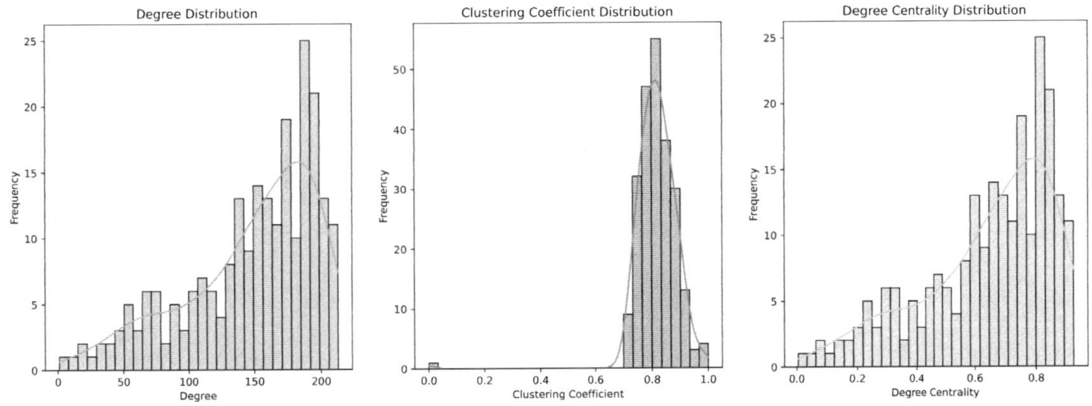

Figure 10: Degree distribution of the *Šāyist nē šāyist* book chapters (chapter 3), with $T_M = 0.5$, Word2Vec.

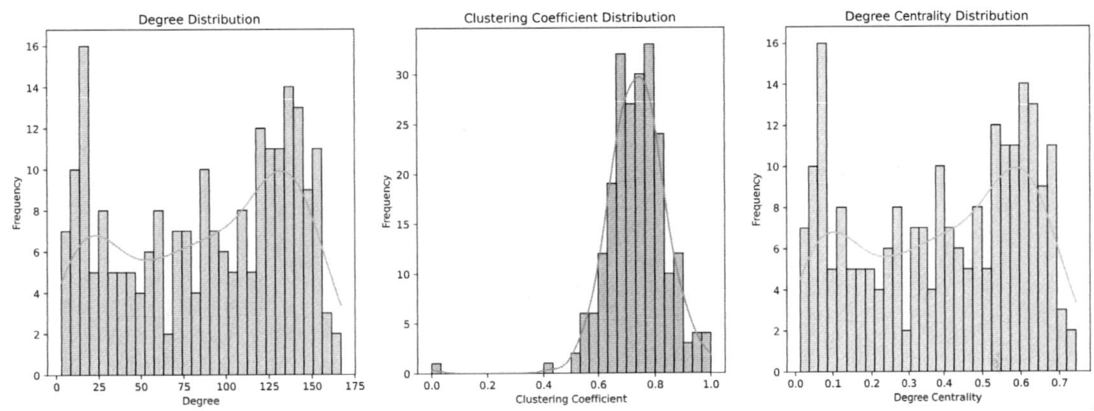

Figure 11: Degree distribution of the *Šāyist nē šāyist* book chapters (chapter 3), with $T_M = 0.65$, Word2Vec.

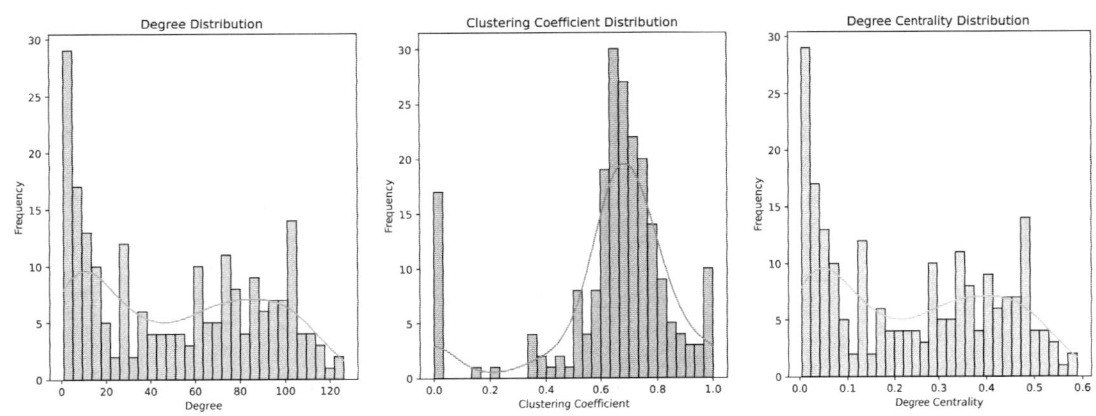

Figure 12: Degree distribution of the *Šāyist nē šāyist* book chapters (chapter 3), with $T_M = 0.75$, Word2Vec.

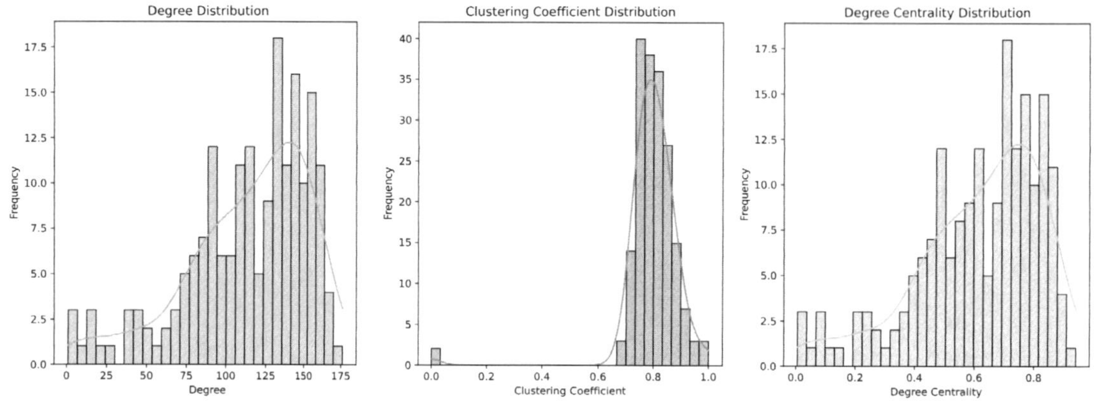

Figure 13: Degree distribution of the *Šāyist nē šāyist* book chapters (chapter 20), with $T_M = 0.5$, Word2Vec.

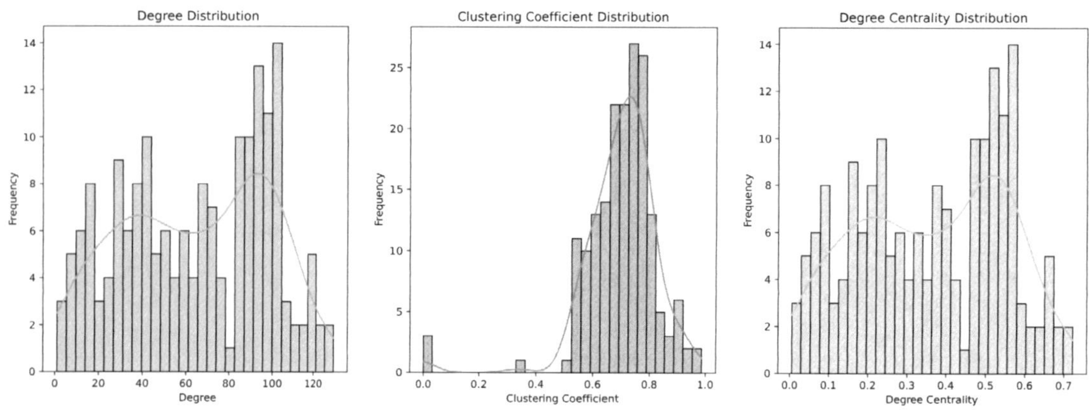

Figure 14: Degree distribution of the *Šāyist nē šāyist* book chapters (chapter 20), with $T_M = 0.65$, Word2Vec.

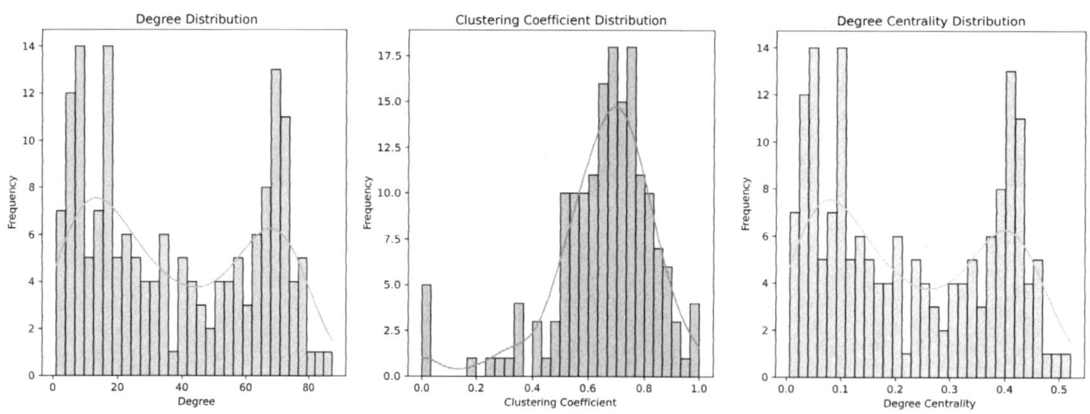

Figure 15: Degree distribution of the *Šāyist nē šāyist* book chapters (chapter 20), with $T_M = 0.75$, Word2Vec.

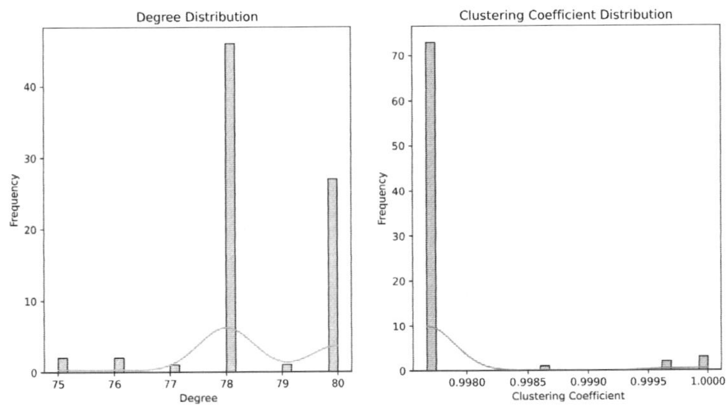

Figure 16: Degree distribution of the *Šāyist nē šāyist* book chapters (chapter 1), with $T_M = 0.5$, FastText.

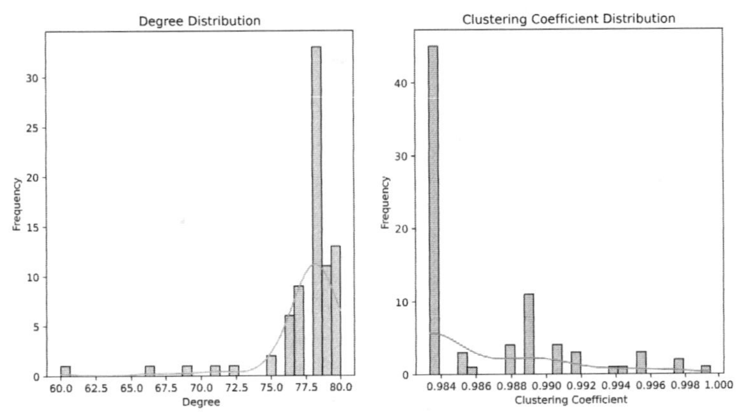

Figure 17: Degree distribution of the *Šāyist nē šāyist* book chapters (chapter 1), with $T_M = 0.65$, FastText.

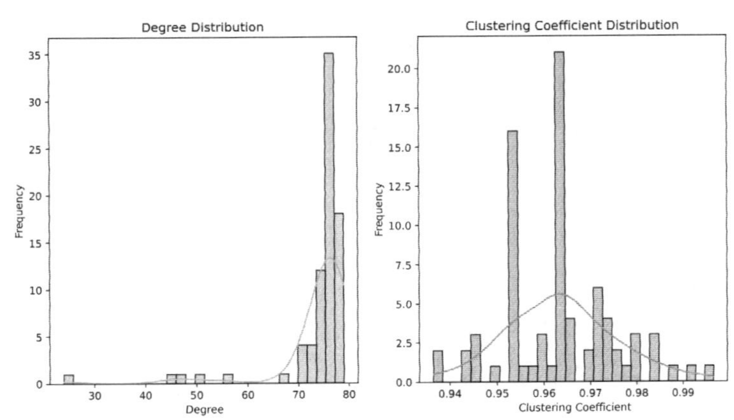

Figure 18: Degree distribution of the *Šāyist nē šāyist* book chapters (chapter 1), with $T_M = 0.75$, FastText.

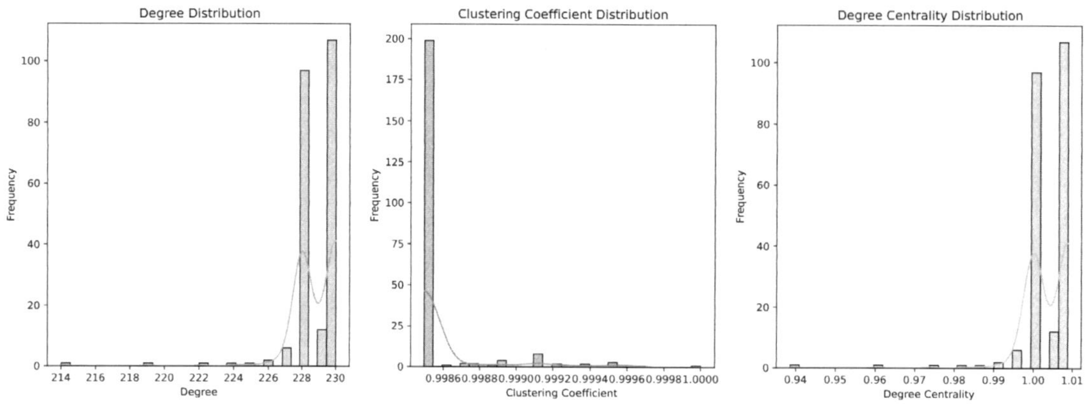

Figure 19: Degree distribution of the *Šāyist nē šāyist* book chapters (chapter 3), with $T_M = 0.5$, FastText.

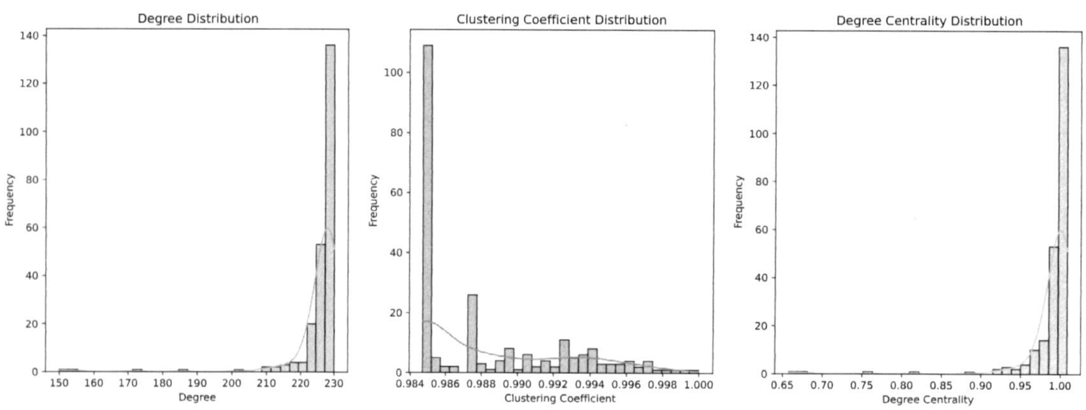

Figure 20: Degree distribution of the *Šāyist nē šāyist* book chapters (chapter 3), with $T_M = 0.65$, FastText.

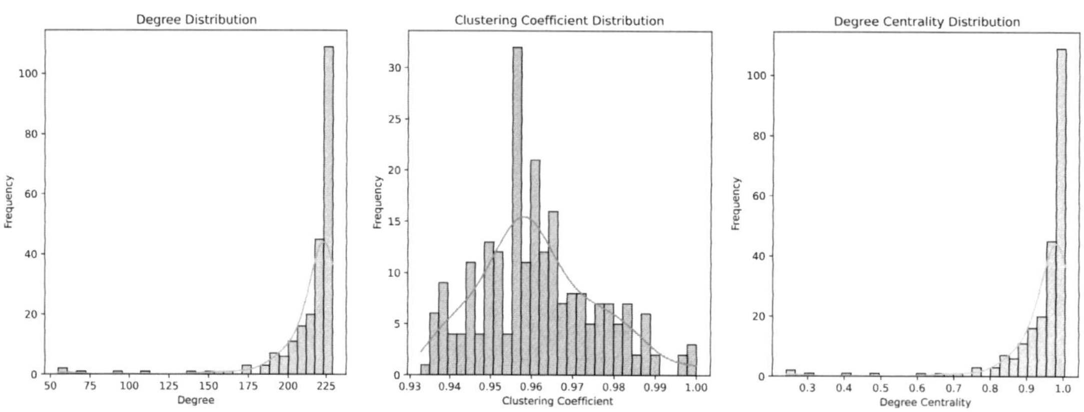

Figure 21: Degree distribution of the *Šāyist nē šāyist* book chapters (chapter 3), with $T_M = 0.75$, FastText.

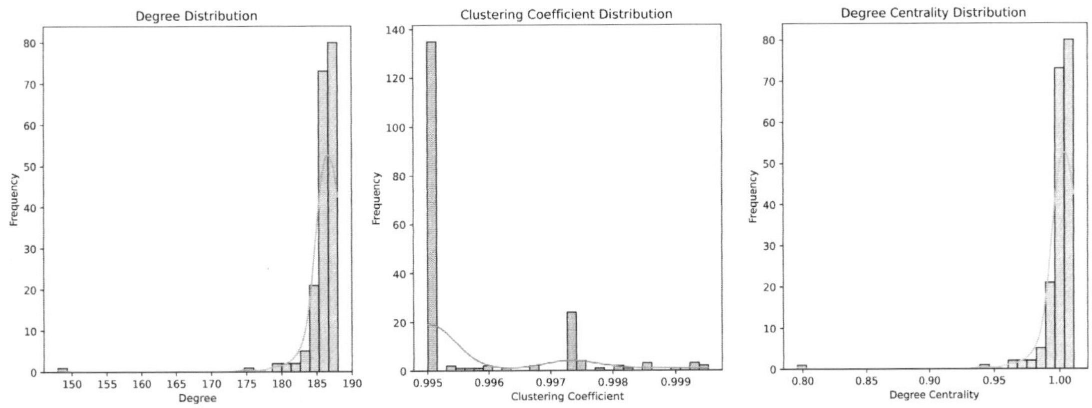

Figure 22: Degree distribution of the *Šāyist nē šāyist* book chapters (chapter 20), with $T_M = 0.5$, FastText.

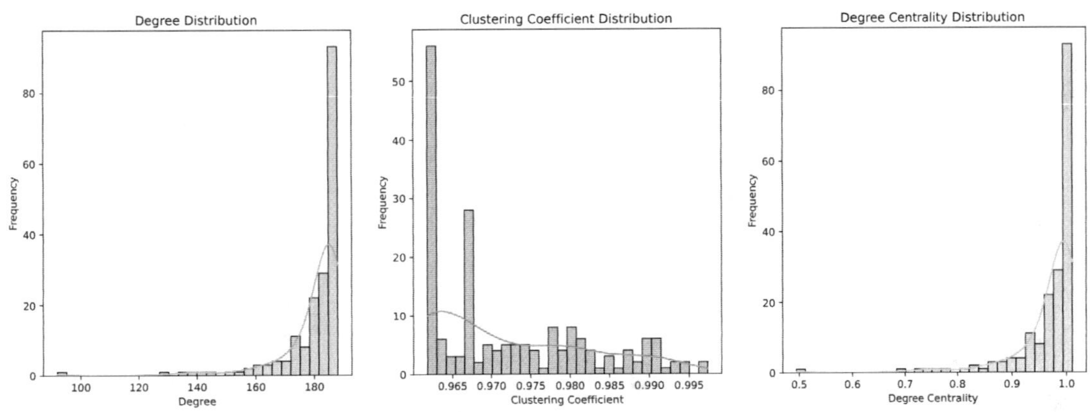

Figure 23: Degree distribution of the *Šāyist nē šāyist* book chapters (chapter 20), with $T_M = 0.65$, FastText.

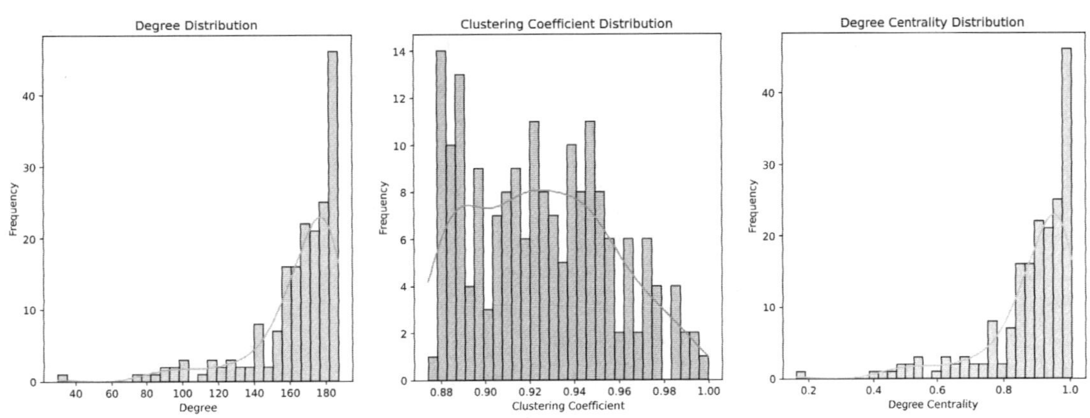

Figure 24: Degree distribution of the *Šāyist nē šāyist* book chapters (chapter 20), with $T_M = 0.75$, FastText.

Multi-stage Training of Bilingual Islamic LLM for Neural Passage Retrieval

Vera Pavlova
rttl labs, UAE
v@rttl.ai

Abstract

This study examines the use of Natural Language Processing (NLP) technology within the Islamic domain, focusing on developing an Islamic neural retrieval model. By leveraging the robust XLM-R_{Base} model, the research employs a language reduction technique to create a lightweight bilingual large language model (LLM). Our approach for domain adaptation addresses the unique challenges faced in the Islamic domain, where substantial in-domain corpora exist only in Arabic while limited in other languages, including English.

The work utilizes a multi-stage training process for retrieval models, incorporating large retrieval datasets, such as MS MARCO, and smaller, in-domain datasets to improve retrieval performance. Additionally, we have curated an in-domain retrieval dataset in English by employing data augmentation techniques and involving a reliable Islamic source. This approach enhances the domain-specific dataset for retrieval, leading to further performance gains.

The findings suggest that combining domain adaptation and a multi-stage training method for the bilingual Islamic neural retrieval model enables it to outperform monolingual models on downstream retrieval tasks.[1]

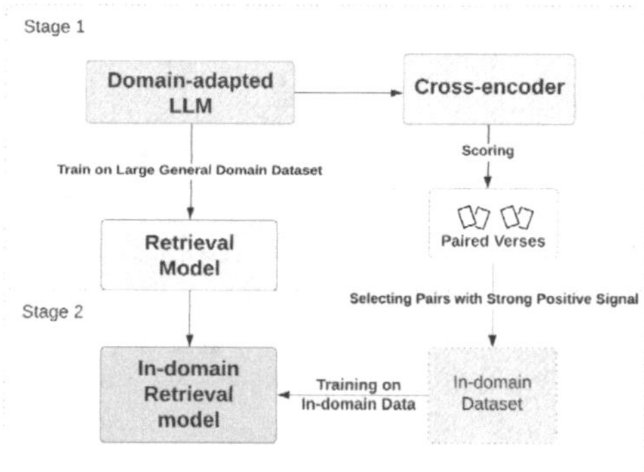

Figure 1: Multi-stage training of Islamic neural retrieval model.

1 Introduction

Despite the advancements in NLP technology, its application in the Islamic domain remains relatively limited. While various fields have harnessed NLP for tasks such as sentiment analysis, language translation, and chatbot development, the rich and complex textual resources within Islamic literature, such as the Holy Qur'an, Hadith, and scholarly articles, have not been fully leveraged.

Information retrieval (IR) plays a crucial role in the exploration of Islamic text. With the vastness of texts spanning centuries, efficient search methods are essential for scholars, researchers, and the general public. The ability to quickly locate specific passages, themes, or authors can significantly enhance understanding and facilitate deeper analysis. Moreover, given the intricate styles and diverse languages in which Islamic texts are written, advanced search tools can help bridge the gap between traditional scholarship and contemporary research needs. Effective retrieval not only saves time but also fosters a richer engagement with the cultural and intellectual heritage contained within Islamic literature (Bashir et al., 2023). One of the significant challenges is the diversity of languages used in Islamic texts, including Arabic, English, Urdu, etc, which complicates the creation of robust NLP tools. Researching and developing multilingual retrieval tools could assist in accessing Islamic literature for Arabic and non-Arabic speakers.

In this work, we study efficient ways to prepare a bilingual Islamic retrieval model. Addressing retrieval in both Arabic and English within the context of Islamic literature offers several significant benefits: firstly, it can increase the accessibility of Islamic literature to a broader audience. Classical

[1]A system is deployed at https://rttl.ai/

Proceedings of the New Horizons in Computational Linguistics for Religious Texts (Coling-Rel), pages 42–52
January 19, 2025.

Arabic (CA) is the language of the Holy Qur'an and plays a crucial role in conducting retrieval tasks involving sacred scripture. English is also widely used for search across various domains, including the Islamic field.

Secondly, the use of multilingual or bilingual models enables cross-lingual transfer, which is crucial when there is insufficient data in some languages. English is a high-resource language, with a wealth of available corpora and pre-trained language models across various domains (Conneau et al., 2020). On the other hand, Arabic has more advantageous resources within the Islamic domain than English due to the availability of large in-domain corpora such as OpenITI (Romanov and Seydi, 2019). To benefit from both languages, we utilize the robust XLM-R_{Base} model, which has undergone extensive training on general domain corpora predominately in English and offers state-of-the-art performance on downstream tasks.

We employ a language reduction technique Abdaoui et al. (2020) that enables the creation of a robust, lightweight bilingual model, preserving most of the performance of the XLM-R_{Base}. This model serves as the backbone for our retrieval system. It is known that retrieval models are sensitive to domain shifts, which can lead to a decline in performance (Thakur et al., 2021b). To address this issue, we perform domain adaptation using available text from Islamic literature and the OpenITI corpus in Arabic.

As a next step, we prepare a retrieval model using a dense retrieval approach (Karpukhin et al., 2020; Izacard et al., 2021). Training a robust retrieval model requires a substantial amount of in-domain labeled data, which is currently not available in the Islamic domain. However, there are large general domain datasets available for training retrieval models. We propose a multi-stage training process for an Islamic neural retrieval model that leverages both the large general domain datasets as well as the small in-domain datasets. (see Figure 1).

Additionally, we enhance our in-domain retrieval dataset in English by employing data augmentation techniques, which further improve the performance of the neural retrieval model. Our experiment showed that this approach improves the result on the evaluation dataset and outperforms strong monolingual baselines.

2 Related Work

Recent studies demonstrate that adapting existing LLMs pre-trained on general corpora for a new domain significantly improves performance on downstream tasks (Lee et al., 2019; Huang et al., 2019). The authors of the SciBERT model (Beltagy et al., 2019) showed that constructing a new Scivocab when pre-training SciBERT further enhances the performance of LLM. While pre-training a domain-specific model from scratch (Gu et al., 2020) allows for the inclusion of domain-specific vocabulary, this approach is costly and often impractical when the domain-specific corpora are limited in size. To avoid the random initialization of weights for new tokens and to expedite the pre-training process Poerner et al. (2020); Sachidananda et al. (2021); Pavlova and Makhlouf (2023) experiment with introducing new vocabulary and pre-training domain-specific models using existing checkpoints.

There are several approaches to reducing model size. Research by Sun et al. (2019), Tang et al. (2019), Sanh et al. (2019), and Li et al. (2020) has demonstrated that distilling transformer-based language models (Vaswani et al., 2017) results in significant size reduction while maintaining adequate performance. Another approach is model quantization, as explored in studies by Guo (2018), Jacob et al. (2017), Bondarenko et al. (2021), and Tian et al. (2023). While quantization can help address model size issues, it often compromises performance.

In contrast, language reduction (Abdaoui et al., 2020) does not lead to substantial performance loss. This method decreases the model size by preserving the encoder weights and only trimming the embedding matrix, eliminating languages that are unnecessary for the specific task at hand.

The survey Zhao et al. (2022) provides a detailed overview of dense retrieval, including various model architectures and training approaches. Other studies focusing on dense retrieval include Karpukhin et al. (2020), Qu et al. (2021), Ren et al. (2021). Thakur et al. (2021a), Wang et al. (2021) and Wang et al. (2022) proposed a data augmentation technique to train retrieval models when there is little data for in-domain training. This approach involves creating synthetic data points that can mimic real in-domain scenarios, enriching the existing dataset, and bridging the gap between limited data availability and the need for high-quality model performance.

3 Bilingual Islamic MLLM

The application of cross-lingual transfer capabilities of MLLMs helped to solve important NLP tasks in low-resource languages (Devlin et al., 2019; Lample and Conneau, 2019). Conneau et al. (2020) introduced the XLM-R and XLM-R_{Base} with an increased model capacity trained on a large CommonCrawls corpus covering 100 languages. He demonstrated that increasing model capacity and adding more languages improves cross-lingual performance on low-resource languages to a certain extent. However, beyond a certain point, the overall performance on both monolingual and cross-lingual benchmarks begin to decline, a notion that he referred to as the "curse of multilinguality."

3.1 Size Reduction of LLM

In this work, we want to explore the performance of the XLM-R_{Base} model after performing the language reduction technique, retaining only two languages (English and Arabic). We hypothesize that trimming the extended vocabulary of the XLM-R base model (250k) by removing languages not needed in the experiment will help reduce the model size, enhance model performance on downstream tasks, and facilitate domain adaptation. One of the main advantages of Language Reduction is that it reduces the number of languages by pruning only the embedding matrix while preserving all encoder weights. Unlike Abdaoui et al. (2020), our language reduction method consists of the following steps (see Figure 2):

1. We select English and Arabic texts from a multilingual variant of the C4 corpus.

2. Train a new SentencePiece BPE tokenizer using this corpus.

3. We identify the intersection between the new tokenizer and the XLM-R_{Base} tokenizer. [2] The tokens in this intersection, along with their corresponding weights, are copied to the new embedding matrix of the XLM-R2 model.

4. The encoder weights from XLM-R_{Base} are transferred directly to the new XLM-R2 model.

3.2 Domain Adaptation of MLLM

Though language reduction allows us to benefit from the extensive training the XLM-R_{Base} model underwent, it gives us an LLM pre-trained for the general domain (XLM-R2). It is essential to note that the performance of retrieval models often declines when faced with domain shifts (Thakur et al., 2021b); since our focus in this study is on retrieval tasks and we apply this model as a backbone for retrieval, implementing domain adaptation is a crucial step to mitigate performance deterioration. In most domains, corpora to pre-train MLLMs are English-centric. However, we encounter a unique situation in the Islamic domain where significant domain-specific corpora are available in Arabic rather than English. Performing domain adaptation on a bilingual model brings certain advantages. On the one hand, the XLM-R_{Base} model was trained on extensive general domain English data, which helps to improve performance on Arabic tasks. On the other hand, the availability of larger Islamic corpora in Arabic also enables better results for domain-specific tasks in English. The Open Islamicate Texts Initiative (OpenITI) (Romanov and Seydi, 2019) has provided a substantial corpus of 1 billion words for pre-training LLMs in Classical Arabic, the language of Arabic Islamic literature (Inoue et al., 2021; Malhas and Elsayed, 2022). While the available text in English is primarily composed of Tafseer and Hadith texts. Utilizing the OpenITI corpus can assist in creating a larger in-domain corpus for pre-training. To ensure the corpus is not overly biased towards Arabic, we randomly selected a subset of the OpenITI corpus containing approximately 50 million words. This subset was combined with the text of Hadeeth and Tafseer in English and Arabic, resulting in a total corpus size of 100 million words for domain adaptation. The corpus size is relatively small; nevertheless, since the weights of the XLM-R2 model are initialized from the XLM-R_{Base} model, we can employ continued pre-training. To tackle the word distribution shift, we incorporate new domain-specific vocabulary.

The steps of domain adaptation are the following (see Figure 2):

1. We train a new SentencePiece BPE tokenizer using a multilingual Islamic Corpus and identify the intersection between the new Islamic tokenizer and the XLM-R2 tokenizer. All the tokens outside of the intersection (2k to-

[2] `https://huggingface.co/FacebookAI/xlm-roberta-base`

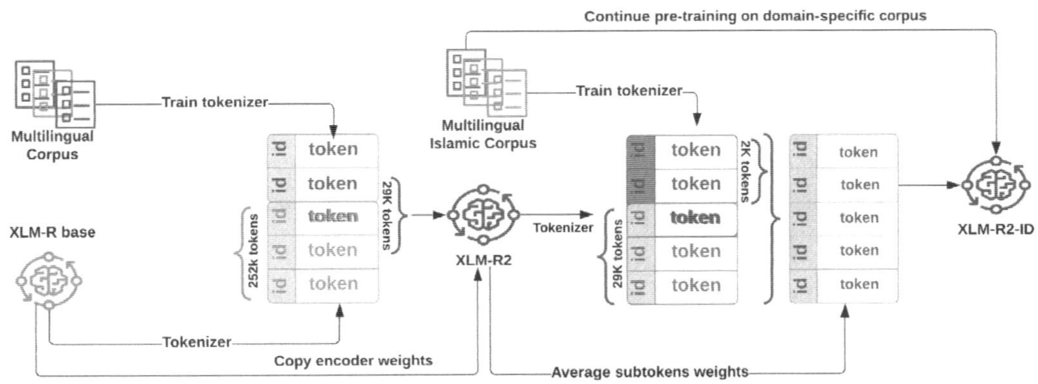

Figure 2: Language Reduction (on the left) gives the XLM-R2 model that goes through Domain Adaptation (on the right) and brings the XLM-R2-ID model. Diagram from Pavlova and Makhlouf (2024) with permission.

kens) are added to the embedding matrix of the XLMR-2 model (domain-specific vocabulary).

2. The weights for new Islamic tokens are assigned by averaging existing weights of subtokens from the XLM-R2 model.

3. We continue pre-training XLM-R2 using the domain-specific corpus, resulting in the XLM-R2-ID (Islamic domain) model. For more details on the hyperparameters, refer to Appendix A.

4 Domain-specific IR

4.1 Datasets, Metrics, and Training Approach

For retrieval, we use a dense retrieval approach (Karpukhin et al., 2020) using the sentence transformer framework that adds a pooling layer on top of LLM embeddings and produces fixed-sized sentence embedding (Reimers and Gurevych, 2019).

We utilize a sizeable general domain dataset (MS MARCO) for the first training stage in our multi-stage approach. The MS MARCO dataset consists of over half a million queries and is paired with a collection of 8.8 million passages (Bajaj et al., 2018). The language dataset is English; Bonifacio et al. (2021) released 13 machine-translated variants for 13 languages, including Arabic. The transfer language for XLM-$\mathrm{R_{Base}}$ is English, while -XLM-R2-ID has been adapted for the Islamic domain, primarily using Arabic. We will experiment with both English and Arabic as transfer languages to assess their effectiveness in addressing the IR task at hand.

The loss function is designed within the framework of contrastive learning, which helps create an embedding space that brings related queries and their relevant passages closer together while distancing queries and irrelevant passages (van den Oord et al., 2018) , and formally defined as:

$$J_{\mathrm{CL}}(\theta) = \frac{1}{M}\sum_{i=1}^{M}\log\frac{\exp\sigma(f_\theta(x^{(i)}), f_\theta(y^{(i)}))}{\sum_{j=1}^{M}\exp\sigma(f_\theta(x^{(i)}), f_\theta(y^{(j)}))}$$

where σ is a similarity function (a cosine similarity), f_θ is the sentence encoder. To enhance training efficiency, we utilize in-batch negatives (Henderson et al., 2017; Gillick et al., 2019; Karpukhin et al., 2020) (for hyperparameter details, see Appendix A).

In-domain training of retrieval model. Training a retrieval model on large-size general domain data would produce a robust model that can distinguish similar passages from dissimilar ones. However, training on a small amount of in-domain data can further enhance the performance (Wang et al., 2022; Lu et al., 2021). For in-domain training for the second stage, we use QUQA (Alnefaie et al., 2023), an Arabic question-answering (QA) dataset based on the Holy Qur'an. It has 3382 pairs, including 1166 pairs from AyaTEC (Malhas and Elsayed, 2020), which we exclude as we use them for evaluation (see below). Some questions relate to more than one verse. We take each relation as a separate anchor-positive pair, which gives us 3252 pairs. The dataset has only an Arabic version; we curate English in-domain training data to improve the in-domain training.

The challenge of limited domain-specific data can often be addressed by augmenting the training data using various methods. These methods include generating synthetic data (dos Santos Tanaka and Aranha, 2019), paraphrasing with synonyms (Wei and Zou, 2019), sampling and recombining new training pairs (Thakur et al., 2021a), employing round-trip translation (Yu et al., 2018; Xie et al., 2020), and utilizing denoising autoencoders (Wang et al., 2021). However, these techniques can distort the data, which is not ideal for religious and heritage datasets. To prevent data distortion, we create anchor-positive pairs based on the verse relations mentioned in Tafseer Ibn Katheer. This method facilitates the creation of relevant, verified, high-quality in-domain data without costly human annotations.

- First, we pair all the verses that have relation mentioned in Tafseer Ibn Katheer.
- Next, we filter out the pairs that may not be interpreted by the model as indicating a strong positive correlation. To filter out these pairs, we scored them using a cross-encoder model trained using the XLM-R2-ID model (for details on cross-encoder training see Appendix A). Cross-encoder is a powerful but expensive approach to identifying similar pairs. Though they are suboptimal to apply in solving real-world retrieval tasks due to high computational overhead, they can help in data augmentation, distillation, and re-ranking without enduring considerable domain shift (Humeau et al., 2020; Wang et al., 2022). Cross-encoder helps to filter out pairs with low similarity scores, leaving us with 2133 pairs for in-domain training.
- Lastly, we combine Arabic QUQA pairs with English pairs, which results in 5385 pairs for training.

Unlike Pavlova (2023), we do not create hard negatives for training the retrieval model. Instead, we apply the same contrastive learning framework, utilizing in-batch negatives as described earlier, to train on in-domain data. We ensure that there are no duplicate entries within the same batch and sample from English and Arabic in-domain datasets in proportion to their respective sizes. This approach allows all samples from each dataset to be utilized.

For evaluation, we combined the train and development split of the QRCD (Qur'anic Reading Comprehension Dataset) (Malhas and Elsayed, 2020) and converted it to the IR dataset (169 queries in total for testing). The QRCD dataset is in Arabic; to conduct evaluations in English, we utilized verified translations of this dataset into English. We use the Holy Qur'an text (Arabic) and Sahih International translation (English) as retrieval collections.[3] The QRCD is designed to retrieve passages composed of verses from the Holy Qur'an. The Holy Qur'an texts mentioned above are organized according to the passages based on the QRCD. We evaluate the models' performance using decision support metric Recall@100 and the order-aware metric MRR@10 (MS MARCO's official metric).

4.2 Baselines and Models

We use two monolingual models as our baselines. For English, we use ST/all-mpnet-base-v2, a robust monolingual model trained with contrastive learning objectives on 1B sentence pairs. [4] For Arabic, we use CL-AraBERT (Malhas and Elsayed, 2022), which was pre-trained on OpenITI corpus, and we fine-tuned as a retrieval model on Arabic MS MARCO and in-domain Arabic data using the same training loss described above (for hyperparameters see Appendix A). This choice of baselines serves two purposes. First, it enables us to evaluate how our bilingual model performs compared to monolingual models. Second, comparing our model against a strong retrieval model that is not domain-adapted (ST/all-mpnet-base-v2) allows us to assess the effects of domain adaptation. Additionally, contrasting it with a retrieval model trained using CL-AraBERT—adapted with the full OpenITI dataset, which consists of about 1 billion words — will help us evaluate the potential of utilizing a smaller corpus for domain adaptation.

As previously mentioned in Section 4.1, we experimented with MS MARCO in both English and Arabic to select which language performs better for retrieval tasks in the Islamic domain. We trained two models, XLM-R2-ID-EN and XLM-R2-ID-AR, which correspond to the first stage of our multi-stage training approach. We selected the model that exhibited superior performance on the evaluation dataset for use in the second stage.

In the second stage, where we train on in-

[3]https://tanzil.net/trans/

[4]https://huggingface.co/sentence-transformers/all-mpnet-base-v2

Models	EN	AR
ST/all-mpnet-base-v2	<u>0.388</u>	-
CL-AraBERT-indomain	-	<u>0.512</u>
XLM-R-in-domain	0.211	0.218
XLM-R-EN	0.302	0.267
XLM-R-AR	0.287	0.264
XLM-R-AR-in-domain	0.308	0.316
XLM-R2-ID-in-domain	0.348	0.465
XLM-R2-ID-EN	0.329	0.416
XLM-R2-ID-AR	0.387	0.498
XLM-R2-ID-AR-in-domain	**0.441**	**0.534**

Table 1: Model performance for MRR@10.

Models	EN	AR
ST/all-mpnet-base-v2	<u>0.619</u>	-
CL-AraBERT-indomain	-	<u>0.756</u>
XLM-R-in-domain	0.451	0.462
XLM-R-EN	0.492	0.496
XLM-R-AR	0.493	0.541
XLM-R-AR-in-domain	0.528	0.584
XLM-R2-ID-in-domain	0.592	0.706
XLM-R2-ID-EN	0.571	0.675
XLM-R2-ID-AR	<u>0.619</u>	0.72
XLM-R2-ID-AR-in-domain	**0.646**	**0.766**

Table 2: Model performance for Recall@100.

domain data, we developed the XLM-R2-ID-AR-in-domain. To evaluate the impact of multi-stage training, we also produced the XLM-R2-ID-in-domain model, which was trained solely on in-domain data without using MS MARCO. We aimed to analyze the performance of the XLM-R2-ID model after implementing domain adaptation and language reduction. To facilitate this analysis, we prepared four additional models trained from the XLM-R_{Base} model for comparison with four models trained from the XLM-R2-ID. These include two models trained on the MS MARCO dataset in English and Arabic (XLM-R-EN and XLM-R-AR), a model trained in a multi-stage approach (XLM-R-AR-in-domain), and a model trained solely on in-domain data (XLM-R-in-domain).

4.3 Model Comparison

For our model comparison, we will examine four key aspects: First, we will compare model performance against a baseline. Second, we will assess how models trained from domain-adapted XLM-R2-ID models perform compared to those trained from general domain XLM-R_{Base}. Third, we will evaluate model performance that was trained in a multi-stage approach against training conducted solely with in-domain datasets (only stage two) or only with large general domain datasets (only stage one). Finally, we will analyze how the models perform on the evaluation dataset in English versus the evaluation dataset in Arabic.

In Tables 1 and 2, the best-performing model is in bold, and the second-best is underlined. In terms of MRR@10 for English (see Table 1), we see that most models perform worse than the baseline monolingual model, all-mpnet-base-v2 (0.388), with the exception of XLM-R2-ID-AR-in-domain (0.441). This model, which was trained using a multi-stage approach, outperforms the baseline. A similar trend is observed for MRR@10 in Arabic.

Table 1 shows that the second stage of in-domain training provides significant benefits for English, resulting in a 12% performance improvement (increasing from 0.387 to 0.441). For Arabic, the second stage yields an improvement of approximately 6%. The same is true for Recall@100 (see Table 2); only the models that utilized a multi-stage training approach were able to surpass a strong monolingual baseline, but the improvement was less pronounced than that observed in MRR@10.

Figures 3 and 4 illustrate the performance comparison between all stages of the models trained from XLM-R_{Base} and the XLM-R2-ID for MRR@10, and Figures 5 and 6 for Recall@100. It is evident that all XLM-R2-ID models outperform the XLM-R_{Base} models in both Arabic and English, with a particularly significant difference in performance observed in Arabic. This indicates that domain adaptation has been especially beneficial for the Arabic language.

Another important observation is that XLM-R_{Base} models do not respond to multi-stage training as effectively as models based on XLM-R2-ID. Additionally, training solely on in-domain data results in competitive models; however, these still fall short compared to models trained using a multi-stage approach, similar to those trained only on general domain data.

Interestingly, although machine-translated, training on the Arabic version of MS MARCO yields better results than training on the original English version of MS MARCO. This trend holds true for evaluations in both Arabic and English. Despite starting the domain adaptation process from the XLM-R_{Base} model, which is an English-

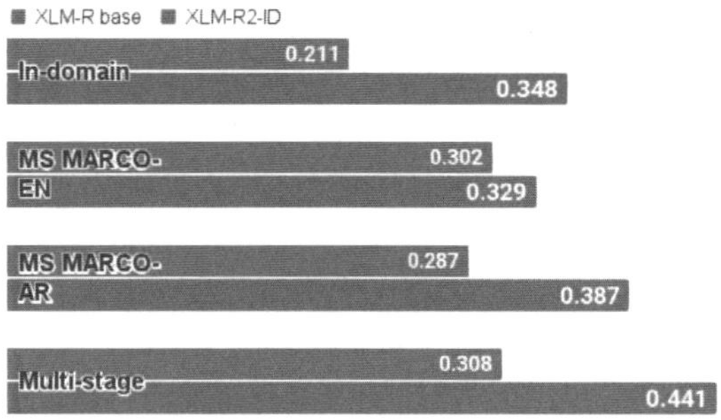

Figure 3: Comparison of the performance of the retrieval models trained from XLM-R_{Base} and XLM-R2-ID for MRR@10 in English.

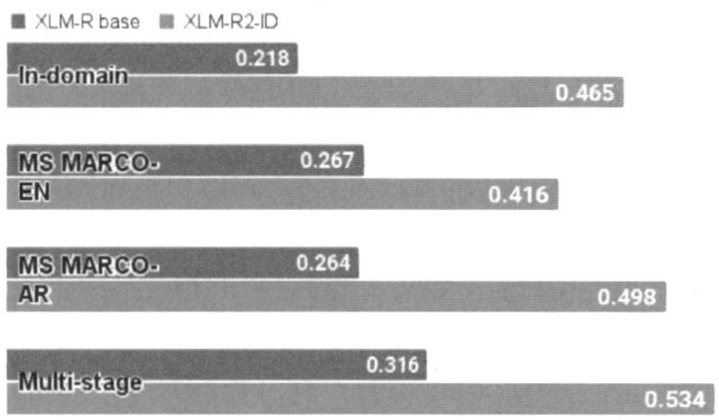

Figure 4: Comparison of the performance of the retrieval models trained from XLM-R_{Base} and XLM-R2-ID for MRR@10 in Arabic.

centric model, training on a small amount of Arabic data and adding domain-specific vocabulary significantly improved the results for the Arabic language.

As a final part of our comparison, we closely examine the performance of models using English and Arabic datasets. Figure 7 (MRR@10) and Figure 8 (Recall@100) demonstrate that the results for Arabic are superior to those for English across all models. The disparity is particularly pronounced in MRR@10, while the difference is less significant for Recall@100.

Overall, our experiments and comparisons reveal several important findings: domain adaptation of LLMs, even with a small corpus, significantly contributes to improved performance on downstream tasks. However, adaptation alone was insufficient to surpass strong monolingual baselines. Instead, the multi-stage training approach enhanced the results, allowing us to outperform the baselines.

Additionally, the XLM-R2-ID-in-domain model outperformed the retrieval model trained on CL-AraBERT, which was developed on a larger corpus.

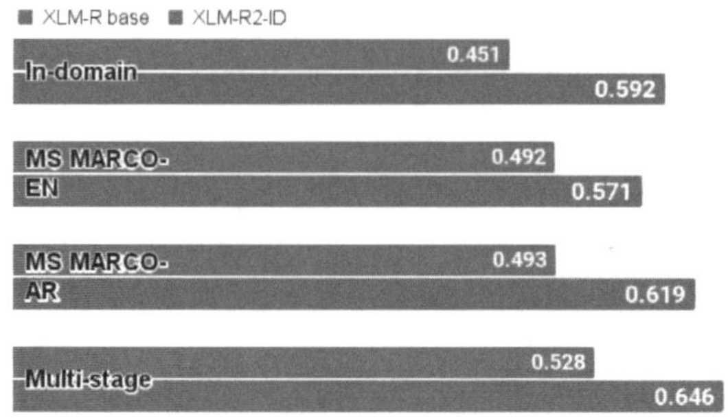

Figure 5: Comparison of the performance of the retrieval models trained from XLM-R_{Base} and XLM-R2-ID for Recall@100 in English.

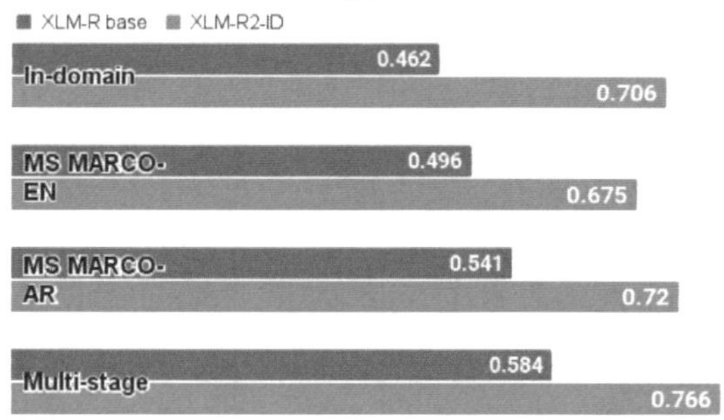

Figure 6: Comparison of the performance of the retrieval models trained from XLM-R_{Base} and XLM-R2-ID for Recall@100 in Arabic.

Models	EN	AR
XLM-R2-ID-AR-in-domain	**0.441**	**0.534**
XLM-R2-ID*-AR-in-domain	0.414	0.498
XLM-R2-ID-in-domain*	0.381	0.521

Table 3: Model performance for MRR@10 with two ablated models.

This suggests that even a small corpus can be effective, especially when leveraging strong XLM-R_{Base} weights for a warm start.

5 Ablation Study

In this section, we conduct an ablation study on various aspects of our highest-performing model, XLM-R2-ID-AR-in-domain, which was trained using domain adaptation with extended corpus and a multi-stage approach with augmented in-domain data. To better understand the relative importance of each component, we examine the effects of removing each one individually.

First, we removed the domain adaptation that involved extending the Islamic corpus with OpenITI. We then used only the available Islamic texts from

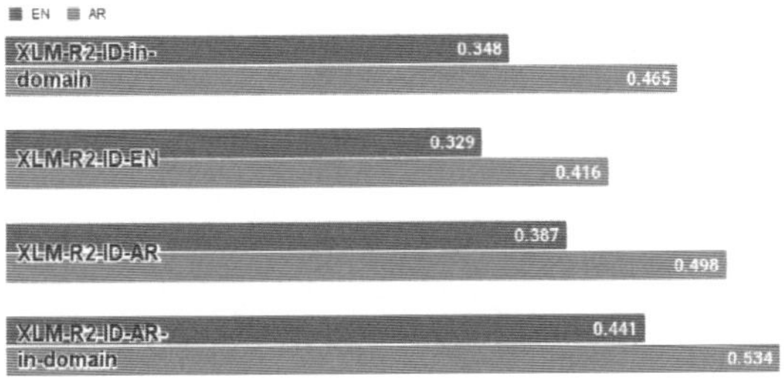

Figure 7: Comparison of results between Arabic and English for MRR@10.

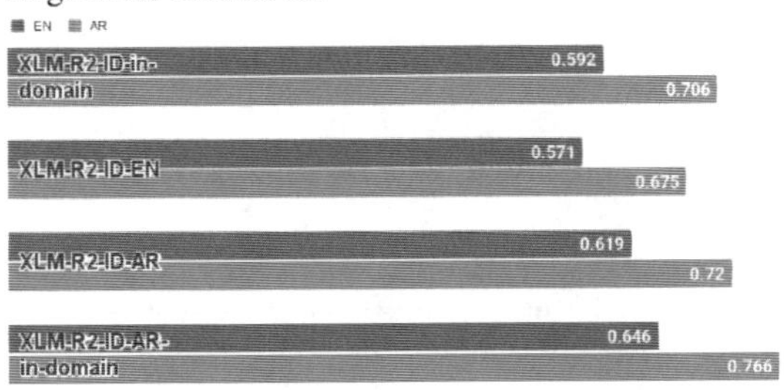

Figure 8: Comparison of results between Arabic and English for Recall@100.

Models	EN	AR
XLM-R2-ID-AR-in-domain	**0.646**	**0.766**
XLM-R2-ID*-AR-in-domain	0.643	0.739
XLM-R2-ID-in-domain*	0.622	0.751

Table 4: Model performance for Recall@100 with two ablated models.

Hadith and Tafseer in English and Arabic, totaling 50 million words. In Tables 3 and 4, we present the performance of the model XLM-R2-ID*-AR-in-domain, which was trained without OpenITI but still employed a multi-stage approach. The results show that MRR@10 decreased by approximately 6% for both Arabic and English. For Recall@100, the difference in performance for English was relatively small, whereas for Arabic, it was about 3.5%.

Next, we removed the augmentation of the in-domain corpus with English data, resulting in the model XLM-R2-ID-in-domain*. As shown in Table 3, this led to a more substantial decline in performance for English — around 14% - while the decrease for Arabic was only about 2.43%. Again, for Recall@100 (Table 4), the difference was less pronounced. This indicates that augmenting the in-domain data with English has a significant impact, especially for performance on retrieval task in English.

Moreover, our findings suggest that expanding the pre-training corpus with OpenITI improved results for both Arabic and English. Since adding additional texts amounting to 50 million words does not significantly prolong pre-training time, we recommend this approach; however, as we demonstrated in the section 4.3, even without pre-training on an extended corpus of 1 billion words, using a relatively small corpus for domain adaptation can still yield significant improvements.

6 Conclusion

This study emphasizes the importance of leveraging domain adaptation to enhance the performance of LLMs on downstream tasks such as retrieval. By combining language reduction with domain adaptation applied to the XLM-R_{Base} model, we developed a lightweight bilingual Islamic LLM (XLM-R2-ID). This model underwent a multi-stage training process and demonstrated improved performance on retrieval tasks, surpassing monolingual models on the evaluation datasets.

Moreover, incorporating an augmented in-domain dataset in English further enhanced the performance of the retrieval model during the second training phase.

Overall, our research demonstrates that combining domain adaptation of LLMs with multi-stage training of neural retrieval models leads to improved results in downstream tasks such as IR.

Limitations

One of the limitations of our study is that we conducted experiments only in English and Arabic; experiments that involve other languages may vary. Additionally, we used machine-translated datasets. While machine translation has not yet reached the quality of expert human translation, our use of the Arabic machine-translated version of MS MARCO has shown promising results.

Ethics Statement

We do not anticipate any considerable risks associated with our work. The data and other related resources in this work are publically available, and no private data is involved.

Acknowledgment

This work would not have been possible without my colleague Mohammed Makhlouf. We extend our thanks to the anonymous Reviewers for their valuable feedback.

References

Amine Abdaoui, Camille Pradel, and Grégoire Sigel. 2020. Load what you need: Smaller versions of mutililingual BERT. In *Proceedings of SustaiNLP: Workshop on Simple and Efficient Natural Language Processing*, pages 119–123, Online. Association for Computational Linguistics.

Sarah Alnefaie, Eric Atwell, and Mohammad Ammar Alsalka. 2023. HAQA and QUQA: Constructing two Arabic question-answering corpora for the Quran and Hadith. In *Proceedings of the 14th International Conference on Recent Advances in Natural Language Processing*, pages 90–97, Varna, Bulgaria. INCOMA Ltd., Shoumen, Bulgaria.

Payal Bajaj, Daniel Campos, Nick Craswell, Li Deng, Jianfeng Gao, Xiaodong Liu, Rangan Majumder, Andrew McNamara, Bhaskar Mitra, Tri Nguyen, Mir Rosenberg, Xia Song, Alina Stoica, Saurabh Tiwary, and Tong Wang. 2018. Ms marco: A human generated machine reading comprehension dataset. *Preprint*, arXiv:1611.09268.

Muhammad Huzaifa Bashir, Aqil M Azmi, Haq Nawaz, Wajdi Zaghouani, Mona Diab, Ala Al-Fuqaha, and Junaid Qadir. 2023. Arabic natural language processing for qur'anic research: A systematic review. *Artificial Intelligence Review*, 56(7):6801–6854.

Iz Beltagy, Kyle Lo, and Arman Cohan. 2019. SciBERT: A pretrained language model for scientific text. In *Proceedings of the 2019 Conference on Empirical Methods in Natural Language Processing and the 9th International Joint Conference on Natural Language Processing (EMNLP-IJCNLP)*, pages 3615–3620, Hong Kong, China. Association for Computational Linguistics.

Yelysei Bondarenko, Markus Nagel, and Tijmen Blankevoort. 2021. Understanding and overcoming the challenges of efficient transformer quantization. In *Proceedings of the 2021 Conference on Empirical Methods in Natural Language Processing*, pages 7947–7969, Online and Punta Cana, Dominican Republic. Association for Computational Linguistics.

Luiz Henrique Bonifacio, Israel Campiotti, Roberto de Alencar Lotufo, and Rodrigo Frassetto Nogueira. 2021. mmarco: A multilingual version of MS MARCO passage ranking dataset. *CoRR*, abs/2108.13897.

Alexis Conneau, Kartikay Khandelwal, Naman Goyal, Vishrav Chaudhary, Guillaume Wenzek, Francisco Guzmán, Edouard Grave, Myle Ott, Luke Zettlemoyer, and Veselin Stoyanov. 2020. Unsupervised cross-lingual representation learning at scale. In *Proceedings of the 58th Annual Meeting of the Association for Computational Linguistics*, pages 8440–8451, Online. Association for Computational Linguistics.

Jacob Devlin, Ming-Wei Chang, Kenton Lee, and Kristina Toutanova. 2019. BERT: Pre-training of deep bidirectional transformers for language understanding. In *Proceedings of the 2019 Conference of the North American Chapter of the Association for Computational Linguistics: Human Language Technologies, Volume 1 (Long and Short Papers)*, pages 4171–4186, Minneapolis, Minnesota. Association for Computational Linguistics.

Fabio Henrique Kiyoiti dos Santos Tanaka and Claus Aranha. 2019. Data augmentation using gans. *Preprint*, arXiv:1904.09135.

Daniel Gillick, Sayali Kulkarni, Larry Lansing, Alessandro Presta, Jason Baldridge, Eugene Ie, and Diego Garcia-Olano. 2019. Learning dense representations for entity retrieval. In *Proceedings of the 23rd Conference on Computational Natural Language Learning (CoNLL)*, pages 528–537, Hong Kong, China. Association for Computational Linguistics.

Yu Gu, Robert Tinn, Hao Cheng, Michael Lucas, Naoto Usuyama, Xiaodong Liu, Tristan Naumann, Jianfeng Gao, and Hoifung Poon. 2020. Domain-specific language model pretraining for biomedical natural language processing. *CoRR*, abs/2007.15779.

Yunhui Guo. 2018. A survey on methods and theories of quantized neural networks. *Preprint*, arXiv:1808.04752.

Matthew Henderson, Rami Al-Rfou, Brian Strope, Yun hsuan Sung, Laszlo Lukacs, Ruiqi Guo, Sanjiv Kumar, Balint Miklos, and Ray Kurzweil. 2017. Efficient natural language response suggestion for smart reply. *Preprint*, arXiv:1705.00652.

Kexin Huang, Jaan Altosaar, and Rajesh Ranganath. 2019. Clinicalbert: Modeling clinical notes and predicting hospital readmission. *CoRR*, abs/1904.05342.

Samuel Humeau, Kurt Shuster, Marie-Anne Lachaux, and Jason Weston. 2020. Poly-encoders: Transformer architectures and pre-training strategies for fast and accurate multi-sentence scoring. *Preprint*, arXiv:1905.01969.

Go Inoue, Bashar Alhafni, Nurpeiis Baimukan, Houda Bouamor, and Nizar Habash. 2021. The interplay of variant, size, and task type in Arabic pre-trained language models. In *Proceedings of the Sixth Arabic Natural Language Processing Workshop*, pages 92–104, Kyiv, Ukraine (Virtual). Association for Computational Linguistics.

Gautier Izacard, Mathilde Caron, Lucas Hosseini, Sebastian Riedel, Piotr Bojanowski, Armand Joulin, and Edouard Grave. 2021. Unsupervised dense information retrieval with contrastive learning. *Trans. Mach. Learn. Res.*, 2022.

Benoit Jacob, Skirmantas Kligys, Bo Chen, Menglong Zhu, Matthew Tang, Andrew Howard, Hartwig Adam, and Dmitry Kalenichenko. 2017. Quantization and training of neural networks for efficient integer-arithmetic-only inference. *Preprint*, arXiv:1712.05877.

Vladimir Karpukhin, Barlas Oguz, Sewon Min, Patrick Lewis, Ledell Wu, Sergey Edunov, Danqi Chen, and Wen-tau Yih. 2020. Dense passage retrieval for open-domain question answering. In *Proceedings of the 2020 Conference on Empirical Methods in Natural Language Processing (EMNLP)*, pages 6769–6781, Online. Association for Computational Linguistics.

Guillaume Lample and Alexis Conneau. 2019. Cross-lingual language model pretraining. *CoRR*, abs/1901.07291.

Jinhyuk Lee, Wonjin Yoon, Sungdong Kim, Donghyeon Kim, Sunkyu Kim, Chan Ho So, and Jaewoo Kang. 2019. BioBERT: a pre-trained biomedical language representation model for biomedical text mining. *Bioinformatics*.

Zhuohan Li, Eric Wallace, Sheng Shen, Kevin Lin, Kurt Keutzer, Dan Klein, and Joseph E. Gonzalez. 2020. Train large, then compress: Rethinking model size for efficient training and inference of transformers. *CoRR*, abs/2002.11794.

Jing Lu, Gustavo Hernandez Abrego, Ji Ma, Jianmo Ni, and Yinfei Yang. 2021. Multi-stage training with improved negative contrast for neural passage retrieval. In *Proceedings of the 2021 Conference on Empirical Methods in Natural Language Processing*, pages 6091–6103, Online and Punta Cana, Dominican Republic. Association for Computational Linguistics.

Rana Malhas and Tamer Elsayed. 2020. Ayatec: building a reusable verse-based test collection for arabic question answering on the holy qur'an. *ACM Transactions on Asian and Low-Resource Language Information Processing (TALLIP)*, 19(6):1–21.

Rana Malhas and Tamer Elsayed. 2022. Arabic machine reading comprehension on the holy qur'an using cl-arabert. *Information Processing and Management*, 59(6):103068.

Vera Pavlova. 2023. Leveraging domain adaptation and data augmentation to improve qur'anic IR in English and Arabic. In *Proceedings of ArabicNLP 2023*, pages 76–88, Singapore (Hybrid). Association for Computational Linguistics.

Vera Pavlova and Mohammed Makhlouf. 2023. BIOptimus: Pre-training an optimal biomedical language model with curriculum learning for named entity recognition. In *The 22nd Workshop on Biomedical Natural Language Processing and BioNLP Shared Tasks*, pages 337–349, Toronto, Canada. Association for Computational Linguistics.

Vera Pavlova and Mohammed Makhlouf. 2024. Building an efficient multilingual non-profit IR system for the islamic domain leveraging multiprocessing design in rust. In *Proceedings of the 2024 Conference on Empirical Methods in Natural Language Processing: Industry Track*, pages 981–990, Miami, Florida, US. Association for Computational Linguistics.

Nina Poerner, Ulli Waltinger, and Hinrich Schütze. 2020. Inexpensive domain adaptation of pretrained language models: Case studies on biomedical NER and covid-19 QA. In *Findings of the Association for Computational Linguistics: EMNLP 2020*, pages 1482–1490, Online. Association for Computational Linguistics.

Yingqi Qu, Yuchen Ding, Jing Liu, Kai Liu, Ruiyang Ren, Wayne Xin Zhao, Daxiang Dong, Hua Wu, and Haifeng Wang. 2021. RocketQA: An optimized training approach to dense passage retrieval for open-domain question answering. In *Proceedings of the 2021 Conference of the North American Chapter of the Association for Computational Linguistics: Human Language Technologies*, pages 5835–5847, Online. Association for Computational Linguistics.

Nils Reimers and Iryna Gurevych. 2019. Sentence-BERT: Sentence embeddings using Siamese BERT-networks. In *Proceedings of the 2019 Conference on Empirical Methods in Natural Language Processing and the 9th International Joint Conference on Natural Language Processing (EMNLP-IJCNLP)*, pages 3982–3992, Hong Kong, China. Association for Computational Linguistics.

Ruiyang Ren, Yingqi Qu, Jing Liu, Wayne Xin Zhao, QiaoQiao She, Hua Wu, Haifeng Wang, and Ji-Rong Wen. 2021. RocketQAv2: A joint training method for dense passage retrieval and passage re-ranking. In *Proceedings of the 2021 Conference on Empirical Methods in Natural Language Processing*, pages 2825–2835, Online and Punta Cana, Dominican Republic. Association for Computational Linguistics.

Maxim Romanov and Masoumeh Seydi. 2019. Openiti: a machine-readable corpus of islamicate texts. *Zenodo, URL: https://doi. org/10.5281/zenodo*, 3082464.

Vin Sachidananda, Jason Kessler, and Yi-An Lai. 2021. Efficient domain adaptation of language models via adaptive tokenization. In *Proceedings of the Second Workshop on Simple and Efficient Natural Language Processing*, pages 155–165, Virtual. Association for Computational Linguistics.

Victor Sanh, Lysandre Debut, Julien Chaumond, and Thomas Wolf. 2019. Distilbert, a distilled version of BERT: smaller, faster, cheaper and lighter. *CoRR*, abs/1910.01108.

Siqi Sun, Yu Cheng, Zhe Gan, and Jingjing Liu. 2019. Patient knowledge distillation for BERT model compression. In *Proceedings of the 2019 Conference on Empirical Methods in Natural Language Processing and the 9th International Joint Conference on Natural Language Processing (EMNLP-IJCNLP)*, pages 4323–4332, Hong Kong, China. Association for Computational Linguistics.

Raphael Tang, Yao Lu, Linqing Liu, Lili Mou, Olga Vechtomova, and Jimmy Lin. 2019. Distilling task-specific knowledge from BERT into simple neural networks. *CoRR*, abs/1903.12136.

Nandan Thakur, Nils Reimers, Johannes Daxenberger, and Iryna Gurevych. 2021a. Augmented SBERT: Data augmentation method for improving bi-encoders for pairwise sentence scoring tasks. In *Proceedings of the 2021 Conference of the North American Chapter of the Association for Computational Linguistics: Human Language Technologies*, pages 296–310, Online. Association for Computational Linguistics.

Nandan Thakur, Nils Reimers, Andreas Rücklé, Abhishek Srivastava, and Iryna Gurevych. 2021b. Beir: A heterogenous benchmark for zero-shot evaluation of information retrieval models. In *Thirty-fifth Conference on Neural Information Processing Systems (NeurIPS 2021) - Datasets and Benchmarks Track (Round 2)*.

Rong Tian, Zijing Zhao, Weijie Liu, Haoyan Liu, Weiquan Mao, Zhe Zhao, and Kan Zhou. 2023. SAMP: A model inference toolkit of post-training quantization for text processing via self-adaptive mixed-precision. In *Proceedings of the 2023 Conference on Empirical Methods in Natural Language Processing: Industry Track*, pages 123–130, Singapore. Association for Computational Linguistics.

Aäron van den Oord, Yazhe Li, and Oriol Vinyals. 2018. Representation learning with contrastive predictive coding. *CoRR*, abs/1807.03748.

Ashish Vaswani, Noam Shazeer, Niki Parmar, Jakob Uszkoreit, Llion Jones, Aidan N. Gomez, Lukasz Kaiser, and Illia Polosukhin. 2017. Attention is all you need. *CoRR*, abs/1706.03762.

Kexin Wang, Nils Reimers, and Iryna Gurevych. 2021. TSDAE: Using transformer-based sequential denoising auto-encoderfor unsupervised sentence embedding learning. In *Findings of the Association for Computational Linguistics: EMNLP 2021*, pages 671–688, Punta Cana, Dominican Republic. Association for Computational Linguistics.

Kexin Wang, Nandan Thakur, Nils Reimers, and Iryna Gurevych. 2022. GPL: Generative pseudo labeling for unsupervised domain adaptation of dense retrieval. In *Proceedings of the 2022 Conference of the North American Chapter of the Association for Computational Linguistics: Human Language Technologies*, pages 2345–2360, Seattle, United States. Association for Computational Linguistics.

Jason Wei and Kai Zou. 2019. EDA: Easy data augmentation techniques for boosting performance on text classification tasks. In *Proceedings of the 2019 Conference on Empirical Methods in Natural Language Processing and the 9th International Joint Conference on Natural Language Processing (EMNLP-IJCNLP)*, pages 6382–6388, Hong Kong, China. Association for Computational Linguistics.

Qizhe Xie, Zihang Dai, Eduard Hovy, Minh-Thang Luong, and Quoc V. Le. 2020. Unsupervised data augmentation for consistency training. *Preprint*, arXiv:1904.12848.

Adams Wei Yu, David Dohan, Minh-Thang Luong, Rui Zhao, Kai Chen, Mohammad Norouzi, and Quoc V. Le. 2018. Qanet: Combining local convolution with global self-attention for reading comprehension. *Preprint*, arXiv:1804.09541.

Wayne Xin Zhao, Jing Liu, Ruiyang Ren, and Ji rong Wen. 2022. Dense text retrieval based on pretrained language models: A survey. *ACM Transactions on Information Systems*, 42:1 – 60.

A Appendix

Computing Infrastructure	1x H100 (80 GB)
Hyperparameter	**Assignment**
number of epochs	60
batch size	128
maximum learning rate	0.0005
learning rate optimizer	Adam
learning rate scheduler	None or Warmup linear
Weight decay	0.01
Warmup proportion	0.06
learning rate decay	linear

Table 5: Hyperparameters for pre-training of XLM-R2-ID model.

Computing Infrastructure	1x H100 (80 GB)
Hyperparameter	**Assignment**
number of epochs	1
batch size	32
learning rate	2e-5
pooling	mean

Table 6: Hyperparameters for training retrieval models.

Cross-encoder training details

In a cross-encoder architecture, a pair of sentences are simultaneously fed into a transformer-like model, allowing attention to be applied across all tokens to generate a similarity score. The model is trained using triples provided by MS MARCO, starting from the XLM-R2-ID model checkpoint, with a classification task and employing Cross Entropy Loss.

Although this approach does not enable end-to-end information retrieval and involves significant computational overhead, it often outperforms other methods in many information retrieval (IR) tasks. Additionally, it can be utilized for mining hard negatives, data augmentation, and reranking.

Automated Translation of Islamic Literature Using Large Language Models: Al-Shamela Library Application

Mohammad Mohammad Khair[1], **Majdi Sawalha**[1,2,3]

[1] International Computing Institute for Quran and Islamic Sciences, USA
[2] College of Engineering, Al Ain University, Abu Dhabi, UAE.
[3] King Abdullah II School of Information Technology,
The University of Jordan, Amman, Jordan.
mohammad.khair@gmail.com, sawalha.majdi@ju.edu.jo

Abstract

Large Language Models (LLM) can be useful tools for translating Islamic literature written in Arabic into several languages, making this complex task technologically feasible, providing high-quality translations, at low cost and high-speed production enabled by parallel computing. We applied LLM-driven translation automation on a diverse corpus of Islamic scholarly works including: the Qur'an, Quranic exegesis (Tafseer), Hadith, and Jurisprudence from the Al-Shamela library. More than 250,000 pages have been translated into English, emphasizing the potential of LLMs to cross language barriers and increase global access to Islamic knowledge. OpenAI's gpt-4o-mini model was used for the forward translation from Arabic to English with acceptable translation quality. Translation quality validation was achieved by reproducing Arabic text via back-translation from English using both the OpenAI LLM and an independent Anthropic LLM. Correlating the original source Arabic text and the back-translation Arabic text using a vector embedding cosine similarity metric demonstrated comparable translation quality between the two models.

1 Introduction

Islam is the religion of more than 1.8 billion people on Earth. Yet, only about 20% of that population speak Arabic as their native language, the language of the Quran, and the rest speak their native languages. Islamic literature and the majority of its scholarly writings have been traditionally authored in Arabic with very limited or scarce translations available into other languages, hindered by the manual translation process complexity and effort that requires translators with multilingual proficiency. There exists a large volume of Arabic books in digital libraries with content extending over the last 1450 years of Islamic literature. Mass translation is feasible today using LLM models with professional-grade translation at a fraction of the cost of human translation.

The advent of Large Language Models has enabled the generation of high-quality translations, maintaining the formatting, style, and context of the original source. Parallel computing enables multi-tasking processing of translation for multiple books or to multiple languages simultaneously. LLM models have resulted in significant cost reductions via a cost-efficient API query for translation prompts.

2 Limitations for Translations

The number and type of languages supported by the LLM during its pretraining is a key criterion for selection of LLM to perform the translation task. The ability to understand Arabic language was also required since most of the Islamic books were written in Arabic.

The cost of hardware associated with servicing translation requests was another key criterion. We

Proceedings of the New Horizons in Computational Linguistics for Religious Texts (Coling-Rel), pages 53–58
January 19, 2025.

were able to load multiple small-size models (1B / 3B / 7B parameters) on a single GPU for hardware acceleration for parallel computing of separate model instances, however; the performance was limited due to the maximum GPU speed. Furthermore, the models loaded were open-source models with limited translation quality due to their small parameters size.

Model size, measured in billions of parameters, significantly affects the quality of the translated text. The smaller size models are less capable for translation and use more basic vocabulary as opposed to a more sophisticated expression style. In some instances, the LLM may revert to producing text in its predominant language that it was trained on rather than the language that was requested in the query. For example, English for Llama 3.2, and Chinese for Qwen 2.5.

Another limitation is that many of the sourced Arabic text books are in image-formatted pdf files, and not available in machine readable formatted pdf files. This necessitates the pre-processing step with Optical Character Recognition (OCR) for the recognition of the Arabic text from these files. OCR technology itself is limited in its success rate, with most existing tools are optimized for the English language, and very few OCR tools are available to process Arabic text at high cost, often missing the preservation of diacritic (tashkeel / harakat) marks in the scanned text.

The availability of LLM longer contextual memory is advantageous for continuous information flow, resulting in better translation quality. By comparison, sentence-by-sentence translation using traditional machine translation systems such as Google Translate or Meta's Seamless models do not retain translation context as compared to a LLM with a large prompt token context size.

3 Detailed Architecture and Design

3.1 LLMs for Translation

LLMs are highly suitable for translation tasks due to several factors: 1) Large context length, typically 4K-128K tokens possible which enables longer scope of text for translation, resulting in less text fragmentation via chunking, and better continuity of information and longer memory due to longer context scope. 2) LLMs support the Transformers architecture with multiple attention heads mechanism enabling it to efficiently map sequence to sequence relationships focusing on key relevant information, making it ideal for translation tasks. 3) Multiple attention heads and deep learning layers are also well suited for parallel computing architectures of GPU hardware enabling computing acceleration. 4) LLMs creates knowledge maps using pre-training on huge volume of text (Trillions of tokens) across multiple languages. 5) Finally, LLMs behavior can be customized using simple prompts, which makes them ideal for ease of use.

3.2 LLM model choice

We subjectively compared translation quality from multiple LLM models that were pretrained on Arabic and other languages, and using different models' parameters sizes. Some of these LLM models are open-source including Llama 3.2 3B, Qwen 2.5 3B, Silma 9B, Jais 13B, and Mistral 7B, and some models are proprietary including OpenAI's "gpt-4o", "gpt-4o-mini", and Anthropic's Claude 3.5 Sonnet and Claude 3.5 Haiku. Finally, the best overall performance LLM "gpt-4o-mini" was selected for low cost, fast response speed, and high quality of translations generated with expressive vocabulary that is contextually relevant and meaningful.

3.3 Prompt Engineering

The LLM prompt query specification is key for driving accuracy and quality in LLM's response to users' requirements. The prompt needs to specify several key elements: 1) Provide detailed proficient translation from Arabic language to English language 2) No transliteration 3) Use Islamic terminology and scientific expressions as possible 4) Keep translation accessible and understandable to the reader 5) Preserve the truthful representation of the source text 6) When translating text from the Quran or Hadith provide both the source Arabic text and its translation 7) Maintain page and paragraph formatting, as well as enumerated or bullet list formatting to ease reading clarity of text structure 8) Use bold headings, and 9) Separate book chapters with a clear heading in bold font and a new page break.

3.4 Parallel Computing Architecture

Accelerating the translation process is key due to the large number of books (more than 50,000 books) available for translation into multiple target languages per book. The main translation process is forked into multithreaded tasks, one task per book per language, whereby each task is responsible for completing translation of all pages of a book in the one of the requested target languages for translation, before picking up another book in sequence. Multiple parallel requests can be made simultaneously as the LLM API requests and responses are uniquely targeted to each subtask process. Using commercially available LLM APIs trades-off the need for significantly high-cost of local GPU hardware with the significantly reduced-cost of remote services, due to scale economics. Figure 1 describes the complete data flow for one translation process task, which is repeated for every page per book per target language. The resulted translations are appended in a Word and Excel output formats, the Word file is finally converted into PDF format as well.

3.5 Database Storage

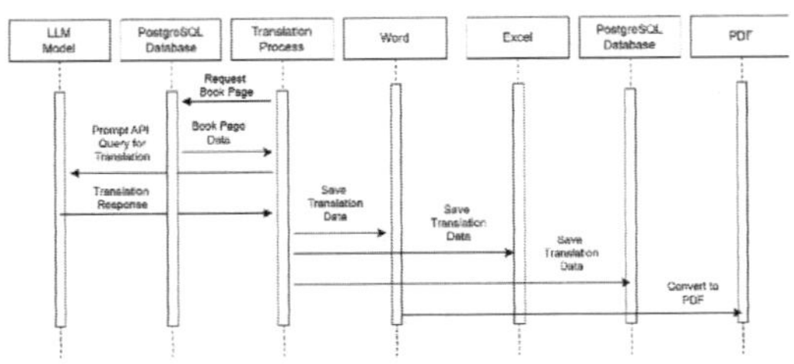

Figure 1: Sequence of Process Steps for Each Translation Task.

All input Arabic books text sources as well as translated output text results was stored in PostgreSQL tables. This allows instant API connectivity to the database tables via python-based SQL scripts. Iteration of all available book pages, one page per record, enables automation of an entire book translation, as well as the translation of multiple books simultaneously, via multi-threaded applications.

All text was stored in Unicode utf-8 format. The database schema was kept simple with the book tables containing one page of text per row, which represented the input to the LLM model prompts.

3.6 Output Formats

All translated books were stored in multiple file formats including PostgreSQL tables (one row per page), Microsoft Word format, Microsoft Excel format, and Adobe pdf format. We also added the ability to optionally create mp3 audio books from the translated text as well using the text-to-speech LLM service of OpenAI's "tts-1-hd" model.

3.7 Optical Character Recognition (OCR)

To enable translation of books in the format of image-based pdf files, an OCR process was performed using a multi-modal LLM, gpt-4o, that accepts as input text and images and produces text as output. Such a multi-modal LLM configuration is ideal to input prompt instructions for processing an image of a pdf page, in order to recognize the text in the image and provide it as an output via the LLM's response to the query.

The pages of each book were first saved in a high-resolution images, and these images were processed with image processing filters to remove background noise, sharpen the text quality of the words, diacritic marks, and punctuations. Then each of these page images were converted into a base64 string that is passed to the prompt query for the LLM along with a text prompt instruction requesting to scan the image; transcribe the Arabic text; maintain diacritic marks if they appear; while preserving the accuracy, and other Quranic symbols such as pause marks.

3.8 Using Retrieval Augmented Generation (RAG) to preserve Quran and Hadith script accuracy.

To preserve the accuracy of transcription of the Quran verses and the Hadith of the Prophet (SAW) is considered critical as any errors could change the meaning significantly. The original Arabic source text of the Ayas from the Quran or the Hadith text is requested to be repeated in the LLM response in addition to the English translation to preserve the reference source in the translated text. The accuracy of the source text for OCR scanned books is also important to ensure its accurate translation steps afterwards. Thus, in order to avoid potential translation errors or OCR processing errors of omission or insertion of a letter or even diacritic marks of the word, we therefore recommend applying Retrieval Augmented Generation (RAG) to the LLM query using trusted validated databases of Quran verses and Hadith source Arabic text for OCR processing or translations for English text. RAG enables search and match using a cosine similarity metric of embedding vectors equivalent to the desired Quran verse or Hadith from a validated trusted database. Once matched, the Quran verse or Hadith in the OCR result are replaced with the RAG equivalent retrieved result. This process ensured the accuracy of the sacred texts of Quran and Hadith.

Furthermore, building this translation application is part of a larger project that aims to build a database of Islamic-specific terminology dictionary that includes translations of the Islamic terms in several languages that can improve the clarity of the translation description when submitted to the LLM via a RAG process. This represents future enhancement to this project's implementation. Finally, incorporating contextual relevance is important for generating accurate translation of ambiguous terms or phrases that could have multiple interpretations in the target language. The ability of an LLM prompt context to recall historical information within the prompt and from past prompts greatly advances the contextual relevance of the translation output. This has demonstrated advantages in contextual accuracy over sentence-by-sentence chunking and translation.

3.9 Languages Translations and Validation

Target languages for translations of interest that the gpt4o-mini LLM is capable of include: Turkish, Persian, Urdu, Malay, Bengali, Indonesian, Swahili, French, German, Russian, Spanish, and English. More languages can be added depending on the proficiency level of the LLM model. Language bias in LLMs output exists when there exists an imbalance in the training languages used, particularly in open-source models. For example, bias towards English in Llama-2.0 (but less so in Llama-3.2) or bias towards Chinese in Qwen-2.5. This can be detected through the response character set and the query retried with emphasis on the target language in the instructions. However, the used commercial LLMs , the OpenAI-4o-mini and the Anthropic's Clause-Haiku-3.0, did not display detectable language bias between Arabic and English. Validation of translation quality is accomplished using both automated and manual methods. The manual method (human-in-the-loop) includes crowd-sourcing reviews and soliciting feedback from interested readers and reviewers proficient in both the Arabic and the target language (English) who provide either acceptance or correction to the translation. Any correction requires at least two separate reviewers to accept it. Once the allowed review period ends, which varies depending on the book length, then we produce a pdf file, which is also secured from further alterations of page deletions or insertions.

The automated method for translation validation requires first using a back-translation step to regenerate Arabic text from the English, and then comparing its semantic similarity to the original source in Arabic. Both the original Arabic and back-translated Arabic are converted to vector embeddings. Then, a cosine similarity metric is applied that produces a score 0-1 for their semantic similarity or equivalence. The back-translation step can be performed either by the same primary model "gpt-4o-mini" or by an independent secondary model, such as Claude 3.5 Haiku or "claude-3-haiku-20240307". Any limitations of equivalence between original source Arabic and back-translation Arabic is primarily due to A) lack of available equivalent semantic expressions or equivalent vocabulary between Arabic and English, and then back to Arabic, B) lack of precision of meaning for words or pronouns across languages, such as words indicating singular vs plural or male vs female, and C) if the secondary model used in back-translation is different than the primary model used in forward-translation, then differences in model pre-training data sources and model design can result in performance differences between forward-translation and back-translation steps.

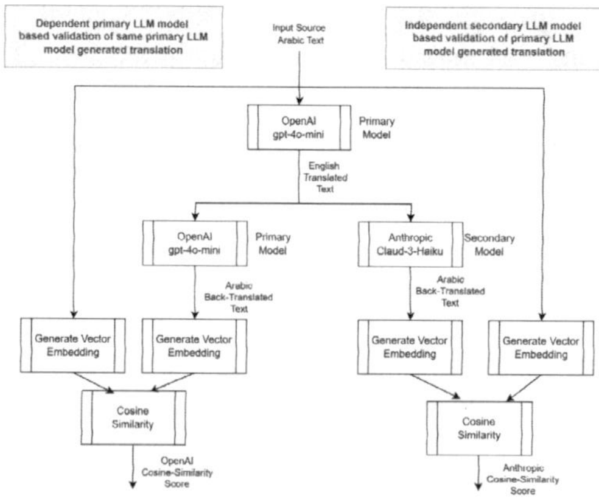

Figure 2: Automated validation of LLM translation

As shown in Figure 2, we applied an analysis using both scenarios of using the same primary model (gpt-4o-mini) for forward-translation and back-translation, and similarly using a different independent model claude-3-haiku-20240307 for back-translation. Both the original source Arabic text and the back-translated Arabic text were converted into vector embeddings and a cosine-similarity is then calculated to evaluate the semantic similarity between them to ensure fidelity of the translation process. A similarity score at or above a threshold level of 0.7-1 indicates the quality of the translation process is acceptable, and below 0.7 is poor similarity, and below 0.2 is a not-accepted outlier due to an error in forward translation. Additionally, the semantic similarity score will depend on the language model design and its pre-training strength and data sources in the Arabic language and the target language (e.g. English). The GPT-4o and the Claude-3.5-Sonnet models are considered the best models for language understanding and expression, while the GPT-4o-mini and the Claude-3.0-Haiku are the cost-effective versions of these models.

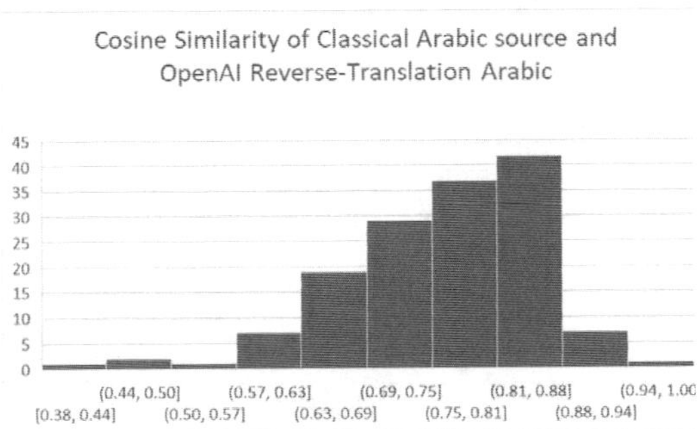

Figure 3: Distribution of OpenAI Back-Translation Cosine Similarity Scores

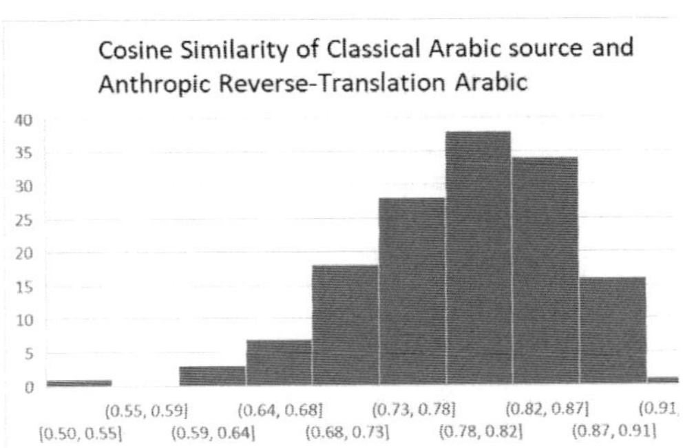

Figure 4: Distribution of Anthropic Back-Translation Cosine Similarity Scores

Furthermore, as shown in Figure 3 and Figure 4, 71% of the OpenAI model results and 86% of the Anthropic model results had cosine similarity scores >= 0.7, acceptable translations quality.

As shown in Figure 5, there exists a correlation in the semantic similarity scores between the OpenAI gpt-4o-mini cosine similarity results and the Anthropic claude-3.0-haiku model cosine similarity results.

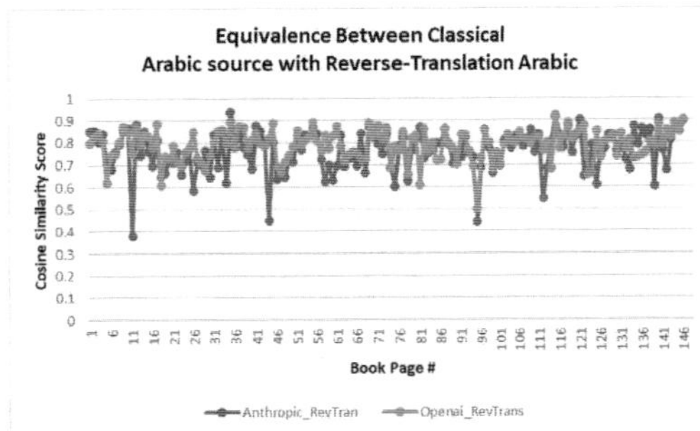

Figure 5: Equivalence Between Classical Arabic source with Back-Translation Arabic (without error outliers with scores < 0.2)

To control cost, quality checks for translation validation can be randomized checks and do not need to be systematic across the entire document being translated.

3.10 Conclusions

LLMs deep learning architectures offer a strong tool for linguistic understanding across wide variety of languages enabling them as ideal tools for translation tasks. Their ability to retain longer historical contextual information, and their attention design to focus on key information enables them to be more capable of producing high-quality translations that are contextually relevant and provide better information continuity. The longer context window also allows us to reduce fragmentation by translating one page at a time instead of one sentence at a time. The availability of a low-cost API interface for querying the LLMs enables us to parallelize the computational loads for translation queries resulting in a faster translation process execution, commercial LLMs economies of scale removes requirements for localized LLM requirements for GPU hardware costs to perform the computations. Translation quality was validated by examining the source Arabic text and the back-translated Arabic text (produced using either OpenAI or Anthropic models) by applying a cosine similarity metric to their vector embeddings, and the results demonstrate high acceptability of translation quality for both models. We therefore highly recommend use of LLMs as reliable translation tools, specifically the OpenAI's GPT-4o-mini and Anthropic's Claude Haiku LLM models.

Acknowledgments

We would like to extend our gratitude to the Al-Shamela Library team of developers who put great care in assembling and preserving the Islamic literature. All literature works used for translation are royalty-free of copyrights, and we thank the authors of these books who granted their knowledge and work to educate the world on Islam.

References

Wenhao Zhu, Hongyi Liu, Qingxiu Dong, Jingjing Xu, Shujian Huang, Lingpeng Kong, Jiajun Chen, Lei Li. 2024. *Multilingual Machine Translation with Large Language Models: Empirical Results and Analysis*. Computing Research Repository, arXiv:2304.04675v4.

https://arxiv.org/abs/2304.04675

Benjamin Marie, Atsushi Fujita, and Raphael Rubino. 2021. *Scientific Credibility of Machine Translation Research: A Meta-Evaluation of 769 Papers*. In Proceedings of the 59th Annual Meeting of the Association for Computational Linguistics, pages 7297-7306.

https://aclanthology.org/2021.acl-long.566/

Philipp Koehn and Rebecca Knowles. 2024. *How Good Are LLMs for Literary Translation, Really?* Computing Research Repository, arXiv:2410.18697v1.

https://arxiv.org/html/2410.18697v1

Ali Albashir Mohammed Alhaj. 2020. Translating Islamic texts into English: *A Practical and Theoretical Guide for Students of Translation*. LAP LAMBERT Academic Publishing, Saarbrücken.

https://www.amazon.com/Translating-Islamic-texts-into-English/dp/6202554258

Ronit Ricci. 2011. *Islam Translated: Literature, Conversion, and the Arabic Cosmopolis of South and Southeast Asia*. University of Chicago Press, Chicago, IL.

https://press.uchicago.edu/ucp/books/book/chicago/I/bo11274031.html

Bradley J. Cook. 2010. *Classical Foundations of Islamic Educational Thought: A Compendium of Parallel English-Arabic Texts*. Brigham Young University Press, Provo, UT.

https://press.uchicago.edu/ucp/books/book/distributed/C/bo11698936.html

Abu Bakr Soliman, Kareem Eisa, and Samhaa R. El-Beltagy. 2017. *AraVec: A set of Arabic Word Embedding Models for use in Arabic NLP*. In Proceedings of the 3rd International Conference on Arabic Computational Linguistics (ACLing 2017), Dubai, UAE.

https://www.sciencedirect.com/science/article/pii/S1877050917321749

Haaya Naushan. 2021. *Arabic Sentence Embeddings with Multi-Task Learning*. Towards Data Science.

https://towardsdatascience.com/arabic-sentence-embeddings-with-multi-task-learning-815801024375

A Supplementary Material

All translations will made accessible at https://QuranComputing.org

Sample translation material available at Github: https://github.com/mohammadkhair7/Translations

Automated Authentication of Quranic Verses Using BERT (Bidirectional Encoder Representations from Transformers) based Language Models

Khubaib Amjad Alam[1,*] , **Maryam Khalid**[2] , **Syed Ahmed Ali**[2] , **Haroon Mahmood**[1]
Qaisar Shafi[2] , **Muhammad Haroon**[2] **and Zulqarnain Haider**[2]
[1] College of Engineering, Al Ain University, UAE
[2] National University of Computer and Emerging Sciences (FAST-NUCES), Pakistan
khubaib.alam@aau.ac.ae

Abstract

The proliferation of Quranic content on digital platforms, including websites and social media, has brought about significant challenges in verifying the authenticity of Quranic verses. The inherent complexity of the Arabic language, with its rich morphology, syntax, and semantics, makes traditional text-processing techniques inadequate for robust authentication. This paper addresses this problem by leveraging state-of-the-art transformer-based Language models tailored for Arabic text processing. Our approach involves fine-tuning three transformer architectures **BERT-Base-Arabic**, **AraBERT**, and **MarBERT** on a curated dataset containing both authentic and non-authentic verses. Non-authentic examples were created using sentence-BERT, which applies cosine similarity to introduce subtle modifications. Comprehensive experiments were conducted to evaluate the performance of the models. Among the three candidate models, **MarBERT**, which is specifically designed for handling Arabic dialects demonstrated superior performance, achieving an F1-score of 93.80%. **BERT-Base-Arabic** also showed competitive F1 score of 92.90% reflecting its robust understanding of Arabic text. The findings underscore the potential of transformer-based models in addressing linguistic complexities inherent in Quranic text and pave the way for developing automated, reliable tools for Quranic verse authentication in the digital era.

1 Introduction

With the rapid spread of Islamic content online, particularly on social media and websites, verifying the authenticity of Quranic verses has become a challenge. There are many verses that are mistakenly shared, without proper checks, which makes it hard for the users to confirm their authenticity. Traditional methods of identifying Quranic verses, such as checking for diacritics or specific phrases, are time-consuming and inefficient (Hakak, 2018). There is a clear need for an automated system that can accurately and quickly authenticate Quranic verses. The complexity of the Arabic language, including its morphological nature and diacritics (Eksell, 1995), further complicates this task. Previous attempts to automate Quranic verse authentication using word embeddings and deep learning have shown promising results, but they often struggle with accurately capturing the full context and intricate meanings of the Quranic text. In contrast, transformer models have proven to be better in dealing with these complexities (Vaswani, 2017). Transformer models, such as BERT (Bidirectional Encoder Representations from Transformers), are designed to capture long-range dependencies in text and model complex linguistic structures through an attention mechanism. This enables them to focus on relevant parts of the input sequence, making them ideal for context-sensitive tasks like Quranic verse authentication, where understanding the meaning behind specific words and phrases is crucial (Shreyashree et al., 2022). In this project, we propose a solution for Quranic verse authentication through the use of models based on the Transformer architecture. We experimented with advanced large language models including **BERT-Base-Arabic**, **AraBERT** and **MarBERT** that are already pre-trained using Arabic datasets. Additionally, to create a more robust non-authentic dataset, we automated the generation of non-authentic verses using **Sentence-BERT** and cosine similarity thresholds, improving the quality of the dataset for training. This study aims to offer a more reliable method for Quranic verse authentication, addressing the limitations of existing techniques and providing an efficient, scalable solution for verifying digital Quranic content. Given the high sensitivity of the Quranic text, it is imperative that authentication tools achieve perfect accuracy. This paper sets the goal of developing error-proof tool to ensure that Quranic content can

Proceedings of the New Horizons in Computational Linguistics for Religious Texts (Coling-Rel), pages 59–66
January 19, 2025. ©2025 Association for Computational Linguistics

be reliably verified. While current models show promising results, future work will focus on further improving the precision and reliability of the system, reducing false positives and false negatives, and extending the methods to handle more diverse datasets.

2 Related Work

In the last decade, several methods have been put forward for verifying Quranic texts through various techniques, especially in the context of preserving their integrity in the digital space. These studies offer diverse methodologies, including word embeddings and machine learning models for automated classification. Kamsin et al. (Kamsin et al., 2014) acknowledged the importance of both Quran and Hadith authentication by creating a central authenticated repository for verifying digital texts. Their approach relies on manual validation, which limits scalability and efficiency. Jarrar et al. (Jarrar et al., 2018) have suggested an Arabic word matching technique based on the use of diacritic marks, mainly emphasizing phonetic shaping. While effective in handling diacritics, this approach emphasizes phonetic accuracy over deeper contextual understanding. Touati-Hamad et al. (Touati-Hamad et al., 2021) used Long Short-Term Memory (LSTM) models to detect Quranic verses that have been altered or reordered. Their model achieved high accuracy using a dataset from the Tanzil website but the only center of attention was sequence reordering, neglecting the semantic variations in the verses. Later, Touati-Hamad et al. (Touati-Hamad et al., 2022) came up with a deep learning method that employs CNN and LSTM models which were used to classify Quranic verses, the specific text is drawn from an Arabic learner corpus for non-authentic text. While effective in distinguishing Quranic verses from regular Arabic text, the simpler Arabic corpus used leaves room for further exploration in addressing subtle variations that closely resemble authentic verses. Muaad et al. (Muaad et al., 2023) performed a survey on Arabic text detection, revolving around the morphology problem of Arabic, which is one of the major challenges, and the necessity of context-aware models. Their review of deep learning techniques underscores the limitations of traditional methods in processing complex Arabic texts. However, these previous techniques are less efficient in dealing with Arabic complexities, like the text bidirectionality and long-range dependencies, in particular, when recognizing verses with slight but significance among variations in the non-authentic sample which is very close to the actual Quranic verses. In contrast to the approaches outlined above, **string-based comparison methods** such as hashing algorithms or text similarity checks are traditional techniques that compare a reference validated source of Quranic text with a target test source. These methods, while effective in identifying exact textual matches, **struggle to detect subtle variations** such as paraphrasing, semantic shifts, or alterations that do not involve significant structural changes. Methods like hashing focus primarily on exact matches.

Despite their effectiveness, the techniques mentioned above (LSTM, CNN, word matching) often rely on simpler models or datasets that do not fully capture the complexities of Arabic text. Similarly, while **sequence reordering** and **CNN-LSTM hybrid models** achieve good performance in detecting certain types of alterations, they may still struggle with the nuanced variations that closely resemble authentic verses. Transformer-based models, particularly BERT-based architectures, address these gaps by being **context-aware** and capable of distinguishing subtle semantic differences. This makes them a **better fit** for the task of authenticating Quranic verses, especially when the alterations are not immediately visible but affect the **underlying meaning**.

In recent years, **deep learning models**, particularly **transformer-based architectures** (Gillioz et al., 2020) emerged as powerful tools for text analysis. These models surpass traditional methods by not only detecting structural changes but also understanding the **context** and **semantics** of the text. The ability of transformer models to process **long-range dependencies** and handle **bidirectional relationships** in text allows them to detect even **subtle semantic alterations** that might evade simpler techniques. Unlike traditional string-based comparison, these models are trained to capture complex relationships between words and phrases, making them more robust for **identifying non-authentic Quranic verses** where minor variations in wording might otherwise go unnoticed.

3 Proposed Methodology

QuranAuthentic aims to address the critical challenge of authenticating Quranic verses by utilizing advanced deep learning techniques, specifically leveraging transformer-based language models. This section outlines the methodology adopted in the development of the QuranAuthentic tool. Our system is designed to identify subtle variations and manipulations in Quranic verses, ensuring the sanctity of the text. The methodology is organized into key components: dataset collection, preprocessing, text representation, and classification. We employed 3 different BERT models such as **BERT-Base-Arabic**, **AraBERT** and **MarBERT**, and explored fine-tuning techniques to ensure accurate detection of non-authentic Quranic verses. Figure 1 illustrates the workflow followed in this approach.

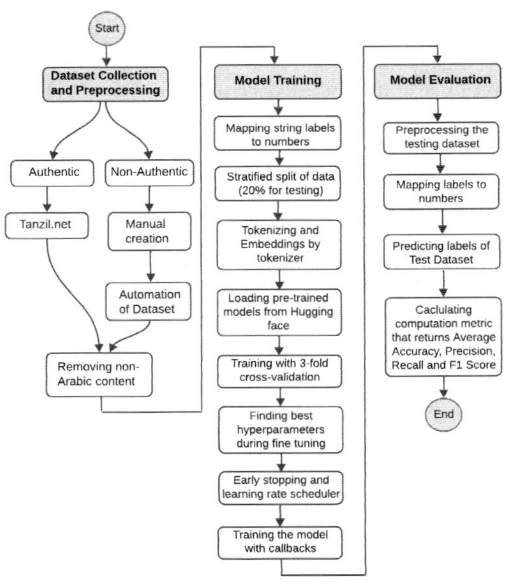

Figure 1: Step-by-step procedure of QuranAuthentic

3.1 Research Questions

This study addresses the following primary research question: **How effective is the QuranAuthentic system in accurately identifying and authenticating Quranic verses, especially when distinguishing between authentic and subtly altered texts using transformer-based language models?**. This research question focuses on evaluating the performance of the QuranAuthentic tool in detecting non-authentic Quranic verses, particularly those with minor alterations, which could resemble authentic verses closely. The study aims to measure the accuracy and reliability of the system compared to traditional methods of Quranic verse verification. Specifically, it explores the use of advanced deep learning models, such as BERT-based architectures (Koroteev, 2021), and how well these models handle the complexities of the Arabic language, including subtle semantic and contextual differences (Alammary, 2022). The goal is to create a more efficient, scalable, and automated solution for Quranic verse authentication in the digital age. This work has the potential to significantly improve the verification of Quranic verses within digital contexts, thus protecting both their authenticity and integrity in light of increasing online distribution (Hakak et al., 2019).

3.2 Dataset Collection

The dataset for our proposed methodology, QuranAuthentic, consists of two main classes: authentic Quranic verses and non-authentic, altered verses. While previous studies have focused on classifying Quranic verses against general Arabic text, no research has specifically addressed distinguishing authentic verses from subtly altered versions that closely resemble the original. In our data collection step, Sentence-BERT (sBE) was employed to compare the similarity between authentic verses and their altered counterparts. A cosine similarity threshold ensured minimal alterations, preserving structural similarity while introducing meaningful contextual differences. This approach aligns with recent advances in semantic textual similarity using transformer-based models (Reimers, 2019). The automated process altered words, phrases, or sentence structures within verses, keeping the difference between authentic and non-authentic text within a controlled range. Natural language processing techniques, such as TF-IDF and WordNet antonym replacement (Fellbaum, 1998), were applied to introduce alterations. The system replaced high-importance words or modified verse structures, and in cases where antonym replacement failed, selective word removal was used. This method ensured non-authentic verses retained close resemblance to their authentic counterparts while introducing subtle but detectable differences. This automated approach significantly enhanced the quality and scalability of the non-authentic dataset, offering a controlled method for generating text that closely mimics authentic Quranic verses with minor, contextually distinct variations.

- **Authentic dataset:** Sourced from tanzil.net[1],

[1]tanzil.net is a Quran initiative founded in 2007 to generate

providing verified Quranic texts.

- **Non-authentic dataset:** Initially, 500 verses were manually altered to create the dataset. This was then expanded through automation using sentence-BERT [2] and cosine similarity, followed by quality checks, resulting in a total of 2068 non-authentic verses.

Given the sensitive nature of the Quranic text, the non-authentic verses generated for this research are labeled as non-authentic and are **kept strictly for internal use.** These altered verses will not be published or shared publicly in any form. They are solely utilized for the purpose of model training and evaluation, and all data handling complies with ethical guidelines to ensure the protection of the Quran's integrity.

3.3 Text Pre-processing

The Quranic dataset comprises 2000 verses labeled as "Authentic", and the non-authentic dataset consists of 2068 lines labeled as "non-Authentic". Since our dataset was sourced from authentic Quranic content which serves as a reliable source provided by **tanzil.net** (Tanzil, 2023), and the non-authentic dataset was manually curated, and further rechecked after automation, it was inherently clean and required minimal preprocessing. However, to ensure that the QuranAuthentic tool can handle real-world data, preprocessing was primarily applied to the unseen test data. This preprocessing was designed to clean and standardize content that might be encountered in online settings. For the unseen real world data, non-Arabic content such as numbers and foreign text, was removed to focus solely on relevant Arabic text. Normalization was conducted to unify variations in the script, particularly different forms of Alef, to reduce ambiguity and improve text consistency. Special symbols, including URLs, emoticons, and extraneous characters, were eliminated to maintain a clean dataset. Additionally, Kashida (Tatweel), often used for text decoration, was removed to prevent interference with text analysis. Such steps are important in handling the complexities of Arabic text, as highlighted in studies like preprocessing pipelines for Arabic NLP (Awajan, 2007). Finally, tokenization was carried out to separate the text into tokens which allows the model to process particular words or characters with a greater efficiency (Alkaoud and Syed, 2020). These techniques made sure that the text data utilized in real-life scenarios was standardized and appropriate for proper model processing.

a thoroughly Unicode Quran text to be utilized in Quranic websites and apps

[2]https://huggingface.co/sentence-transformers

3.4 Model Training

In recent years, models based on transformer architecture have set the benchmark for multiple natural language processing tasks. Based on a thorough analysis of the existing body of knowledge (Alammary, 2022), we considered experimenting with the most outperforming BERT models for Arabic text which include **BERT-Base-Arabic**, **AraBERT** and **MarBERT**. Our aim was to utilize their sophisticated language understanding capabilities for accurately distinguishing between authentic and altered Quranic verses. **BERT-Base-Arabic** was chosen for its general applicability and strong performance in a wide range of Arabic text processing tasks. **BERT-Base-Arabic** is pre-trained on a large Arabic corpus, making it well-suited for understanding context and semantics in Arabic. It serves as an excellent baseline for Quranic verse authentication by detecting semantic shifts and structural changes, which are essential for distinguishing authentic from altered verses. **AraBERT**, trained on a large corpus of Modern Standard Arabic (MSA) text, was selected due to its strong performance in various Arabic NLP tasks (Antoun et al., 2020). While **AraBERT** does not have the same specialized focus on Quranic text as other models, its understanding of standard Arabic syntax and semantics makes it an important baseline model in this study. We employed **MarBERT** for its specialized focus on Arabic text, particularly in identifying textual discrepancies. Given its training on a large Arabic corpus and different Arabic dialects (AlKhamissi et al., 2021), **MarBERT** is highly effective at recognizing slight deviations in text structure and style, allowing it to detect alterations in Quranic verses that may compromise their authenticity. All models were fine-tuned through hyperparameter tuning, including adjustments to learning rates, batch sizes, and the number of training epochs to achieve optimal performance. Training was conducted using the balanced dataset of authentic and non-authentic Quranic verses described in the previous section. The results of this model training and testing are evaluated in the subsequent sections.

4 Experimental Setup

This section is divided into different subsections that explain the collection of datasets, preparation of dataset for authentic and non-authentic classes, the evaluation metrics used for finding and working out the results and then the implementation and experimentation of the models. These steps ensure a robust and accurate evaluation of the Quranic verse classification system.

4.1 Data Preparation

For this study, the dataset consists of two classes: authentic Quranic verses and non-authentic, altered verses. The authentic dataset was sourced from *Tanzil.net*, a verified repository of Quranic texts. The non-authentic dataset was generated automatically by introducing controlled alterations to the authentic verses using **sentence-BERT** and cosine similarity threshold. The dataset statistics are as follows:

Authentic Dataset: 2000 Quranic verses from *Tanzil.net*.

Non-authentic Dataset: 2068 Non-Authentic text generated by modifying authentic verses, ensuring a cosine similarity threshold that maintains structural resemblance but introduces contextual changes.

The dataset was divided into training and testing sets, with 20% of the data reserved for testing. This separation ensures the model's performance is evaluated on unseen data, reflecting potential real-world performance. Further, the training data underwent Stratified K-Fold cross-validation with three splits, where approximately 1/3 of the training data serves as the validation set in each fold. This method preserves the percentage of samples for each class, crucial for maintaining class distribution consistency across training and validation subsets. The rotational use of data for validation in each fold facilitates effective hyperparameter tuning and model validation without a separate dedicated validation dataset.

Table 1: Dataset Division

Class	Train	Validation	Test	Total
Authentic	1067	533	400	2000
Non-Authentic	1101	553	414	2068
Total	2168	1086	814	4068

4.2 Evaluation Metrics

To evaluate the performance of the models, we utilized the following metrics:

- **Accuracy**: The proportion of correctly classified verses.
- **Precision**: The ratio of true positive predictions to the total predicted positives.
- **Recall**: The ratio of true positive predictions to the actual positives.
- **F1-Score**: The harmonic mean of precision and recall, balancing the trade-off between the two.

These metrics provide a comprehensive view of the models' effectiveness in distinguishing between authentic and non-authentic Quranic verses.

4.3 Experimental Evaluation

For the experimentation of the QuranAuthentic system, we employed three transformer-based models: **BERT-Base-Arabic**, **MarBERT**, and **AraBERT**. After preprocessing, we merged two datasets of Quranic verses, ensuring no missing values. We split the data into training (80%) and test (20%) set using stratified sampling to maintain class distribution. Tokenization was performed using the respective BERT tokenizer, and the pretrained models from Hugging Face were fine-tuned with hyperparameters given in Table 2. We implemented 3-fold stratified cross validation to evaluate model performance. Each fold involved tokenizing the data, compiling the model with the Adam optimizer, and applying early stopping and learning rate scheduling. We calculated precision, recall, F1-score, and accuracy after training on the validation sets. Finally, the model was tested on the unseen dataset to evaluate the model. The models were fine-tuned using varying hyperparameters. Table 2 shows the configurations used during the training process:

Table 2: Hyperparameter Configuration

Model	Learning Rate	Epochs	Batch Size
BERT-Base-Arabic	5e-5	10	8
MarBERT	3e-5	12	16
AraBERT	4e-5	15	8

It is worth mentioning that this process was repeated for several variations of BERT-based models. However, **MarBERT** and **BERT-Base-Arabic** both consistently exhibited the most promising results due to its specialized training on Arabic text. Each model's performance was measured based on average accuracy, precision, recall, and F1 score and the results are detailed in the following section.

5 Results and Analysis

To address the defined research question, we conducted a thorough systematic literature review followed by rigorous experimentation, implementation and analysis to select the best performing models for arabic language (Alrajhi et al., 2022). In order to evaluate the effectiveness of the QuranAuthentic system, we conducted a comprehensive set of experiments on each of the transformer-based models, namely **BERT-Base-Arabic**, **MarBERT**, and **AraBERT**. These experiments aimed to address the research question. The performance of each model was evaluated using average accuracy, precision, recall, and F1-score as the primary metrics. The primary research question revolved around assessing the performance of these models on a specialized dataset comprised of Quranic verse classifications. Our evaluation of models revealed nuanced differences in performance across these models. Notably, **BERT-Base-Arabic** and **MarBERT** demonstrated significantly better performances. In contrast, **AraBERT**, while showing lower precision and overall test accuracy, suggesting a greater tendency for false positives. The results underscore the importance of selecting appropriate models that align with the linguistic and syntactic demands of the text. Table 3 will detail the comparative results of these models under a specific set of configurations, highlighting their respective strengths and limitations in the context of Quranic verse classification.

Table 3: Model Performance on the Test Set

Model	Accuracy	Precision	Recall	F1-Score
MarBERT	93.73%	91.25%	96.50%	93.80%
BERT-Base-Arabic	92.75%	89.56%	96.50%	92.90%
AraBERT	57.99%	53.92%	99.75%	70.00%

The detailed performance metrics for each model reveal significant insights into their capabilities in processing Quranic text authentication. **MarBERT** and **BERT-Base-Arabic** both show exemplary performance, with **MarBERT** slightly leading in terms of precision and overall F1-score. **MarBERT**, with an accuracy of 93.73% and an F1-score of 93.80%, demonstrates a strong balance between precision and recall. This model's focused training on Arabic language content clearly enhances its ability to accurately authenticate Quranic verses while minimizing false positives. Such performance is essential for applications where the authenticity of the text is paramount, like in digital platforms for religious texts. **BERT-Base-Arabic**, while trailing slightly behind **MarBERT**, still presents impressive results with an accuracy of 92.75% and an F1-score of 92.90%. Its high recall rate, in particular, suggests it is highly effective at identifying authentic texts, though its precision indicates some challenges in minimizing false positives. Nonetheless, the improved metrics suggest that even general-purpose models, with appropriate tuning, can offer robust solutions for specialized tasks like Quranic text authentication. Conversely, **AraBERT** displays an unmatched recall of 99.75%, highlighting its strength in identifying relevant verses. However, its lower precision points to a high rate of false positives, limiting its practical utility in scenarios where both identification and precision are critical. This underperformance can be attributed to several factors. First, AraBERT, primarily trained on Modern Standard Arabic (MSA), is suitable for general Arabic tasks (Antoun et al., 2020). However, it does not fully capture the linguistic nuances of Quranic texts, which include classical Arabic features and unique stylistic elements. In contrast, **MARBERT**, trained on both MSA and Arabic dialects, benefits from its ability to handle linguistic diversity, making it better equipped to address text variations and subtle alterations often encountered in Quranic verse authentication. **BERT-Base-Arabic**, while also trained on MSA, performs better than **AraBERT** in this task due to its robust handling of formal Arabic text and stronger generalization capabilities in tasks requiring contextual understanding. Additionally, **AraBERT** struggles with dialectal variations, as its training corpus does not encompass the specific differences in pronunciation and word choice found in Quranic dialects, such as those associated with Qira'at. To enhance AraBERT's performance in Quranic verse authentication, future work should focus on fine-tuning the model on Quran-specific datasets, incorporating dialectal and Qira'at variations, and optimizing hyperparameters to improve precision and reduce false positives.

In summary, the performance of **MarBERT** and **BERT-Base-Arabic** underscores the effectiveness of specialized and appropriately tuned models in enhancing the accuracy and reliability of Quranic verse authentication systems. Their robust capabilities demonstrate significant potential for real-world applications, ensuring the integrity and authenticity of Quranic verses in digital formats. To enhance AraBERT's utility and address its underperformance in Quranic verse authentication tasks, several strategies can be implemented. First, incorporating dialectal Arabic and Qira'at variations in the training data would allow AraBERT to handle the **linguistic diversity** and recitation styles characteristic of Quranic Arabic. This approach would enhance its precision across diverse representations. Furthermore, data augmentation techniques, such as generating varied non-authentic verses and introducing subtle textual changes (e.g., paraphrasing or simulated typographical errors), would improve the model's robustness against real-world variations. In the future, we can employ these methods to provide a comprehensive framework to enhance AraBERT's performance in Quranic text-related tasks.

6 Limitations of the Current Study

Despite the promising outcomes of this research, several limitations warrant consideration:

Dependency on a Single Data Source: The authentic dataset is sourced exclusively from **tanzil.net**[3]. While this source is verified and widely regarded as reliable, it may not cover some of the canonical Quranic variations which are from the different Qira'at or recitation styles. This dependency limits the generalizability of the model to other verified Quranic texts.

Reproducibility Challenges: The fine-tuning process utilized in this study, including hyperparameter optimization, is highly dependent on computational resources. The results achieved may not be easily replicable without having similar hardware configurations and pretrained models, thus limiting the embracing of these methods.

Performance Under Resource Constraints: Despite excellent performance of BERT-based Language Model, their deployment in real environments is resource intensive. However, inference optimization need to be carried out in order to have efficiency and scalability in such environments which has not been dealt with in this paper. These limitations underscore the need of future research that addresses these limitations which relate to dataset diversity, reproducibility issues, and optimal model performance in practical applications.

7 Conclusion

This paper highlights the effectiveness of transformer-based deep learning models in authenticating Quranic verses in Arabic text. We employed three models: **BERT-Base-Arabic**, **MarBERT**, and **AraBERT** which are fine-tuned to classify verses as authentic or non-authentic. Despite the inherent complexities of the Arabic language and subtle alterations in verses, the models achieved notable performance especially the two models **BERT-Base-Arabic** and **MarBERT**. From these experimental analysis, we can conclude that Transformer models can accurately differentiate between authentic and non-authentic Quranic verses, with **MarBERT** and **BERT-Base-Arabic** delivering the promising results. The findings indicate that the specialized models like **MarBERT** and **BERT-Base-Arabic** provide better context and semantic understanding, making them ideal for tasks like religious text authentication. This work offers a potential solution for Quranic verses verification, addressing concerns about unverified verses online. In the future, we aim to enhance the model's performance and create a real-time tool for authenticating Quranic verses. Furthermore, we plan to expand the dataset to include diverse sources and variations, particularly by incorporating multiple **Qira'at (canonical recitations)**, which will ensure that the model is more robust and comprehensive. This will be achieved by collaborating with specialized Qira'at databases and employing data augmentation techniques to simulate variations across different recitation styles. This approach can also be extended to authenticate religious texts in other languages or domains. By fine-tuning pre-trained transformer models like mBERT (Wang et al., 2019) or XLM-R (Goyal et al., 2021) on domain-specific datasets, such as the Bible or the Torah, these models can be adapted to handle the unique linguistic features and structural intricacies of other religious texts. Additionally, data augmentation and transfer learning (Torrey and Shavlik, 2010) can be employed to adapt the model for new languages or domains with limited data. By training on multilingual datasets and incorporating cultural and linguistic nuances, this approach can be extended beyond Quranic texts to other religious and historical contexts, ensuring

[3]https://tanzil.net/download/

robust performance across various languages and traditions.

References

Semantic textual similarity using sbert. Accessed: November 2024.

Ali Saleh Alammary. 2022. Bert models for arabic text classification: a systematic review. *Applied Sciences*, 12(11):5720.

Mohamed Alkaoud and Mairaj Syed. 2020. On the importance of tokenization in arabic embedding models. In *Proceedings of the fifth Arabic natural language processing workshop*, pages 119–129.

Badr AlKhamissi, Mohamed Gabr, Muhammad El-Nokrashy, and Khaled Essam. 2021. Adapting marbert for improved arabic dialect identification: Submission to the nadi 2021 shared task. *arXiv preprint arXiv:2103.01065*.

Wafa Abdullah Alrajhi, Hend Al-Khalifa, and Abdulmalik AlSalman. 2022. Assessing the linguistic knowledge in arabic pre-trained language models using minimal pairs. In *Proceedings of the Seventh Arabic Natural Language Processing Workshop (WANLP)*, pages 185–193.

Wissam Antoun, Fady Baly, and Hazem Hajj. 2020. Arabert: Transformer-based model for arabic language understanding. *arXiv preprint arXiv:2003.00104*.

Arafat Awajan. 2007. Arabic text preprocessing for the natural language processing applications. *Arab Gulf Journal of Scientific Research*, 25(4):179–189.

Kerstin Eksell. 1995. Complexity of linguistic change as reflected in arabic dialects. *Studia Orientalia Electronica*, 75:63–74.

Christiane Fellbaum. 1998. Wordnet: An electronic lexical database. *MIT Press google schola*, 2:678–686.

Anthony Gillioz, Jacky Casas, Elena Mugellini, and Omar Abou Khaled. 2020. Overview of the transformer-based models for nlp tasks. In *2020 15th Conference on computer science and information systems (FedCSIS)*, pages 179–183. IEEE.

Naman Goyal, Jingfei Du, Myle Ott, Giri Anantharaman, and Alexis Conneau. 2021. Larger-scale transformers for multilingual masked language modeling. *arXiv preprint arXiv:2105.00572*.

Saqib Hakak, Amirrudin Kamsin, Omar Tayan, Mohd Yamani Idna Idris, and Gulshan Amin Gilkar. 2019. Approaches for preserving content integrity of sensitive online arabic content: A survey and research challenges. *Information Processing & Management*, 56(2):367–380.

Saqib Iqbal Hakak. 2018. *Authenticating Sensitive Diacritical Texts Using Residual, Data Representation and Pattern Matching Methods*. Ph.D. thesis, University of Malaya (Malaysia).

Mustafa Jarrar, Fadi Zaraket, Rami Asia, and Hamzeh Amayreh. 2018. Diacritic-based matching of arabic words. *ACM Transactions on Asian and Low-Resource Language Information Processing (TALLIP)*, 18(2):1–21.

Amirrudin Kamsin, Abdullah Gani, Ishak Suliaman, Salinah Jaafar, Rohana Mahmud, Aznul Qalid Md Sabri, Zaidi Razak, Mohd Yamani Idna Idris, Maizatul Akmar Ismail, Noorzaily Mohamed Noor, et al. 2014. Developing the novel quran and hadith authentication system. In *The 5th International Conference on Information and Communication Technology for The Muslim World (ICT4M)*, pages 1–5. IEEE.

Mikhail V Koroteev. 2021. Bert: a review of applications in natural language processing and understanding. *arXiv preprint arXiv:2103.11943*.

Abdullah Y Muaad, Shaina Raza, Usman Naseem, and Hanumanthappa J Jayappa Davanagere. 2023. Arabic text detection: a survey of recent progress challenges and opportunities. *Applied Intelligence*, 53(24):29845–29862.

N Reimers. 2019. Sentence-bert: Sentence embeddings using siamese bert-networks. *arXiv preprint arXiv:1908.10084*.

S Shreyashree, Pramod Sunagar, S Rajarajeswari, and Anita Kanavalli. 2022. A literature review on bidirectional encoder representations from transformers. *Inventive Computation and Information Technologies: Proceedings of ICICIT 2021*, pages 305–320.

Tanzil. 2023. Tanzil quran navigator. Accessed: 2023-10-09.

Lisa Torrey and Jude Shavlik. 2010. Transfer learning. In *Handbook of research on machine learning applications and trends: algorithms, methods, and techniques*, pages 242–264. IGI global.

Zineb Touati-Hamad, Mohamed Ridda Laouar, and Issam Bendib. 2021. Authentication of quran verses sequences using deep learning. In *2021 International Conference on Recent Advances in Mathematics and Informatics (ICRAMI)*, pages 1–4. IEEE.

Zineb Touati-Hamad, Mohamed Ridda Laouar, Issam Bendib, and Saqib Hakak. 2022. Arabic quran verses authentication using deep learning and word embeddings. *The International Arab Journal of Information Technology*, 19(4):681–688.

A Vaswani. 2017. Attention is all you need. *Advances in Neural Information Processing Systems*.

Zihan Wang, Stephen Mayhew, Dan Roth, et al. 2019. Cross-lingual ability of multilingual bert: An empirical study. *arXiv preprint arXiv:1912.07840*.

MASAQ Parser: A Fine-grained MorphoSyntactic Analysis for the Quran

Majdi Sawalha [a, b], Faisal Al-Shargi [c], Sane Yagi [d, e], Abdallah T. AlShdaifat [f], Bassam Hammo [b, g]

[a] King Abdullah II School of Information Technology, The University of Jordan, Amman, Jordan.
[b] College of Engineering, Al-Ain University, Abu Dhabi, UAE.
[c] Amazon Robotics, New York, USA.
[d] Department of Foreign Languages, University of Sharjah, Sharjah, UAE.
[e] English Department, The University of Jordan, Amman, Jordan.
[f] College of Arts and Languages, Mohamed bin Zayed University for Humanities, Abu Dhabi, UAE.
[g] School of Computing Sciences, Princess Sumaya University for Technology, Amman, Jordan.

sawalha.majdi@ju.edu.jo, falsharg@amazon.com, saneyagi@yahoo.com, abdallah.alshdaifat@mbzuh.ac.ae, b.hammo@ju.edu.jo

Abstract

This paper introduces the Morphological and Syntactical analysis for the Quran text. In this research we have constructed the MASAQ dataset, a comprehensive resource designed to address the scarcity of annotated Quranic Arabic corpora and facilitate the development of advanced Natural Language Processing (NLP) models. The Quran, being a cornerstone of classical Arabic, presents unique challenges for NLP due to its sacred nature and complex linguistic features. MASAQ provides a detailed syntactic and morphological annotation of the entire Quranic text that includes more than 131K morphological entries and 123K instances of syntactic functions, covering a wide range of grammatical roles and relationships. MASAQ's unique features include a comprehensive tagset of 72 syntactic roles, detailed morphological analysis, and context-specific annotations. This dataset is particularly valuable for tasks such as dependency parsing, grammar checking, machine translation, and text summarization. The potential applications of MASAQ are vast, ranging from pedagogical uses in teaching Arabic grammar to developing sophisticated NLP tools. By providing a high-quality, syntactically annotated dataset, MASAQ aims to advance the field of Arabic NLP, enabling more accurate and more efficient language processing tools. The dataset is made available under the Creative Commons Attribution 3.0 License, ensuring compliance with ethical guidelines and respecting the integrity of the Quranic text.

1 Introduction

This paper introduces MASAQ, a new dataset for Arabic Natural Language Processing (NLP). MASAQ focuses on the Quran, which presents unique challenges for NLP due to its sacred nature and complex linguistic features. While the Quran is a cornerstone of Classical Arabic and offers rich opportunities for NLP research, no existing resource provides the structured data necessary for computational analysis.

The MASAQ dataset addresses this gap by providing a detailed syntactic and morphological annotation of the entire Quranic text, using over 131,000 morphological entries and 123,000 instances of syntactic functions. These annotations cover a wide range of grammatical roles and relationships. MASAQ is particularly valuable for tasks such as: dependency parsing, grammar checking, machine translation, and text summarization.

Previous work on Arabic dependency parsing has resulted in several treebanks. Some of them, e.g., the Arabic Treebank by the University of Pennsylvania, the Prague Arabic Dependency Treebank (PADT), and the Columbia Arabic Treebank, have focused on Modern Standard Arabic (MSA) and news texts. However, these treebanks often use different annotation schemes, and access to some is restricted.

The Quranic Arabic Corpus, developed at the University of Leeds, is one example of a project that uses Quranic Arabic. However, no existing resource faithfully reflects the detail and nuances of traditional Arabic i'rab in a computationally friendly format. MASAQ seeks to address this need, making the sophisticated syntactic analysis found in the Arabic heritage accessible for NLP research and applications.

MASAQ's creation involved the following:

Proceedings of the New Horizons in Computational Linguistics for Religious Texts (Coling-Rel), pages 67–75
January 19, 2025.

- Source Text: The raw data for MASAQ came from the Tanzil Quran text, known for its high accuracy and authenticity.
- Annotation: A team of Arabic native speakers with expertise in traditional Arabic syntactic analysis annotated the text. They used a comprehensive tagset of 71 syntactic roles to capture the grammatical information found in classical grammar treatises.
- Annotation Tool: A custom annotation application was developed to streamline the process, presenting verses for context and breaking down words into their constituent morphemes.

MASAQ will be a valuable resource for advancing both academic and practical applications in Arabic NLP, including:

- Pedagogical Uses: Simplifying the teaching of Arabic grammar.
- NLP Tool Development: Enhancing tools like part-of-speech taggers and parsers.
- Linguistic Research: Providing valuable syntactic analysis for research purposes.
- Cross-linguistic Research: Supporting efforts like Universal Dependencies and facilitating multilingual NLP tool development.

We released MASAQ under the Creative Commons Attribution 3.0 License, and ensured compliance with ethical guidelines and respecting the integrity of the Quranic text.

2 Background Review

The Quran, as the central religious text of Islam, holds immense significance in the Arabic language. It has long been a cornerstone for linguistic studies and, more recently, has emerged as a valuable resource for NLP tasks. Its rich linguistic structure and extensive historical analysis make it an ideal candidate for supervised learning in NLP.

While traditional Quranic parsing resources offer a wealth of linguistic insights, their format and style present significant challenges for computational analysis. These resources often lack a formal, structured representation, relying instead on prose descriptions that assume a deep understanding of Arabic grammar. This reliance on implicit knowledge makes it difficult to automate the extraction of syntactic information. Moreover, inconsistencies in terminology and varying levels of detail further hinder the development of standardized annotation schemes. To address these limitations and enable the application of NLP techniques to Quranic text, there is a pressing need for a structured and consistent dataset like MASAQ.

2.1 Previous Arabic Dependency Datasets

There are several valuable Arabic dependency treebanks that preceded our work and demonstrated considerable efforts in Arabic syntactic analysis. However, these treebanks have left a gap. They exhibit different annotation schemes, restricted access, and a lack of focus on traditional Arabic i'rab. MASAQ addresses these limitations, providing a unique and open resource for the computational analysis of Quranic Arabic.

Many worthy initiatives in Arabic dependency parsing, such as the Arabic Treebank by the University of Pennsylvania (Maamouri, et al., 2006), the Prague Arabic Dependency Treebank (Hajic, et al., 2004; Smrz, Bielicky, and Hajic, 2008), and the Columbia Arabic Treebank (Habash & Roth, 2009), focused on Modern Standard Arabic (MSA) and news texts. These treebanks often used different annotation schemes, making it difficult to compare and integrate their data. Access to some of these treebanks, such as the University of Pennsylvania's, is restricted, requiring a subscription or institutional affiliation.

Other projects focused on Classical Arabic, specifically the language of the Quran. The Quranic Arabic Corpus (Dukes, 2011), developed at the University of Leeds, pioneered the incorporation of i'rab into its framework. The Arabic Poetry Treebank (Al-Ghamdi, Al-Khalifa, & Al-Salman, 2021), focusing on poetic Classical Arabic, faced challenges with errors in tokenization, POS tagging, and dependency relation labeling due to using a parser designed for MSA.

The Camel Lab Treebank (Taji & Habash, 2020) stands out for its coverage of a diverse range of text types, including classical literature, modern news articles, and user-generated content, and its open-access policy. However, it uses a simplified set of syntactic categories and relations based on traditional Arabic grammar but not identical to it.

The I'rab Dependency Treebank (Halabi, Fayyoumi, & Awajan, 2021), while adopting a traditional Arabic grammatical theory approach, is limited in size, containing only 601 sentences sampled from the Prague Arabic Dependency Treebank (Hajic, et al., 2004; Smrz, Bielicky, and Hajic, 2008).

The limitations of existing Arabic dependency datasets underscore the need for a resource like MASAQ, which focuses specifically on traditional Arabic i'rab and provides a comprehensive and consistent annotation scheme in an open-access format.

The Quran, as a cornerstone of Classical Arabic, offers a rich resource for NLP research due to its complex syntax and semantics. The intricate nature of Quranic Arabic necessitates utmost accuracy in NLP tasks related to it. MASAQ addresses this challenge by providing a detailed and carefully annotated dataset specifically designed for dependency parsing of the Quran (Sawalha, et al., 2024).

2.2 Significance of Quranic Arabic for NLP

The Quran's language, Classical Arabic (CA), is vital for datasets aiming to capture the nuances of this Arabic variety. Its complex syntax, semantics, morphology, and phonology provide an excellent resource for testing and refining NLP algorithms. This is especially true given the Quran's meticulous preservation and standardization, ensuring a consistent and reliable corpus for machine learning and linguistic research.

Beyond the text itself, thousands of authoritative works explore facets of the Quran, including interpretation, translation, morphology, syntax, jurisprudence, and the subject matter of over 30 branches of Islamic sciences. These scholarly resources offer detailed analyses that can inform the development of robust NLP datasets.

Despite its value, the Quran poses unique challenges for Arabic NLP, particularly in morphological analysis and parsing. Due to its sacred nature, Muslims expect utmost accuracy in NLP tasks related to the Quran, often approaching 100%. This necessitates careful attention to detail, including sourcing the raw text from authenticated sources, developing a comprehensive and well-justified annotation scheme, and engaging annotators with high expertise in Arabic morphology, syntax, and Quranic interpretation.

The Quran's value is demonstrated by its use in a range of NLP projects. The Quranic Arabic Corpus, for example, utilizes the text for syntactic and morphological analysis. Other projects have leveraged the Quran to improve machine translation systems, text classification, information retrieval, sentiment analysis, and speech recognition and synthesis systems for various Arabic dialects. Additionally, the Quran has been used for tasks like phrase-break prediction and IPA phonemic transcription.

In conclusion, while the Quran presents challenges for NLP research, its linguistic richness, standardization, and extensive body of scholarly work make it an invaluable resource for developing and refining sophisticated NLP tools and resources.

2.3 Limitations of Traditional Quranic Parsing

Traditional Quranic parsing resources, despite their richness and depth, are not suitable for NLP due to limitations primarily that stem from format and style, which make it difficult to adapt such resources for computational analysis.

Lack of Formal Representation: Traditional resources lack a formal, structured representation suitable for computational modeling. Instead, syntactic analyses are presented in prose, assuming a high level of reader expertise in Arabic grammar. This reliance on assumed knowledge leads to abbreviated descriptions that hinder computational analysis. For example, instead of a detailed breakdown, a phrase might simply be labeled as a "prepositional phrase," which is insufficient for training and testing language models.

Inconsistencies and Ambiguity: Traditional resources often exhibit inconsistencies in terminology when describing grammatical functions. For instance, "na't" and "sifa" are both used for "adjective," while "maf'ul bihi" and "maf'ul" both refer to "object". These varying terms introduce ambiguity and make it difficult to develop a standardized annotation scheme for NLP purposes. Additionally, the level of detail in parsing can vary significantly across resources, further complicating computational analysis.

MASAQ as a Solution: The limitations of traditional resources underscore the need for a systematic and structured approach specifically designed for Quranic Arabic. The MASAQ dataset addresses these challenges by providing a consistent representation of Quranic syntax suitable for NLP research. Its standardized syntactic tagset and detailed annotations enable computational analysis and facilitate the development of automatic parsers for Arabic.

3 Syntactic Parsing

Parsing is the process of analyzing textual content to determine its grammatical structure and the relationships between its components. In syntactic analysis, parsing involves examining the structure of a sentence to identify parts of speech (like nouns, verbs, adjectives) and their roles within the sentence, e.g., subject, predicate, object, etc. Parsing is crucial for such NLP tasks as machine translation, speech recognition, and text-to-speech processing.

I'rab is one type of syntactic parsing. It involves grammatically dissecting verses to understand their structure, nuances, and linguistic implications. It encompasses three key aspects: (1) Identifying the grammatical function of a word within a sentence, e.g., subject (مبتدأ *mubtada'*), predicate (خبر *khabar*), circumstantial qualifier (حال *ḥāl*), etc. (2) Specifying the case of the word (e.g., nominative, accusative, genitive inflection) based on its function. (3) Noting any additional context or information associated with the word's phrasal affiliation. Religious scholars use *i'rab* to understand the exact meaning of verses and to resolve grammatical ambiguities in the Quran. Computer scientists may use it for information retrieval and machine translation. Here, Figure 1, is an example of the *i'rab* of the Quran, verse 1:

	Word			***I'rab***	**Phrasal I' rab** *(function of embedded phrases)*
Sentence	1	الْحَمْدُ	*al-ḥamdu*	*mubtada'*	
	2	لِلَّهِ	*li-Allāhi*	Prep. + Noun	**Predicate** (khabar)
	3	رَبِّ	*rabbi*	Adj.	
	4	الْعَالَمِينَ	*al-'ālamīna*	Poss. Comp.	
	5	الرَّحْمَٰنِ	*al-raḥmāni*	Adj.	
	6	الرَّحِيمِ	*al-raḥīmi*	Adj.	
	7	مَالِكِ	*māliki*	Adj.	
	8	يَوْمِ	*yawmi*	Poss. Comp.	
	9	الدِّينِ	*al-dīni*	Poss. Comp.	

Figure 1: *I'rab* for One Quranic Verse

3.1 Constituency vs. Dependency Parsing

Syntactic analysis may be in the form of constituency parsing or dependency parsing. These approaches to syntactic analysis have distinct methodologies and applications. Constituency parsing utilizes context-free grammars to create hierarchical trees that divide sentences into phrasal constituents, such as noun and verb phrases, whereas dependency parsing represents syntax through directed edges in a graph, capturing dependencies between words with a single root, typically the verb. Parsing natural language presents challenges due to ambiguity, often requiring supervised machine learning models trained on annotated data to resolve multiple valid interpretations. The choice between constituency and dependency parsing depends on the application, with dependency parsing being advantageous for information extraction and free word order languages, and constituency parsing preferable for extracting sub-phrases.

I'rab is a type of Arabic dependency rather than constituency parsing since it is focused on identifying the grammatical relationships between words in a sentence, such as subject-verb relationships, while constituency parsing is focused on identifying the phrase and sub-phrase constituents.

4 MASAQ Dataset: Composition and Annotation

MASAQ can be characterized by the composition and structure of its raw data, as well as by its annotations (Sawalha, et al., 2024).

4.1 Composition and Structure of MASAQ

The MASAQ dataset is built upon the foundation of a verified Quranic text that has been enriched through a layered annotation process.

Raw Data Source: The foundation of MASAQ is the Tanzil Quran text, selected for its high accuracy and verification standards. The Tanzil project uses a three-step verification process to ensure accuracy, including: automatic text extraction, rule-based verification, and manual verification against the Medina Mushaf.

This rigorous process makes the Tanzil version widely acclaimed for its lack of errors. The text is available in both the Uthmani and imla'i scripts, with the Uthmani script being the most authoritative and the imla'i offering a modernized representation.

The Tanzil version adheres to the 1924 Cairo edition of the Quran, endorsed by Al-Azhar University. This edition standardized the *Ḥafṣ 'an 'Āṣim* reading and established the commonly accepted verse numbering and chapter ordering. MASAQ utilizes this text in accordance with the Creative Commons Attribution 3.0 License.

Annotation Structure: MASAQ enhances this raw text by adding a layer of comprehensive syntactic analysis. Table 1 provides a profile of the dataset, showing the number of dataset entries to be 130K morphemes, instances of syntactic functions (*i'rab*) 123K, and Quran words (before morphemic analysis) 77,408 words.

The annotated data in MASAQ follows a specific structure. Each row represents a word or word part (morpheme) from a specific verse and chapter (*sūra*) of the Quran. The data is organized sequentially, starting with the first word of the Quran and proceeding to the last. Each word or segment is aligned with morphological, syntactic, and semantic tags to describe its features and function within the sentence.

MASAQ's Raw and Annotated Data: To understand the structure of MASAQ, it is helpful to consider the distinction between the raw data and the added annotations:

- Raw Data: This refers to the Quranic text itself, taken from the Tanzil project. It is the base layer upon which the annotations are built.
- Annotated Data: This layer adds value to the raw text by providing detailed linguistic information about each word or word part. The annotations include morphological details (e.g., root, prefixes, suffixes and their types), syntactic roles (e.g., subject, object, preposition), and semantic information.

Table 1 gives further details about the composition of the MASAQ dataset, including information about:

- The breakdown of words based on the number of morphemes they contain.
- The number of definite article tokens, reflecting a key feature of Arabic grammar.

Table 1: Profile Summary of MASAQ

Type	Count
Dataset entries (Morphemes)	131,930
Instances of syntactic functions (*i'rab*)	123,565
Quran words (before morphemic analysis)	77,408
Words composed of one morpheme	34,909
Words composed of two morphemes	31,997
Words composed of three morphemes	9,175
Words composed of four morphemes	1,154
Words composed of five morphemes	152
Words composed of six morphemes	21
Definite article tokens	8,365

These details offer a glimpse into the complexity of the Quranic language and the challenges of analyzing it computationally.

4.2 The Full Tagset

The full tagset encompasses a comprehensive list of 71 syntactic roles assigned to words, word parts, and phrases within the dataset. These tags are essential for understanding the relationship between syntactic units in a Quranic sentence. Each tag encapsulates the grammatical information that classical grammar treatises prescribed for the Quranic text; wherever there is difference of opinion on the grammatical function of an item or unit, the simplistic interpretation is favored. What makes this tagset especially valuable is that it fixes how syntactic roles are referred to.

These tags are meant to account for all syntactic functions of significance that are used in classical literature on the i'rab of the Quran. Here are a few notes to comment on the tags that might not be highly frequent in Arabic Computational Linguistics or whose English translation might not be familiar.

EXPLET: Expletive, when a word or phrase is inserted into a sentence without being necessary for the expression of the basic meaning of the sentence. It is a placeholder. Expletives can serve rhetorical, emphatic, or stylistic functions. The term originates from the Latin word expletivus, meaning "serving to fill out or take up space". For example, اسم لا محل له من الإعراب *'ism lā maḥalla lahu min al-ʾiʿrāb.*

DEM_GEN: Demonstrative in the Genitive Case. The demonstratives in Arabic are called *'ism ishāra.*

SUBJ_COP_PART: Subject of a Copula Particle. The first term in a stative sentence may change case as a result of the effect induced by كان *kāna* and إنّ *inna* and their sisters, which are referred to here as copula particles. There are a few tags that involve the copula in its various forms, as a particle and as a verb: perfect, imperfect, and imperative (كان *kāna*, يكون *yakūnu*, كُنْ *kun*).

An interjection is a word or phrase that is grammatically independent from the words around it and it mainly expresses feeling rather than meaning. It's a part of speech used to express a spontaneous emotion or reaction, such as surprise, excitement, or disgust. Interjections are common in everyday speech and informal writing but they are also present in the most cultivated forms of written language. As a single word or phrase, they may be used on their own or as part of a sentence. They often take the form of an imperative verb (INTERJ_CV, اسم فعل أمر, as in هَلُمَّ *halumma*), an imperfect verb (INTERJ_IV, اسم فعل مضارع, as in وَيْ *wayy*; أُفٍ *'uffin*), or a perfect verb (INTERJ_PV, اسم فعل ماض, as in هيهاتَ *hayhāta*).

A Comitative Object refers to the use of a grammatical construction that expresses the idea of "accompaniment" or "togetherness" with another entity. In Arabic, the comitative object (مفعول معه) is a noun that indicates an entity accompanying the action of the verb, typically introduced by the conjunction "و" and placed in the accusative case.

Driven by curiosity, let us briefly examine the syntactic nature of the Quran. The most frequent 50 syntactic tags are presented in Figure 4.

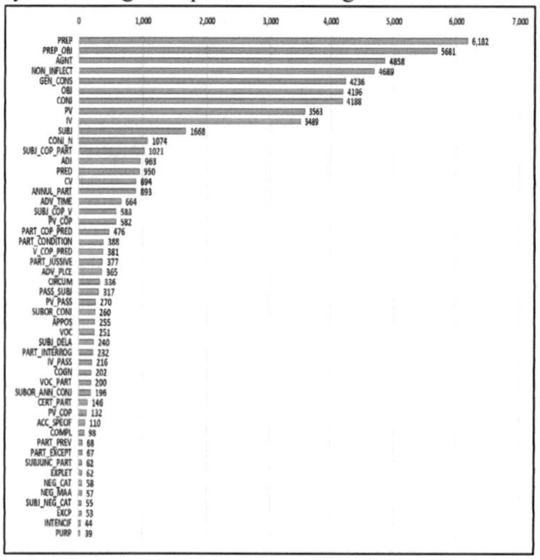

Figure 4: The most frequent 50 tags in the MASAQ Corpus

Figure 4 presents the 50 most frequent syntactic functions in MASAQ. The tag PREP (preposition) appears as the most frequent, followed by PREP_OBJ (prepositional object). One might expect their frequencies to match, since they typically form a governor-governed pair. However, the discrepancy can be explained by syntactic embedding, where a clause can serve as the governed element instead of a single word or phrase; therefore, its surface dependency parsing will not allocate a PREP_OBJ tag to the embedded clause.

Notably frequent is AGENT, which is assigned case by the verb that governs it. The frequency of verbs governing AGENT appears significantly lower because these verbs are split between the tags PV (Past Verb) and IV (Imperfect Verb).

There is clear prevalence of NON_INFLECTing particles, the GEN_CONS (genitive construct), and OBJ (object) which represents the theme and patient roles.

Among the least frequent grammatical functions are PURP (Purpose Adjunct), INTENSIF (Intensifier), EXCP (Exceptus), NEG_CAT (Categorical Negation), along with its related dependent elements.

Another view of the syntactic nature of the Quran dataset is to study some of its inflectional morphology. Let us consider Table 2.

Table 2: Frequency of Case/Mode Markers

Index	Description		Count
1	*Sukūn*	السكون	17677
2	*Fatḥa*	الفتحة	14492
3	*kasra*	الكسرة	6392
4	*ḍamma*	الضمة	4978
5	*nūn*	ثبوت النون	1008
6	elided *nūn*	حذف النون	788
7	implied *fatḥa*	فتحة مقدرة	707
8	implied *ḍamma*	ضمة مقدرة	627
9	*yā'*	الياء	539
10	*wāw*	الواو	236
11	implied *kasra*	الكسرة المقدرة	153
12	elided vowel	حذف حرف العلة	149
13	diptote *fatḥa*	الفتحة ممنوع من الصرف	114
14	*'alif*	الألف	43

Case and mode are expressed in Arabic either through diacritical marks or through such grammatical features as the vowels and "نون" (*nūn*). The high frequency of "سكون" (*sukūn*) is the result of it being the jussive mode and imperative mode marker, as well as the marker of some particles and indeclinables, and a cliticization necessity. Similarly, "فتحة" (*fatḥa*) is the marker of the subjunctive mode for verbs, the accusative case for nouns, as well as the ending diacritic of several particles and indeclinables. Both are crucial for proper pronunciation of cliticized verbs.

Notice also that the frequencies of the vowel and "نون" (*nūn*) markers are relatively low.

One possible implication for the facts presented in this section is pedagogical. School curriculum developers should avoid deterring pupils from learning Arabic by the complexity of the grammar metalanguage. Clearly, the focus of any grammar instruction, if at all, should be on the teaching of verbal and stative sentences and the basic concepts of the part of speech: noun, verb, particle, and the syntactic roles of agent, object, prepositional phrase, genitive construct, adjective, and adverb.

4.3 Annotation Process

The annotation process in MASAQ involved a multi-faceted approach, considering the complexities of Quranic Arabic and its *i'rab*. Due to Arabic's rich morphology, a single word can be composed of multiple morphemes (meaningful units), each potentially serving a distinct grammatical role. Therefore, the annotation in MASAQ had to address both the word and sub-word levels, capturing both morphological details and syntactic relationships within each sentence.

A team of Arabic native speakers proficient in *i'rab* was assembled. Their expertise comes from holding postgraduate degrees in Arabic, with a focus on morphology or syntax. Annotators applied the centuries-old methodology of *i'rab* using our comprehensive tagset. This approach facilitated efficient annotation, as the team was already familiar with the concepts. It also enhanced accuracy and consistency, minimizing the need for extensive training.

To further streamline the process and reduce potential discrepancies, a dedicated annotation application was developed. This tool presented verses (sentences) for context, allowing annotators to understand the grammatical relationships within the sentence. It also displayed words sequentially and it automatically broke them down into their constituent morphemes to simplify the annotators' task. While the tool presented morpheme-level breakdowns, the annotators assigned grammatical functions to only stems and clitics, i.e., at both word and sub-word levels, reflecting the nuances of traditional i'rab. Table 3 illustrates how one verse was morphologically and syntactically analyzed.

The prevalence of embedded phrases in Quranic Arabic posed a challenge for annotation. While not fully accounted for in MASAQ (due to cost constraints), the significance of embedding was acknowledged for future work. In conclusion, the annotation of MASAQ involved a rigorous process conducted by experts. They used a systematic approach, aided by a custom-built application, to provide a detailed and consistent analysis of the Quran's syntactic structure, laying the groundwork for further NLP research and applications.

Table 3: A Morphologically and Syntactically Analyzed Phrase from one Quranic verse 2:76

Word	Morpheme			Grammatical Function	English Gloss
ليحاجوكم	ل	Proc.	SUBJUNC_PART	SUBJUNC_PART	*so*
	ي	Pref.	IMPERF_PREF	-	
	حاج	Stm	IV	IV	*challenge*
	و	Suff.	SUBJ_PRON	AGNT	*they*
	كم	Enc.	OBJ_PRON	OBJ	*you*
به	ب	Stm	PREP	PREP	*with*
	ه	Enc.	PRON_3MS	PREP_OBJ	*it*
عند	عند	Stm	ADV	ADV_PLCE	*before*
ربكم	رب	Stm	NOUN_CONCRETE	GEN_CONS	*Lord*
	كم	Enc.	POSS_PRON	GEN_CONS	*your*

5 Development of the MASAQ Parser

To develop the parser, a comprehensive system was built using NLP techniques and machine learning algorithms. The parser processes Arabic text, by extracting linguistic features and parsing each word into its corresponding grammatical tags. The dataset used for training comprises annotated Quranic words, with each word linked to its verse, chapter, and grammatical tags. The tags include grammatical and syntactic roles such as nouns, verbs, adjectives, and constructs like possessive phrases, nominal sentences, etc.

The parser leverages word-level features, including single letter prefixes, suffixes, positional attributes, and adjacent words, to predict grammatical tags accurately. A pipeline integrating a feature vectorizer and a Linear Support Vector Classifier is employed for classification. Additional preprocessing functions handle linguistic nuances, such as identifying numeric content and checking word shapes.

The model was trained and tested on a dataset consisting of Quranic text. Features were engineered to account for contextual relationships between words, such as preceding and following words, enabling the parser to capture complex syntactic patterns. The trained model achieved a high degree of accuracy and was saved for efficient deployment. This system provides a robust foundation for parsing Quranic text and could be adapted to other Arabic text corpora for similar linguistic analysis.

Example: A parsed phrase from Quranic verse 20:114:

Sentence: وَقُل رَّبِّ زِدْنِي عِلْمًا
Analysis:

- وَ: حرف عطف
- قُل: فعل_أمر
- رَّبِّ : منادى
- زِدْنِي: فعل_أمر + مفعول_به
- عِلْمًا: مفعول_به

This example illustrates the parser's ability to accurately identify the grammatical roles of words within a Quranic verse.

5.1 Evaluation

The evaluation of three classification algorithms—LinearSVC, Logistic Regression, and Random Forest—was conducted to determine the most accurate model. The results of the experiments revealed distinct performance levels among the tested algorithms. LinearSVC achieved an accuracy of 98.23%, showcasing its capability to handle the classification task effectively. Logistic Regression, while robust, performed comparatively lower with an accuracy of 88.0%. On the other hand, Random Forest outperformed the other models with an accuracy of 99.0%, making it the best-performing algorithm in this evaluation. The results highlight Random Forest as the most suitable model for achieving high accuracy in this task. Figure 5 shows the achieved accuracy of the three models used for syntactically parsing Arabic text.

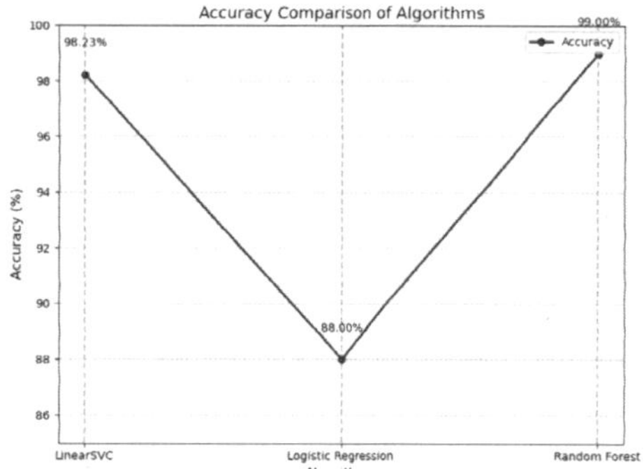

Figure 5: Achieved Accuracy of the Three Models

Example 1: A parsed phrase from Quranic verse 20:114

Sentence	وقل رب زدني علما
Analysis	و: حرف عطف قل: فعل_أمر رب: منادى زدني: فعل_أمر + مفعول_به علما: مفعول_به

6 Ethical Considerations in MASAQ

The development of MASAQ, while guided by rigorous methodology and expert annotation, encountered inherent limitations and required careful navigation of ethical considerations. One key limitation stems from the inherent ambiguity of i'rab, which is tied to the interpretation of meaning in the Quran. This subjectivity introduces potential inconsistency in the annotations. Another challenge lies in the complexity of structural embedding in Quranic Arabic, which MASAQ did not fully address due to cost constraints.

Despite these limitations, MASAQ prioritizes ethical compliance. The use of the verified Tanzil Quran text ensures accuracy and integrity, and adherence to the Creative Commons Attribution 3.0 license guarantees proper usage of resources. The research focuses solely on linguistic analysis, avoiding ethical concerns related to sensitive personal data. The authors emphasize fairness and adopt a rigorous methodology to minimize bias and enhance the dataset's reliability for future NLP research.

Acknowledgements

We are deeply thankful to the Deanship of Scientific Research at the University of Jordan for financially supporting this project through a research grant awarded to the principal investigator, Prof. Bassam Hammo.

References

Habash, N., & Roth, R. (2009). Catib: The columbia arabic treebank. Proceedings of the ACL-IJCNLP 2009 conference short papers,

Hajic, J., Smrz, O., Zemánek, P., Šnaidauf, J., & Beška, E. (2004). Prague Arabic dependency treebank: Development in data and tools. Proc. of the NEMLAR Intern. Conf. on Arabic Language Resources and Tools,

Halabi, D., Fayyoumi, E., & Awajan, A. (2021). I3rab: A new Arabic dependency treebank based on Arabic grammatical theory. Transactions on Asian Low-

Resource Language Information Processing, 21(2), 1-32.

Maamouri, M., Bies, A., Buckwalter, T., Diab, M. T., Habash, N., Rambow, O., & Tabessi, D. (2006). Developing and Using a Pilot Dialectal Arabic Treebank http://www.lrec-conf.org/proceedings/lrec2006/summaries/543.html

Sawalha, Majdi; Al-Shargi, Faisal; Yagi, Sane; AlShdaifat, Abdallah T.; Hammo, Bassam; Belajeed, Mariam; Al-Ogaili, Lubna R. (2025) Morphologically-analyzed and syntactically-annotated Quran dataset, Data in Brief, https://doi.org/10.1016/j.dib.2024.111211.

Sawalha, Majdi; Yagi, Sane; Alshargi, Faisal; Hammo, Bassam; Alshdaifat, Abdallah (2024), "MASAQ: Morphologically-Analyzed and Syntactically-Annotated Quran Dataset", Mendeley Data, V7, doi: 10.17632/9yvrzxktmr.7

Sawalha, Majdi; Brierley, Claire; Atwell, Eric (2012). Prosody Prediction for Arabic via the Open-Source Boundary-Annotated Qur'an Corpus, Journal of Speech Sciences 2 (2), 175-191.

Sawalha, Majdi; Brierley, Claire and Atwell, Eric (2014) "Automatically generated, phonemic Arabic-IPA pronunciation tiers for the Boundary Annotated Qur'an Dataset for Machine Learning (version 2.0)", in: Proceedings of LRE-Rel 2: 2nd Workshop on Language Resource and Evaluation for Religious Texts, LREC 2014 post-conference workshop 31st May 2014, Reykjavik, Iceland

Silveira, N., Dozat, T., De Marneffe, M. C., Bowman, S. R., Connor, M., Bauer, J., & Manning, C. D. (2014). A gold standard dependency corpus for English. Proceedings of the 9th International Conference on Language Resources and Evaluation, LREC 2014,

Smrz, O., Bielický, V., Kourilová, I., Krácmar, J., Hajic, J., & Zemánek, P. (2008). Prague Arabic dependency treebank: A word on the million words. Proceedings of the workshop on Arabic and local languages (LREC 2008),

Taji, D., Habash, N., & Zeman, D. (2017). Universal dependencies for Arabic. Proceedings of the Third Arabic Natural Language Processing Workshop,

Taji, D., & Habash, N. (2020). PALMYRA 2.0: A Configurable Multilingual Platform Independent Tool for Morphology and Syntax Annotation. Proceedings of the Fourth Workshop on Universal Dependencies (UDW 2020),

Tanzil Project. (n.d.). Tanzil project. Retrieved from https://tanzil.net/docs/tanzil_project

Zhao, Y., Zhou, M., Li, Z., & Zhang, M. (2020). Dependency Parsing with Noisy Multi-annotation Data. Lecture Notes in Computer Science (including subseries Lecture Notes in Artificial Intelligence and Lecture Notes in Bioinformatics),

Zaki, Y., Hajjar, H., Hajjar, M., & Bernard, G. (2016). Survey of syntactic parsers of Arabic language. ACM International Conference Proceeding Series.

Leveraging AI to Bridge Classical Arabic and Modern Standard Arabic for Text Simplification

Shatha Altammami
King Saud University
Riyadh, Saudi Arabia
shaltammami@ksu.edu.sa

Abstract

This paper introduces the Hadith Simplification Dataset, a novel resource comprising 250 pairs of Classical Arabic (CA) Hadith texts and their simplified Modern Standard Arabic (MSA) equivalents. Addressing the lack of resources for simplifying culturally and religiously significant texts, this dataset bridges linguistic and accessibility gaps while preserving theological integrity. The simplifications were generated using a large language model and rigorously verified by an Islamic Studies expert to ensure precision and cultural sensitivity. By tackling the unique lexical, syntactic, and cultural challenges of CA-to-MSA transformation, this resource advances Arabic text simplification research. Beyond religious texts, the methodology developed is adaptable to other domains, such as poetry and historical literature. This work underscores the importance of ethical AI applications in preserving the integrity of religious texts while enhancing their accessibility to modern audiences.

1 Introduction

Automatic text simplification (TS) is the process of reducing the linguistic complexity of a text to improve its readability and accessibility while preserving its original meaning and core information (Saggion and Hirst, 2017). TS serves a wide range of purposes, including aiding readers with low literacy levels, second-language learners, and children (Alhafni et al., 2024). It is particularly valuable for facilitating the understanding of religious texts, which often feature intricate linguistic structures, symbolic expressions, and culturally specific content that can pose challenges for contemporary audiences (Brown, 2017).

When simplifying religious texts, it is crucial to address the unique characteristics of the source material. Strategies such as elaborative modification or adjusting linguistic form to enhance clarity are essential (Siddharthan, 2014). This need is particularly pronounced for Classical Arabic (CA), the language of foundational Islamic texts, including the Quran and Hadith. CA is renowned for its rich linguistic structures, characterized by complex syntax and vocabulary that is often symbolic or archaic (Kadaoui et al., 2023). In contrast, Modern Standard Arabic (MSA), which evolved from CA, offers a simpler and more standardized linguistic framework, making it more accessible for modern communications (Habash, 2010).

Simplifying Hadith texts requires addressing not only linguistic and syntactic differences but also sensitivity to cultural and theological nuances. These texts carry profound religious significance, necessitating methods that safeguard their authenticity while enhancing accessibility. Moreover, many words and grammatical structures in CA have no direct equivalents in MSA or modern Arabic dialects, posing an additional layer of complexity (Kadaoui et al., 2023).

Recent advancements in natural language processing (NLP) have facilitated the use of machine learning and large language models (LLMs) for tasks like text simplification (Al-Thanyyan and Azmi, 2023; Alhafni et al., 2024; Khallaf and Sharoff, 2022; Nassiri et al., 2022; Elneima et al., 2024). However, LLMs trained on modern data often lack exposure to the archaic vocabulary and syntax of CA, as many of its linguistic features are absent in MSA or contemporary dialects (Kadaoui et al., 2023). To address this gap, this study introduces the Hadith Simplification Dataset, consisting of 250 Hadith texts simplified from CA to MSA[1]. Although the dataset is relatively small, it aligns well with the capabilities of current LLMs,

[1] https://github.com/ShathaTm/CA_MSA

Proceedings of the New Horizons in Computational Linguistics for Religious Texts (Coling-Rel), pages 76–85
January 19, 2025.

which can learn effectively from a few high-quality examples, as demonstrated by the promise of few-shot in-context learning. This approach leverages semantic alignment and contextual examples to enable LLMs to perform effectively on low-resource languages (Cahyawijaya et al., 2024).

The primary contribution of this work is not only the introduction of the Hadith Simplification Dataset but also the development of a versatile framework for producing similar datasets. Although the focus here is on religious texts, the framework is adaptable to other domains, such as poetry, historical documents, legal texts, and classical literature, where simplifying Classical Arabic (CA) to Modern Standard Arabic (MSA) can enhance accessibility and comprehension. For example, simplifying pre-Islamic Arabic poetry could make its rich imagery and cultural insights more understandable to modern readers, while converting legal texts written in CA into MSA could improve their usability for contemporary legal practice.

Moreover, it is undeniable that large language models (LLMs) are increasingly being used to answer critical questions (Dam et al., 2024), including those on sensitive religious and cultural topics (Alan et al., 2024; Benkler et al., 2023). Given the widespread adoption of these technologies, it is no longer feasible to prevent people from using LLMs for such purposes. Therefore, it is essential to take a proactive approach to ensure these models are guided toward accuracy and authenticity. Training LLMs with carefully curated datasets, including the one introduced in this paper, is not aimed at replacing scholars but at mitigating the risks of these models inadvertently disseminating misinformation. This effort is especially important as many users, regardless of their age or background, may lack the expertise to identify inaccuracies in the responses provided (Chen and Shu, 2023). By equipping LLMs with reliable data, the goal is to enable them to serve as complementary tools to Islamic scholarship, fostering a well-informed and responsible digital discourse while preserving the integrity of religious knowledge in an era increasingly influenced by artificial intelligence.

2 Related Work

The field of Text Simplification (TS) has seen a significant advancement through the creation of various corpora aimed at simplifying texts across different languages. One of the most prominent datasets is the English Wikipedia (EW) and Simple English Wikipedia (SEW) corpus, which provides 137,000 aligned sentence pairs between English Wikipedia articles and their simplified counterparts in Simple English (Coster and Kauchak, 2011). Another English-based resources are Zhu et al. (2010); Kajiwara and Komachi (2016) with more than 50K sentence pairs. These dataset are widely used due to its scale and the lexical and syntactic diversity it provides.

Beyond English, TS research in other languages has also benefited from various datasets. For example, the Simplext corpus (Saggion et al., 2015) is a Spanish dataset with 200 simplified news texts, covering domains such as national and international news, culture, and society. In Italian, the SIMPITIKI corpus (Brunato et al., 2016) provides 1,166 aligned sentences and combines semi-automatically and manually simplified texts, making it a useful resource for rule-based syntactic simplification research. In French, the Alector corpus (Gala et al., 2020) comprising 79 texts with simplified versions adapted for young readers, Alector is designed to improve readability in primary school education and is simplified at morpho-syntactic, lexical, and discourse levels.

Although recent resources mark progress in text simplification (TS) across various languages, research and resources for Arabic TS remain comparatively limited, especially given the language's range, including Classical Arabic (CA), Modern Standard Arabic (MSA), and various regional dialects. One of the newer datasets in this area is the Saaq al-Bambuu Corpus (Khallaf and Sharoff, 2022), which includes 2,980 parallel sentences from the Arabic novel Saaq al-Bambuu, aligned between complex and simplified versions. This corpus represents MSA rather than CA, focusing on narrative simplifications and lacking the religious and traditional stylistic elements found in Hadith literature. Consequently, while it offers valuable data for syntactic and lexical simplification, its structure, vocabulary, and themes differ considerably from those in CA

Hadith, which embodies distinct stylistic and lexical patterns.

Another resource is the Arabic EW-SEW (English Wikipedia–Simple English Wikipedia) and Arabic WikiLarge (Al-Thanyyan and Azmi, 2023) datasets are machine-translated Arabic adaptations of popular English text simplification resources (Coster and Kauchak, 2011). The Arabic EW-SEW contains 82,585 sentence pairs and is primarily based on general encyclopedic content, aligning complex and simplified forms on a wide variety of topics. Both datasets primarily address contemporary MSA content, thus differing significantly from CA Hadith in both thematic focus and linguistic style. The Hadith texts involve highly specialized religious content and formal syntax, which require preserving theological and moral nuances, a complexity less emphasized in the encyclopedic datasets.

Each of these resources, while valuable for general Arabic text simplification, does not address the unique complexities involved in simplifying Classical Arabic (CA) Hadith to Modern Standard Arabic (MSA). CA contains many words and grammatical structures that no longer appear in MSA or Arabic dialects, and large language models (LLMs) trained primarily on modern data have limited exposure to these structures, which impacts their performance on such data (Kadaoui et al., 2023).

Simplifying religious texts like Hadith requires precision to preserve theological accuracy, religious sensitivity, and the formal, traditional style specific to Hadith literature. The proposed Hadith simplification dataset aligns CA Hadith with their simplified MSA versions, carefully maintaining the semantic integrity of each Hadith while enhancing readability. This alignment contributes uniquely to Arabic text simplification, filling a critical gap for resources that address the specific demands of religious and CA with high fidelity.

3 Data Collection

The dataset of Classical Arabic (CA) hadith was collected using a structured approach to ensure the selection of relevant, authentic, and concise hadith texts for effective simplification into Modern Standard Arabic (MSA). Below are the detailed steps taken during data collection:

3.1 Source of Hadith

Hadith were sourced from the LK Hadith Corpus[2] (Altammami et al., 2020). In this corpus, Matn (actual Hadith teaching) is separated from Isnad (chain of narrators), allowing for the extraction of only the Matn, which is the primary focus for simplification.

3.2 Selection Criteria

Hadith were selected exclusively from the Sahih Al-Bukhari and Sahih Muslim collection to ensure authenticity, given that other collections within the corpus include hadith with varying levels of authenticity. Random sampling was then applied to achieve a diverse and representative dataset, prioritizing hadith with 100 words or fewer to maintain manageable text lengths for analysis and simplification (Al-Shameri and Al-Khalifa, 2024). Furthermore, duplicate hadith were identified and removed, ensuring that each entry in the dataset is unique and distinct.

3.3 Preprocessing

Diacritics were systematically removed from the Matn text to ensure consistency and focus on the core linguistic structure, minimizing variations that arise from diacritical marks. This approach aligns with findings from previous research, which indicated that removing diacritics from CA texts generally enhances translation accuracy, as models tend to interpret meanings inaccurately when diacritics are present (Kadaoui et al., 2023)

4 Methodology

4.1 Using a large Language Model

Closed-source language models, while limiting access to their underlying architecture and training data, continue to be attractive due to their exceptional performance on a wide range of natural language processing tasks (Bang et al., 2023). Particularly, GPT-4 (OpenAI, 2023), a powerful language model known for its ability to generate human-quality text, was chosen as the primary tool for this task.

4.2 Prompt Engineering

To enhance the quality of the simplifications, task-specific instructions and domain-specific knowl-

[2]https://github.com/ShathaTm/LK-Hadith-Corpus

edge were incorporated into the prompts provided to the model. This approach, inspired by previous research (Peng et al., 2023; Gao et al., 2023), guided the LLM towards more accurate and contextually relevant outputs. The following lines show the prompt given to the LLM:

```
Please simplify the following
hadith from Classical Arabic to
clear formal Modern Standard Arabic.
Start directly with the main content,
omitting any chain of narrators.
Use straightforward language,
replacing any archaic terms
with widely understood MSA vocabulary.
For religious or specialized terms,
provide simple explanations or
add clarifying words in parentheses
where needed. Keep the original
dialogue structure and retain all
essential details.
```

4.3 Self-correction

A self-correction mechanism was employed to mitigate potential errors introduced by the LLM itself. By asking the language model to review and refine its own responses, the overall quality of the generated text was improved. This is particularly aligned with other studies (Lu et al., 2023)

4.4 Using English prompt

To optimize the model's performance, a concise and direct English prompt was adopted for the experiments. This approach, supported by previous research (Khondaker et al., 2023), provided clear instructions to the LLM and maximized its capabilities.

4.5 Few-shot learning

Inspired by recent research on enhancing the performance of large language models (LLMs) (Kadaoui et al., 2023), a few-shot learning approach was employed to guide the LLM in generating simplified versions of Classical Arabic (CA) Hadith texts into Modern Standard Arabic (MSA). Few-shot learning involves presenting the model with a small, carefully selected set of annotated examples to demonstrate the desired task and output structure. In this study, five examples of CA Hadith, paired with their human-generated MSA simplifications, were incorporated into the prompts to clearly define the task. This approach leverages the model's in-context learning capability, enabling it to adapt its responses by recognizing and replicating the patterns, structures, and stylistic nuances present in the provided examples.

5 Human Verification

To ensure the accuracy and reliability of the Hadith simplification process from Classical Arabic (CA) to Modern Standard Arabic (MSA) performed by the large language model (LLM), a human verification step was incorporated. This verification was conducted by an Islamic Studies graduate with a strong background in interpreting religious texts. The primary responsibility of the annotator was to carefully review the simplified MSA version of each Hadith and compare it to its original CA counterpart. The annotator was asked to refer to external sources of exegesis if necessary. The annotation was done through a Google Form interface.

The verification process focused on ensuring that the meaning, context, and theological accuracy of the Hadith were preserved in the MSA version. In cases where discrepancies were identified, the annotator would rewrite the Hadith text to ensure alignment with the original meaning. The involvement of an annotator was crucial to maintaining the integrity and authenticity of the Hadith, particularly given the sensitive nature of religious texts. As shown in Figure 1, a significant number of Hadith simplifications required modification by the human annotator. These modifications ranged from minor word choice adjustments to more substantial rephrasing to accurately convey the original meaning. For example, the simplification of the word فتمعكت was not correct and needed to be revised. In other cases, the AI model struggled with complex grammatical structures or nuanced meanings, leading to inaccuracies in the simplified text. The human annotator's role was essential in identifying and correcting these errors, ensuring that the simplified Hadith remained faithful to the original text.

6 Evaluation

Traditional readability metrics for Arabic, as described in the literature, rely heavily on surface-level linguistic features. For example, Al-Dawsari (2004) developed a formula based on

	CA Hadith	AI Generated MSA Hadith	Correct?	Human modified MSA Hadith	Type of mistake
1	جاء رجل إلى عمر بن الخطاب، فقال: إني أجنبت فلم أصب الماء. فقال عمار بن ياسر لعمر بن الخطاب: أما تذكر أنا كنا في سفر، أنا وأنت، فأما أنت فلم تصل، وأما أنا فتمعكت فصليت، فذكرت للنبي صلى الله عليه وسلم، فقال النبي صلى الله عليه وسلم: إنما كان يكفيك هكذا. فضرب النبي صلى الله عليه وسلم بكفيه الأرض، ونفخ فيهما، ثم مسح بهما وجهه وكفيه.	هذا ليس النص الأصلي للحديث، بل تفسير مبسط له: جاء رجل إلى عمر بن الخطاب وقال: "أصابتني جنابة ولم أجد ماء. " فقال عمار بن ياسر: هل تذكر أننا كنا في سفر، ولم تصل أنت، أما أنا فتوسخت أو اتسخت ثم صليت؟ وعندما أخبرت النبي ، قال: كان يكفيك أن تفعل هكذا . ثم ضرب النبي ﷺ كفيه على الأرض، ونفخ فيهما ، ومسح بهما وجهه وكفيه.	No	هذا ليس النص الأصلي للحديث، بل تفسير مبسط له: جاء رجل إلى عمر بن الخطاب وقال: "أصابتني جنابة (أي حالة تتطلب الغسل) ولم أجد ماء". عندها تذكر عمار بن ياسر وقال لعمر: "هل تذكر أننا كنا في سفر، وأنت لم تصل، بينما أنا تمرغت (تقلبت في التراب لتطهير نفسي) ثم صليت؟ وعندما أخبرت النبي صلى الله عليه وسلم بذلك، قال: كان يكفيك أن تفعل هكذا". ثم ضرب النبي كفيه على الأرض، ونفخ فيهما، ومسح بهما وجهه وكفيه.	تفسير معنى كلمة تمعكت
2	عن عائشة، أن هند بنت عتبة، قالت يا رسول الله إن أبا سفيان رجل شحيح، وليس يعطيني ما يكفيني وولدي، إلا ما أخذت منه وهو لا يعلم فقال خذي ما يكفيك وولدك بالمعروف .	هذا ليس النص الأصلي للحديث، بل تفسير مبسط له: جاءت هند بنت عتبة إلى النبي وقالت: يا رسول الله، إن أبا سفيان رجل بخيل، فهل يجوز لي أن آخذ من ماله لإطعام عائلتنا؟" فأجابها النبي ﷺ: "نعم، لكن بما هو معروف ومعتدل بما يكفي للحاجة فقط)."	No	هذا ليس النص الأصلي للحديث، بل تفسير مبسط له: جاءت هند بنت عتبة إلى النبي وقالت: يا رسول الله، إن أبا سفيان رجل بخيل، ولايعطينى مايكفيني أنا وولدي فهل يجوز لي أن آخذ من ماله وهو لايعلم " فأجابها النبي ﷺ: "نعم، لكن بما هو معروف ومعتدل بما يكفي للحاجة فقط)."	عدم اتمام المعنى المقصود
3	اوصاني خليلي بثلاث لا ادعهن حتى اموت: صوم ثلاثة ايام من كل شهر، وصلاة الضحى، ونوم على وتر.	هذا ليس النص الأصلي للحديث، بل تفسير مبسط له: قال النبي صلى الله عليه وسلم: أوصاني خليلي بثلاثة أمور لن أتركها حتى أموت: صيام ثلاثة أيام من كل شهر، وصلاة الضحى، وختم الليل بصلاة الوتر.	No	هذا ليس النص الأصلي للحديث، بل تفسير مبسط له: قال أبو هريرة رضى الله عنه أوصانى خليلي وهو النبي صلى الله عليه وسلم بثلاثة أمور لن أتركها حتى أموت: صيام ثلاثة أيام من كل شهر، وصلاة الضحى، وختم الليل بصلاة الوتر.	قائل هذا الحديث أبو هريرة
4	من اعتق شقصا له في عبد، اعتق كله، ان كان له مال، والا يستسع غير مشقوق عليه.	هذا ليس النص الأصلي للحديث، بل تفسير مبسط له: من حرر نصيبًا له في عبد، يُعتق العبد بالكامل إذا كان لديه مال لدفع باقي قيمته. وإن لم يكن لديه مال، يعمل العبد لسداد باقي قيمته دون تحميله مشقة.	No	هذا ليس النص الأصلي للحديث، بل تفسير مبسط له: إذا اشترك رجلين في ثمن عبد فدفع كل منهم نصف ثمنه ثم بعد ذلك أراد واحد منهم أن يحرر العبد في نصيبه فقط هنا أمر النبي صلى الله عليه وسلم بأن يُحرر العبد بالكامل إذا كانت هناك مقدرة مالية للعاتق فوق احتياجته الأساسية، وإن لم يكن لديه المقدرة يعمل العبد لسداد باقي قيمته دون تحميله مشقة	عدم التوضيح
5	اذا كان يوم الجمعة، كان على كل باب من ابواب المسجد الملائكة، يكتبون الاول فالاول، فاذا جلس الامام طووا الصحف، وجاؤوا يستمعون الذكر.	عندما يأتي يوم الجمعة، تقف الملائكة عند أبواب المسجد، يكتبون أسماء القادمين بالترتيب. فإذا جلس الإمام لبدء الخطبة، طووا الصحف وجلسوا يستمعون للذكر.	No	هذا ليس النص الأصلي للحديث، بل تفسير مبسط له: عندما يأتي يوم الجمعة، تقف الملائكة عند أبواب المسجد، يكتبون أسماء القادمين بالترتيب. فإذا جلس الإمام لبدء الخطبة، تركت كتابة من يأتي بعد ذلك ، وجلسوا ليستمعوا للخطبة.	عدم تبسيط بعض الكلمات
6	قال النبي صلى الله عليه وسلم: الجنة اقرب الى احدكم من شراك نعله	هذا ليس النص الأصلي للحديث، بل تفسير مبسط له: قال النبي صلى الله عليه وسلم: "الجنة قريبة من أحدكم بقدر قرب شراك نعله" (وهو الحزام الذي يثبت النعل على القدم).	Yes	-	-
7	عن رسول الله ﷺ قال يتبع الميت ثلاثة، فيرجع اثنان ويبقى معه واحد: يتبعه أهله وماله وعمله، فيرجع أهله وماله، ويبقى عمله.	هذا ليس النص الأصلي للحديث، بل تفسير مبسط له: يتبع الميت ثلاثة أشياء: أهله، وماله، وعمله. فيرجع أهله وماله، ويبقى معه عمله.	Yes	-	-
8	كنت عند النبي صلى الله عليه وسلم إذ جاءه رسول إحدى بناته، وعنده سعد وأبي بن كعب ومعاذ، أن ابنها يجود بنفسه، فبعث إليها: لله ما أخذ ولله ما أعطى، كل بأجل، فلتصبر ولتحتسب.	هذا ليس النص الأصلي للحديث، بل تفسير مبسط له: جاء رسول إحدى بنات النبي صلى الله عليه وسلم يخبره أن ابنها يحتضر. فقال النبي صلى الله عليه وسلم: "لله ما أخذ، ولله ما أعطى، وكل شيء عنده بأجل محدد. فلتصبر ولتحتسب."	Yes	-	-

Figure 1: Examples of CA Hadith Simplified to MSA using LLM, then verified and corrected if necessary by a Human annotator

five features, such as average word length, sentence length, and word frequency. Similarly, Al Tamimi et al. (2014) introduced AARI, which calculates readability using seven features, including the number of characters, words, sentences, and difficult words. On the other hand, El-Haj and Rayson (2016) proposed the OSMAN metric, which leverages Modern Standard Arabic (MSA) script markers and syllable counts derived from automatic diacritization. While these methods provide valuable insights into general readability, they are less likely to account for the nuanced linguistic simplifications involved in simplifying religious texts like Hadith from CA to MSA.

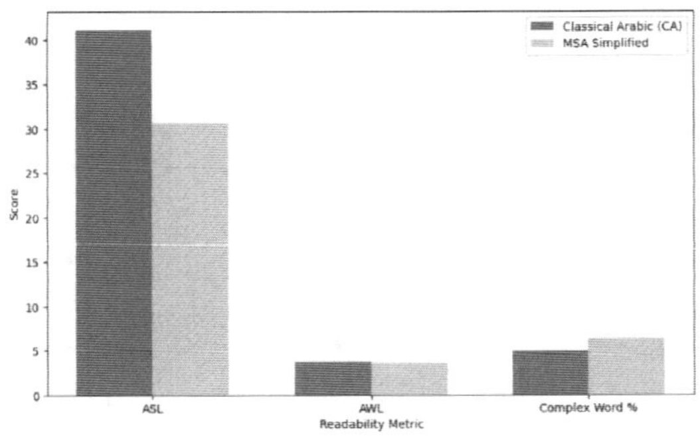

Figure 2: Comparison of traditional features used in readability metrics

This limitation is evident in the data presented in Figure 2, which shows metrics such as Average Word Length (AWL) and the percentage of complex words. Although AWL remains relatively stable, the increase in the percentage of complex words highlights the inadequacy of these traditional measures for this task. This is because the process of simplifying Hadith often involves explaining archaic terms, which can lead to an increase in the overall word count and a higher number of words exceeding six characters. Consequently, traditional metrics, which rely on surface-level features like sentence and word length, are less likely to reflect deeper shifts in linguistic style and register. Hence, these methods do not fully encapsulate the readability improvements achieved through the simplification of CA Hadith to MSA texts.

In contrast, the SAMER readability metric is specifically designed to address the unique linguistic features of Arabic, making it particularly

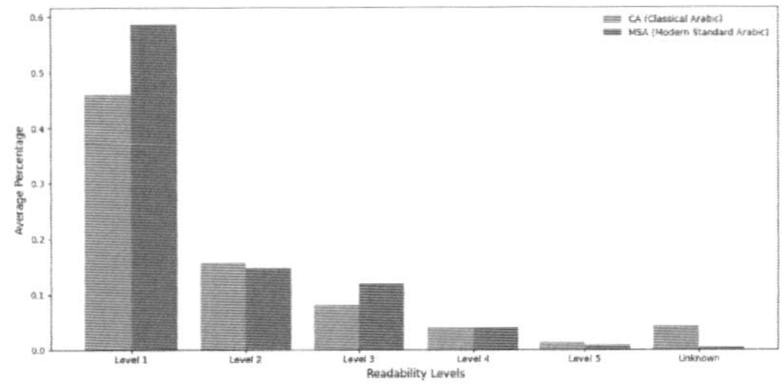

Figure 3: SAMER readability scores of Hadith texts in their Classical Arabic (CA) and Modern Standard Arabic (MSA)

suitable for evaluating the simplification process of Hadith texts. Unlike traditional metrics, SAMER goes beyond surface-level features by incorporating the morphological richness and syntactic complexity inherent in Arabic. SAMER evaluates readability by analyzing lexical, syntactic, and morphological features, mapping them to predefined readability levels.

The SAMER tool is underpinned by the SAMER Arabic Text Simplification Corpus, a resource created from 15 publicly available Arabic fiction novels. These texts were manually simplified into parallel versions representing specific readability levels. This enables SAMER to capture the linguistic shifts involved in simplifying CA to MSA, such as replacing archaic terms and restructuring sentences to enhance readability. Therefore, it is used to measure the readability of the CA hadiths and and their simplified meaning to MSA. An example of how the SAMER tool analyzes text is shown in Figures 4 and Figure 5 where words are color coded to show which level of readability it falls into.

SAMER has developed a five-level readability scale. This scale categorizes words based on their frequency and complexity, facilitating the adaptation of texts to appropriate reading levels. The levels are defined as follows:

- Level 1: Contains the most basic and frequently used words in MSA, suitable for beginners.
- Level 2: Includes slightly more complex words that are still common, appropriate for early intermediate learners.

- Level 3: Comprises words of moderate complexity, intended for intermediate learners.
- Level 4: Features less common and more complex words, suitable for advanced learners.
- Level 5: Consists of the most complex and least frequent words, appropriate for proficient readers.

Figure 3 illustrates the SAMER readability scores of the Hadith Simplification Dataset by comparing their CA and MSA scores, showcasing the effectiveness of simplification. The distribution highlights a significant shift in readability levels, with MSA texts displaying a higher proportion of words categorized in Level 1, indicating simpler and more accessible content. Meanwhile, the percentage of words in higher complexity levels, such as Level 4 and Level 5, is notably reduced in the MSA version compared to CA. This transformation reflects the effort to clarify and simplify archaic terms and dense sentence structures in the original CA Hadith.

7 Conclusion and Future Work

This paper introduces the framework for developing the Hadith Simplification Dataset, which comprises 250 pairs of Classical Arabic (CA) Hadith texts and their simplified Modern Standard Arabic (MSA) equivalents. Unlike general-purpose Arabic corpora, this specialized dataset preserves the semantic integrity of culturally and religiously significant Hadith texts while enhancing accessibility for MSA readers. By addressing the intricate lexical, syntactic, and cultural challenges inherent in transforming CA into MSA, this resource makes a substantial contribution to Arabic text simplification research, particularly in domains requiring precision, cultural sensitivity, and semantic fidelity, such as religious texts.

This research represents an ongoing effort to explore how computational tools can responsibly contribute to addressing sensitive topics in religious studies. With the growing reliance on AI systems for religious and ethical guidance, it is crucial to address their limitations and refine methodologies in this space. Avoiding this domain entirely could exacerbate the issue, as individuals are unlikely to refrain from using AI and chatbots for religious inquiries despite their current shortcomings. By proactively developing approaches to manage large language models (LLMs) within this context, the potential for misinformation can be mitigated, ensuring that AI systems handle religious topics with greater accuracy, responsibility, and cultural respect.

Future directions include expanding the dataset by incorporating more annotators and a wider selection of text pairs to increase its robustness and applicability. Additionally, feedback from the Coling-Rel workshop's community will be instrumental in refining and extending this initiative. A collaborative and iterative approach will help tackle the challenges posed by AI in religious contexts, creating solutions that harmonize technological innovation with ethical and cultural responsibilities.

Ethical Note

The creation of a dataset for Hadith simplification from Classical Arabic (CA) to Modern Standard Arabic (MSA) entails significant ethical considerations due to the theological and cultural importance of Hadith. Any simplification effort must maintain theological accuracy, respect the integrity of the original texts, and avoid altering their essential meaning or spiritual significance. To address these concerns, the simplifications generated by GPT-4 have been rigorously reviewed by an Islamic studies graduate to ensure their fidelity to the original texts.

This work not only aims to make Hadith more accessible to non-specialists and modern readers who may find CA challenging but also contributes to the field of Natural Language Processing (NLP) by providing a carefully validated dataset. This dataset serves as a resource for training models dedicated to Arabic text simplification, emphasizing the ethical responsibility to preserve the meaning and sanctity of religious texts while advancing AI applications.

By bridging the gap between traditional Islamic texts and contemporary understanding, this research exemplifies a commitment to ethical rigor in AI-based religious text processing. It highlights the importance of ensuring that technological advancements respect cultural and theological values, while also addressing the under-representation of

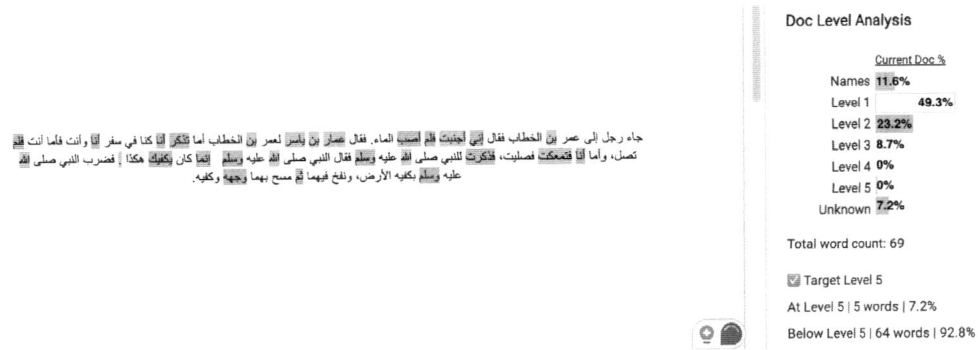

Figure 4: Original CA Hadith analyzed using SAMER readability metric

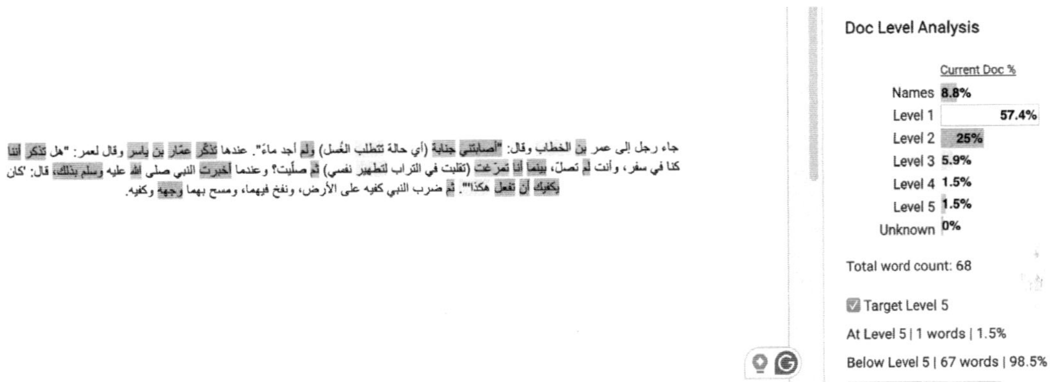

Figure 5: The simplified Hadith analyzed using SAMER readability metric

CA in NLP applications.

Acknowledgments

I thank the anonymous reviewers for their valuable feedback, which greatly enhanced this paper. I also express gratitude to the annotator for their dedication in ensuring the dataset's accuracy and theological integrity, which were essential to this work

References

M Al-Dawsari. 2004. The assessment of readability books content (boys-girls) of the first grade of intermediate school according to readability standards. *Sultan Qaboos University, Muscat.*

Noora Al-Shameri and Hend Al-Khalifa. 2024. Arabic paraphrased parallel synthetic dataset. *Data in Brief*, page 111004.

Abdel Karim Al Tamimi, Manar Jaradat, Nuha Al-Jarrah, and Sahar Ghanem. 2014. Aari: automatic arabic readability index. *Int. Arab J. Inf. Technol.*, 11(4):370–378.

Suha S Al-Thanyyan and Aqil M Azmi. 2023. Simplification of arabic text: A hybrid approach integrating machine translation and transformer-based lexical model. *Journal of King Saud University-Computer and Information Sciences*, 35(8):101662.

Ahmet Yusuf Alan, Enis Karaarslan, and Ömer Aydin. 2024. A rag-based question answering system proposal for understanding islam: Mufassirqas llm. *arXiv preprint arXiv:2401.15378.*

Bashar Alhafni, Reem Hazim, Juan Piñeros Liberato, Muhamed Al Khalil, and Nizar Habash. 2024. The samer arabic text simplification corpus. *arXiv preprint arXiv:2404.18615.*

Shatha Altammami, Eric Atwell, and Ammar Alsalka. 2020. The arabic-english parallel corpus of authentic hadith. *International Journal on Islamic Applications in Computer Science And Technology*, 8(2).

Yejin Bang, Samuel Cahyawijaya, Nayeon Lee, Wenliang Dai, Dan Su, Bryan Wilie, Holy Lovenia, Ziwei Ji, Tiezheng Yu, Willy Chung, et al. 2023. A multitask, multilingual, multimodal evaluation of chatgpt on reasoning, hallucination, and interactivity. arxiv. *arXiv preprint arXiv:2302.04023.*

Noam Benkler, Drisana Mosaphir, Scott Friedman, Andrew Smart, and Sonja Schmer-Galunder. 2023. Assessing llms for moral value pluralism. *arXiv preprint arXiv:2312.10075.*

Jonathan AC Brown. 2017. *Hadith: Muhammad's legacy in the medieval and modern world.* Simon and Schuster.

Dominique Brunato, Andrea Cimino, Felice Dell'Orletta, and Giulia Venturi. 2016. Paccss-it: A parallel corpus of complex-simple sentences for automatic text simplification. In *Proceedings of the 2016 Conference on Empirical Methods in Natural Language Processing*, pages 351–361.

Samuel Cahyawijaya, Holy Lovenia, and Pascale Fung. 2024. Llms are few-shot in-context low-resource language learners. *arXiv preprint arXiv:2403.16512.*

Canyu Chen and Kai Shu. 2023. Can llm-generated misinformation be detected? *arXiv preprint arXiv:2309.13788.*

William Coster and David Kauchak. 2011. Simple english wikipedia: a new text simplification task. In *Proceedings of the 49th Annual Meeting of the Association for Computational Linguistics: Human Language Technologies*, pages 665–669.

Sumit Kumar Dam, Choong Seon Hong, Yu Qiao, and Chaoning Zhang. 2024. A complete survey on llm-based ai chatbots. *arXiv preprint arXiv:2406.16937.*

Mahmoud El-Haj and Paul Rayson. 2016. Osman—a novel arabic readability metric. In *Proceedings of the Tenth International Conference on Language Resources and Evaluation (LREC'16)*, pages 250–255.

Ashraf Hatim Elneima, AhmedElmogtaba Abdelmoniem Ali Abdelaziz, and Kareem Darwish. 2024. Osact6 dialect to msa translation shared task overview. In *Proceedings of the 6th Workshop on Open-Source Arabic Corpora and Processing Tools (OSACT) with Shared Tasks on Arabic LLMs Hallucination and Dialect to MSA Machine Translation@ LREC-COLING 2024*, pages 93–97.

Núria Gala, Anaïs Tack, Ludivine Javourey-Drevet, Thomas François, and Johannes C Ziegler. 2020. Alector: A parallel corpus of simplified french texts with alignments of misreadings by poor and dyslexic readers. In *Proceedings of the Twelfth Language Resources and Evaluation Conference*, pages 1353–1361.

Yuan Gao, Ruili Wang, and Feng Hou. 2023. How to design translation prompts for chatgpt: An empirical study. *arXiv preprint arXiv:2304.02182.*

Nizar Y Habash. 2010. *Introduction to Arabic natural language processing.* Morgan & Claypool Publishers.

Karima Kadaoui, Samar M Magdy, Abdul Waheed, Md Tawkat Islam Khondaker, Ahmed Oumar El-Shangiti, El Moatez Billah Nagoudi, and Muhammad Abdul-Mageed. 2023. Tarjamat: Evaluation of bard and chatgpt on machine translation of ten arabic varieties. *arXiv preprint arXiv:2308.03051.*

Tomoyuki Kajiwara and Mamoru Komachi. 2016. Building a monolingual parallel corpus for text simplification using sentence similarity based on alignment between word embeddings. In *Proceedings of COLING 2016, the 26th International Conference on Computational Linguistics: Technical Papers*, pages 1147–1158.

Nouran Khallaf and Serge Sharoff. 2022. Towards arabic sentence simplification via classification and generative approaches. *arXiv preprint arXiv:2204.09292.*

Md Tawkat Islam Khondaker, Abdul Waheed, El Moatez Billah Nagoudi, and Muhammad Abdul-Mageed. 2023. Gptaraeval: A comprehensive evaluation of chatgpt on arabic nlp. *arXiv preprint arXiv:2305.14976.*

Qingyu Lu, Baopu Qiu, Liang Ding, Liping Xie, and Dacheng Tao. 2023. Error analysis prompting enables human-like translation evaluation in large language models: A case study on chatgpt.

Naoual Nassiri, Safae Berrichi, Abdelhak Lakhouaja, Violetta Cavalli-Sforza, and Azzeddine Mazroui. 2022. Lexical simplification of arabic educational texts through a classification approach. In *The International Conference on Artificial Intelligence and Smart Environment*, pages 581–587. Springer.

OpenAI. 2023. Gpt-4 technical report. `https://openai.com/research/gpt-4`.

Keqin Peng, Liang Ding, Qihuang Zhong, Li Shen, Xuebo Liu, Min Zhang, Yuanxin Ouyang, and Dacheng Tao. 2023. Towards making the most of chatgpt for machine translation. *arXiv preprint arXiv:2303.13780*.

Horacio Saggion and Graeme Hirst. 2017. *Automatic text simplification*, volume 32. Springer.

Horacio Saggion, Sanja Štajner, Stefan Bott, Simon Mille, Luz Rello, and Biljana Drndarevic. 2015. Making it simplext: Implementation and evaluation of a text simplification system for spanish. *ACM Transactions on Accessible Computing (TACCESS)*, 6(4):1–36.

Advaith Siddharthan. 2014. A survey of research on text simplification. *ITL-International Journal of Applied Linguistics*, 165(2):259–298.

Zhemin Zhu, Delphine Bernhard, and Iryna Gurevych. 2010. A monolingual tree-based translation model for sentence simplification. In *Proceedings of the 23rd International Conference on Computational Linguistics (Coling 2010)*, pages 1353–1361.

Word boundaries and the morphology-syntax trade-off

Pablo Mosteiro
Utrecht University, the Netherlands
p.mosteiro@uu.nl

Damián Blasi
Pompeu Fabra University, Spain
Harvard University, USA
dblasi@fas.harvard.edu

Abstract

This paper investigates the relationship between syntax and morphology in natural languages, focusing on the relation between the amount of information stored by word structure on the one hand, and word order on the other. In previous work, a trade-off between these was observed in a large corpus covering over a thousand languages, suggesting a dynamic 'division of labor' between syntax and morphology, as well as yielding proof for the efficient coding of information in language. In contrast, we find that the trade-off can be explained by differing conventions in orthographic word boundaries. We do so by redefining word boundaries within languages either by increasing or decreasing the domain of wordhood implied by orthographic words. Namely, we paste frequent word-pairs together and split words into their frequently occurring component parts. These interventions yield the same trade-off within languages across word domains as what is observed across languages in the orthographic word domain. This allows us to conclude that the original claims on syntax-morphology trade-offs were spurious and that, more importantly, there does not seem to exist a privileged wordhood domain where within- and across-word regularities yield an optimal or optimized amount of information.

1 Introduction

Few taxonomic distinctions in the study of language are as storied as that of 'syntax' and 'morphology', in spite of the numerous conceptual and technical obstacles in defining them. Glossing over theory-specific approaches to these two levels of description, as a first approximation syntax can be regarded as the study of combinations *between* words into grammatical phrases and sentences, whereas morphology is the study of processes that hold *within* words. Thus, linguistic phenomena such as word order, phrasal and constituency structure fall within syntax, whereas inflectional paradigms and allomorphy are uncontroversially assigned to morphology.[1] Whether these two levels involve truly different linguistic processes is a matter of controversy (Tallman and Auderset, 2023), and the descriptions of many linguistic phenomena, such as noun incorporation, seem to sit right between the two. Many attempts to distinguish between syntax and morphology need first to tackle the challenge of embracing some definition of wordhood, which is no less complex a task. Circularity of definition (e.g. by defining 'word' as the maximal domain of morphological processes), complicated cases (can clitics be words? should collocations be treated as words?) and reliance on phonological, morphosyntactic, psycholinguistic, etc. criteria have led to a seemingly inescapable situation where only a few solutions are available. According to Haspelmath (2023), we can either (1) drop the term 'word' altogether, perhaps along with the syntax-morphology distinction, (2) ignore the problem with the definition and hope that our results will be robust regardless of minutiae with the definition, (3) regard certain words as prototypical, or (4) come up with a potentially awkward and unpractical technical definition that covers much of the effective uses of the term.

Yet some patterns in language seem to provide independent support to the morphology-syntax divide (and with it, perthaps, to the notion of a 'true' wordhood). One such pattern is the celebratred trade-off between the amount of information conveyed by morphology (word structure) versus syntax (word order) (Crystal, 2010), i.e. the notion that if one system is flexible and arbitrary in its rules, the other will compensate through the enrichment

[1] We acknowledge that the definitions of syntax and morphology are more nuanced than those provided here. We merely chose simple definitions because those are the ones that give rise to the operationalizations we employed of word-order information and word-structure information. These come from Koplenig et al. (2017) and will be discussed in Section 2.

Proceedings of the New Horizons in Computational Linguistics for Religious Texts (Coling-Rel), pages 86–93
January 19, 2025.

of its relevant rules.

A statistical corpus study found the trade-off to be observable across many languages (Koplenig et al., 2017), using the Parallel Bible Corpus (Mayer and Cysouw, 2014): languages seem to rely more on word order or more on word structure in order to convey information.

In the present study, we address the following research questions: *Can the morphology-syntax trade-off be explained by orthographic conventions?* In other words, if the word boundaries are re-defined, does a language now distribute information differently across morphology and syntax? And *do languages* optimise *the amount of information conveyed by the sum of morphology and syntax?* In other words, how much redundancy is there in the information conveyed by morphology and syntax?

We find that the morphology-syntax trade-off can be reproduced by manipulations of the word boundaries. In a single language, changes to the word boundaries causes the information distribution to change in the word-order/word-structure plane. Our contribution is to show that specific previous evidence for the morphology-syntax trade-off (Koplenig et al., 2017) can be reproduced by manipulations of word boundaries, and that therefore this evidence should not be considered as supporting the claim that morphology and syntax are separate cognitive processes.

2 Related Work

Using mathematical tools to quantify the amount of information conveyed by sequences of symbols starts with the seminal work of Shannon (1948). The metric *entropy* as defined therein has been widely used to compute the information content in sequences of language (Arora et al., 2022; Bentz et al., 2022; Gutierrez-Vasques et al., 2021; Ferrer-i Cancho and Martín, 2011; Jaeger, 2010). A popular approach to computing Shannon's entropy is to *plug in* empirical probabilities into the formula. However, this underestimates the entropy (Miller, 1955). Several corrections to Shannon's entropy were proposed to mitigate this (Arora et al., 2022). However, those corrected formulas still depend crucially on estimating the probabilities of text sequences. Doing this empirically is already unreliable for sequences of length five (Schürmann and Grassberger, 1996). To avoid this problem altogether, we followed previous work on estimating Shannon's entropy using the key insight from a compression algorithm (Kontoyiannis et al., 1998).

This estimation method was previously used to estimate the entropy per word in books in multiple languages, which led to the proposal of a linguistic universal: the amount of information per word that is encoded by word ordering is the same across all languages (Montemurro and Zanette, 2011). This study used different texts for different languages. One way to make the study more robust is to use a parallel corpus such as the Parallel Bible Corpus (Mayer and Cysouw, 2014). Using this corpus and the compression-algorithm-based entropy estimation method, Bentz et al. (2017) confirmed the finding of the linguistic universal.

Along these same lines, Koplenig et al. (2017) studied the trade-off between word order information and word structure information (both in bytes per character) using the Parallel Bible Corpus. The word-order information and word-structure information are operationalizations of the information contained in syntax and morphology, respectively. As mentioned previously, their study is cross-language, and in the present work we extend it by analyzing each language individually, varying the amount of common word-pairs that are pasted together and words that are split into component parts.

Gibson et al. (2019) have reviewed the various ways in which the question of a morphology-syntax trade-off has been studied. They conclude that evidence for an efficient trade-off between these quantities puts pressure on the theories of the evolutionary origins of language. They also suggest that cognitive processes could be associated with the different ways in which we communicate information, but they do not claim any causal relationships.

On the machine-learning end, Abdou et al. (2022) have found that language models that presumably produce state-of-the-art results using shuffled sentences (Sinha et al., 2021) are actually employing sub-word information (e.g., morphology). They stress the importance of word-order information in language.

As for the observation by Koplenig et al. (2017) that languages tend to *optimize* their position along the morphology-syntax trade-off, Jaeger (2010) proposed the principle of Uniform Information Density: language production is affected by a preference to distribute information uniformly across the linguistic signal.

3 Data

We use the Parallel Bible Corpus (Mayer and Cysouw, 2014). It contains 2000 translations[2] of the Bible in 1460 languages in a verse-aligned parallel structure, covering over 40 language families from the Americas, Europe, Africa, Asia and Oceania. Each translation is tokenized and Unicode-normalized, with spaces inserted between words and both punctuation marks and non-alphabetic symbols. We follow the same pre-processing steps as Koplenig et al. (2017). Namely, we lowercase all text following the Unicode Standard (The Unicode Consortium, 2022) using the Python `str.lower` method. We then split each bible translation into different books of the bible, treating each book as a different text sample. We focus on the same six books of the New Testament studied by Koplenig et al. (2017): the four Gospels (Matthew, Mark, Luke, John), the Book of Acts and the Book of Revelation. Restricting our dataset to translations that contain at least one verse of at least one of the aforementioned books leaves 1962 bible translations in 1444 languages. This dataset is appropriate to answer our research question because it is available in many languages across multiple families, so that any findings cannot be ascribed to specific features of a given language.

We remove 4 bible translations because of the presence of a character that cannot be processed by the entropy calculator (which will be described in Section 4).[3] We remove a further 2 bibles because they contain a verse with incorrectly repeated text that leads to mistakes in the entropy calculations.[4] As a result, we have 1956 bible translations in 1442 languages.

4 Methods

We follow most of the methodology employed by Koplenig et al. (2017) to compute word-order and word-structure information, and then apply some manipulations to the word boundaries.

[2]The Parallel Bible Corpus is an evolving project. We use the version from 21st October 2021, corresponding to commit c64117d in `git@github.com:cysouw/paralleltext.git`

[3]A solution to this problem is to manually replace the troublesome character by some known character that is not used anywhere in that bible. We leave this for future work.

[4]Nevertheless, we ran the analysis with these 2 bibles included, and we found entirely consistent results.

4.1 Word-order and word-structure information

Consider a single book from a single translation of the bible, as described in Section 3, to be a sequence b of N characters. The entropy per symbol H^b is the average amount of information that is needed in order to describe b, per unit character (Shannon, 1948). We estimate entropy using a non-parametric method built upon the Lempel-Ziv compression algorithm (Wyner and Ziv, 1989). This method converges to the entropy at the limit of long texts (Kontoyiannis et al., 1998). The formula for the entropy is

$$H^b = \left[\frac{1}{N} \sum_{i=2}^{N} \frac{l_i}{\log i} \right] \quad (1)$$

where l_i is the length of the shortest substring starting at position i of b that is not also a substring of the part of the book before this position. We use the implementation of this calculation by Koplenig et al. (2017), and we write an independent implementation to verify it[5].

Following Koplenig et al. (2017), we compute the entropy on three variants of the bible books:

1. H^b_{original} is computed on the original book
2. H^b_{order} is computed on a version of the book in which word order has been deliberately destroyed by shuffling all tokens within each verse
3. $H^b_{\text{structure}}$ is computed on a version of the book in which word structure has been deliberately destroyed by replacing every word type in the book by a randomly generated sequence of characters of the same length

This allows us to define $D^b_{\text{order}} = H^b_{\text{order}} - H^b_{\text{original}}$, i.e., the amount of information contained in word ordering; similarly, we define $D^b_{\text{structure}} = H^b_{\text{structure}} - H^b_{\text{original}}$, i.e., the amount of information contained in word structure.

With the setup described, it is possible to compute, for a given book of the bible, the quantities D^b_{order} and $D^b_{\text{structure}}$ for every translation available. We expand the methodology by performing *word-pasting* and *word-splitting* experiments.

[5]See `11_validate_bpw.ipynb` in `anonymous.4open.science/r/WordOrderBibles-0F4F`

4.2 Word-pasting experiment

We start with the word-pasting experiment: take the single most commonly occurring pair of words and turn it into a word, then repeat the process iteratively. Given a book of the bible in a given translation b, we define b_{P0} as the version of this book as provided in the Parallel Bible Corpus. We compute $D^{b_{P0}}_{\text{order}}$ and $D^{b_{P0}}_{\text{structure}}$ on b_{P0}. We then find the most common pair of consecutive tokens in the book, and redefine these to be a new word, including the space. For example, if the most common pair of words in a given book is *this book*, we redefine "this book" as a single word. We call this new version b_{P1}. Thereafter, we create the order-destroyed and structure-destroyed versions of the book as defined in the previous section, and obtain new quantities $D^{b_{P1}}_{\text{order}}$ and $D^{b_{P1}}_{\text{structure}}$. We iterate this procedure and obtain, for a given book in a given translation, a sequence of pairs of quantities $(D^{b_{Pi}}_{\text{order}}, D^{b_{Pi}}_{\text{structure}})$, where i is the index of the iteration, i.e., how many times we have redefined the most common token pair as a new token and the P stands for *pasting*. By placing all these dots on a word order versus word structure plot, we can see how the two quantities vary as we redefine the word boundaries in this given language.

4.3 Word-splitting experiment

The previous section explained how we paste common word pairs together and redefine them as tokens. In our word-splitting experiment, the goal is to split words into commonly occurring sub-words. We design our word-splitting experiment in a reverse manner, by starting from characters, and then using Byte-Pair Encoding (BPE) (Gage, 1994) to iteratively paste commonly occurring pairs together.

Given a book of the bible in a given translation b, we define b_{S0} as the version of this book as provided in the Parallel Bible Corpus. We compute $D^{b_{S0}}_{\text{order}}$ and $D^{b_{S0}}_{\text{structure}}$ on b_{S0}. We then train a BPE tokenizer using the Huggingface `BpeTrainer`[6] with a `WhitespaceSplit` tokenizer, which matches the tokenization in the PBC. We give the trainer a maximum vocabulary size of 10 000 or 30 000 words, depending on the bible translation, to ensure that the training reaches completion, i.e., all words in the original text are regenerated from the component characters. We save the training history and then read it backwards, which allows us to create a history of the splitting of the most common word parts.

For each point in the reverse history, we can create the order-destroyed and structure-destroyed versions of the book as defined in Section 4.1, and obtain new quantities $D^{b_{Si}}_{\text{order}}$ and $D^{b_{Si}}_{\text{structure}}$, where i is the index of the iteration, i.e., how many times we have split a token into two component parts, and the S stands for *splitting*. By placing all these dots on a word order versus word structure plot, we can see how the two quantities vary as we redefine the word boundaries in this given language.

4.4 Implementation

For a given book in a given translation, called b, we compute the sequences $\{(D^{b_{Pi}}_{\text{order}}, D^{b_{Pi}}_{\text{structure}})\}$ at 10 points between 0 and 1 000 merges, and at 10 points between 0 and 10 000 merges. We also compute the sequences $\{(D^{b_{Si}}_{\text{order}}, D^{b_{Si}}_{\text{structure}})\}$ at 10 equidistant points between 0 and the maximum number of splits, and at 10 equidistant points between the last two of the aforementioned points.[7] The experiment was carried on in a parallel computing cluster, where each translation was run on a separate CPU. Thanks to the efficiency of the entropy calculator mentioned in Section 4, the entire experiment was run over a few days without requiring GPUs.

We then combine the information from the two experiments on the same plot. The two experiments join at $D^{b_{S0}}_{\text{order}} = D^{b_{P0}}_{\text{order}}$ and $D^{b_{S0}}_{\text{structure}} = D^{b_{P0}}_{\text{structure}}$. This is because both $S0$ and $P0$ are defined as the original books, without any merges or splits, respectively.

To understand our methodology in a different way, in a sense, BPE is doing our word-pasting experiment, but starting from characters.[8] The joining point is where BPE has created the original text, after which we continue the process by pasting words together.

We note that this methodology of splitting and pasting words can naturally generate certain known phenomena at the morphology-syntax interface. Two notable examples are:

[6] `https://huggingface.co/docs/tokenizers/api/trainers`

[7] To see why the further refinement in some of the areas of the parameter space was necessary, refer to Figure 1.

[8] A perhaps better alternative would be to start by converting all words to phonological forms using a text-to-phonetics converter, and then apply BPE and word-pasting on those phonological forms. Because we are comparing with previous work that operated at the character level, we opted to work at the character level.

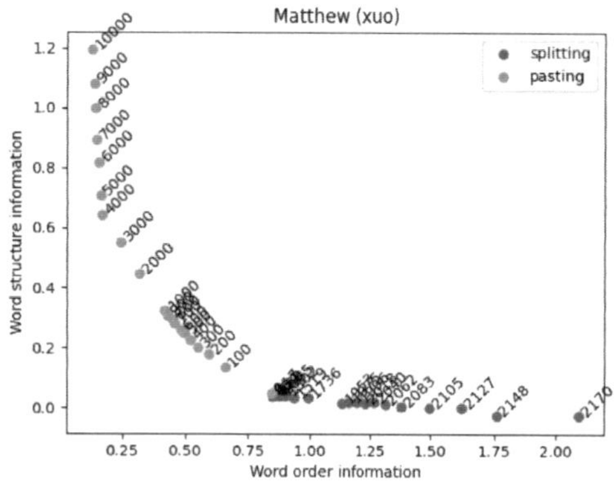

Figure 1: Word-order and word-structure information trade-off for the book of Matthew in the language xuo, in word-pasting and word-splitting experiment. The point labels indicate how many token pairs have been merged or split up to that point.

- compound nouns are separate words in English, but not in German or Dutch; word-splitting can turn German or Dutch compound nouns into pairs of words; word-pasting can turn English compounds into single words
- agglutinative affixes in Turkish are not considered words. Our splitting methodology can naturally turn long Turkish words into sub-parts.

5 Experimental Results

For every one of the six books considered (the four testaments, plus Acts and Revelation), and for every translation available in the Parallel Bible Corpus, we produce two a plot of $D^{b_i}_{\text{structure}}$ *vs* $D^{b_i}_{\text{order}}$. An example plot is shown on Figure 1, for a single translation-book pair. The results are qualitatively similar for all books considered, for all translations available, and can be found in our repository[9].

In all plots, the datapoint at the center, where the experiments join, corresponds to the original dataset, with no word-pairs pasted. As we paste increasingly more words, the datapoints move towards the top left. As we split increasingly more words, the datapoints move towards the bottom right. In other words, as we paste more common word-pairs, more information is encoded in the word structure, and less information is encoded in the word order; as we split words into more common sub-parts, more information is encoded in the word order, and less information is encoded in the word structure. This suggests that redefining the word boundaries is sufficient to reproduce the word-order vs word-structure trade-off observed previously in the literature.

To evaluate the significance of the correlations, we first join the results of the word-pasting and word-splitting experiments by assigning a negative value to the numbers of word-pairs merged in word-pasting experiments. In this way we can identify every datapoint with a single identifier which, if positive, represents a number of splits and, if negative, represents a number of merges.

Figure 2 is a histogram of the Spearman rank correlation coefficient between the number of splits and the word-order information, for all bible translations and books studied. Because the Spearman correlation coefficient is high and positive, we conclude there is a positive correlation between the number of splits and the amount of information carried by word order. Figure 3 is a histogram of the Spearman rank correlation coefficient between the number of splits and the word-structure information, for all bible translations and books studied. Because the Spearman correlation coefficient is close to -1, we conclude there is a negative correlation between the number of splits and the amount of information carried by word structure. Figure 4 is the histogram of Spearman correlation coefficients between the word-order and word-structure information, for all bible translations and books. Because the Spearman correlation coefficient is close to -1, we conclude there is a negative correlation between the amount of information carried by word structure and the amount of information carried by word order. This is the same observation as was made for a specific bible translation and book by looking at Figure 1.

6 Discussion and Future Work

Our study reveals that the trade-off between morphology and syntax in language observed by Koplenig et al. (2017) can be generated by manipulation of word structure, specifically by joining and splitting words. This finding challenges the notion that the use of morphology or syntax in language necessarily reflects distinct mechanisms for conveying information. Rather, the position of a language on the morphology-syntax trade-off appears to be

[9] `https://anonymous.4open.science/r/WordOrderBibles-0F4F`

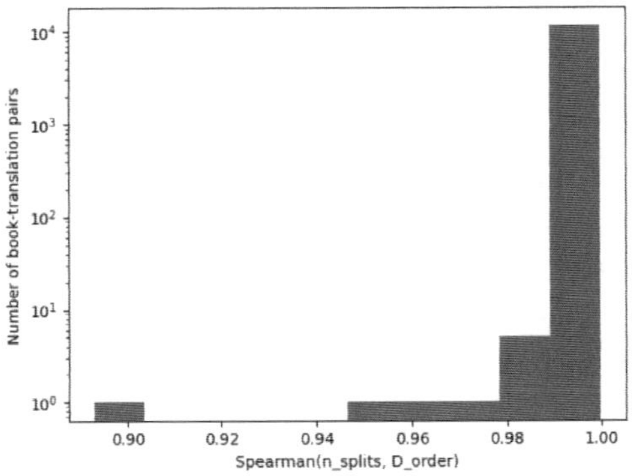

Figure 2: Histogram of the Spearman rank correlation coefficient between word-order information and the number of word-pairs split, for all bible translations and books studied. Word-pasting and word-splitting experiments are joined together by assigning a negative number to the number of word-pairs merged in the word-pasting experiments.

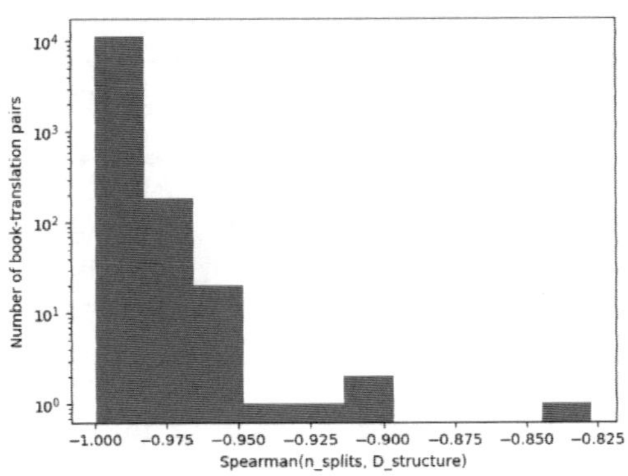

Figure 3: Histogram of the Spearman rank correlation coefficient between word-structure information and the number of word-pairs split, for all bible translations and books studied. Word-pasting and word-splitting experiments are joined together by assigning a negative number to the number of word-pairs merged in the word-pasting experiments.

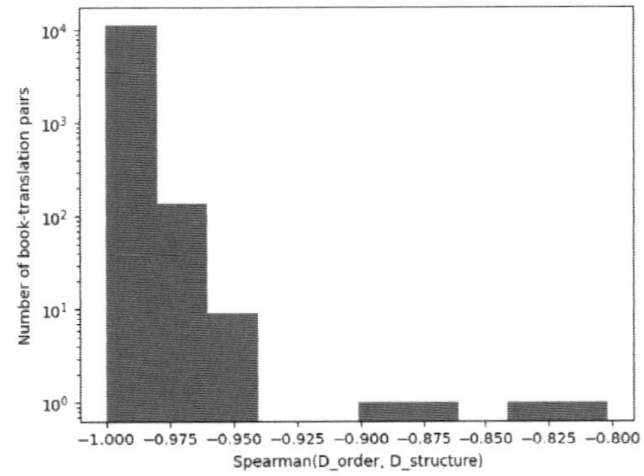

Figure 4: Histogram of the Spearman rank correlation coefficient between word-structure information and word-order information, for all bible translations and books studied. Word-pasting and word-splitting experiments are joined together by assigning a negative number to the number of word-pairs merged in the word-pasting experiments.

determined by how words are constructed. Nevertheless, our results suggest that languages have optimized this trade-off, indicating that a balance between these two mechanisms is preferred. While it may be possible to convey information through either morphology or syntax, the prevalence of the morphology-syntax trade-off across languages suggests that this balance is indeed optimal.

Based on the implications of our findings, there are several avenues for future research that could build upon our work. For example, one possible direction is to investigate whether the balance between morphology and syntax may be subject to change over time. Previous work (Koplenig et al., 2017) has found that the word-order and word-structure information can *evolve* with time; with our methodology, we could verify if this evolution could simply be ascribed to changes in the definition of word boundary. Another potential avenue is to explore the theoretical implications of our findings for our understanding of the relationship between language structure, language use, and cognitive processing (Tallman and Auderset, 2023). Finally, it would be worthwhile to verify the robustness of our methodology by investigating more novel approaches to entropy estimation, such as fine-tuning a pre-trained multi-lingual language model on the Parallel Bible Corpus, and then computing sequence probabilities using this language model.

7 Conclusion

In this paper, we have investigated two research questions concerning the morphology-syntax trade-off. Firstly, we examined whether orthographic conventions, rather than cognitive processes, can account for the trade-off observed by Koplenig et al. (2017). Secondly, we explored whether languages optimise the amount of information conveyed by the sum of morphology and syntax. Our word-pasting and word-splitting experiments showed that a morphology-syntax trade-off can be explained by purely conventional definitions, such as the definition of a word. This would mean that the statistical morphology-syntax trade-off is not necessarily due to a fundamental difference between the cognitive processes responsible for morphology and syntax (Levshina and Moran, 2021). Furthermore, the similarity between the trade-off patterns observed in previous studies and in our experiment suggests that languages do indeed optimise the trade-off between morphology and syntax.

8 Limitations

Like Koplenig et al. (2017), we used six specific books of the bible for which a large number of translations were available, and which were reasonably long for the methodology to work. A natural extension to our work would be to apply the same methodology to all the books of the bible, not just the six books considered here.

Because we restricted our dataset to translations that contain at least one verse of at least one of the aforementioned books, there are some book-translation pairs for which only a single verse or a few verses are available. This is presumably not enough for the entropy estimator we used to approximate the entropy. In future iterations, we shall restrict our analysis only to book-translation pairs for which a sufficient number of verses is available.

Furthermore, we applied the analysis independently to each book because by doing so we ensure that all texts within a given analysis have the same content, avoiding the problem whereby a bible translation does not contain all six books. It would be appropriate to combine at least several of the books together and repeat the analysis.

Finally, the PBC is an evolving project, and there are currently more bible translations available than there were at the time of beginning this study. It would be interesting to look at those new bible translations and seeing if the results hold.

On a more fundamental level, the Parallel Bible Corpus consists mostly of translations, not original texts. This means that the individual bibles used might not reflect natural language in those languages (Baets et al., 2020). We believe this is a minor limitation, since we are only exploring the effect of redefining word boundaries on the morphology-syntax trade-off. Furthermore, Kann (2024) has observed that the PBC displays similar word-order statistics to original texts. Still, it would be interesting to re-do our calculations in non-translated corpora. One possible corpus is TeDDi (Moran et al., 2022).

We focused only on demonstrating that there is a correlation between the word-order and word-structure information when performing manipulations on word boundaries in a single translation-book. In a further study, we will analyze whether the functional forms of the word-order vs word-structure distributions match those found by Koplenig et al. (2017) across bible translations.

Acknowledgements

The authors thank Alexander Koplenig and Marcelo Montemurro for providing details regarding previous studies, and Michael Cysouw for providing access to the Parallel Bible Corpus.

Ethical Considerations

In the context of this study, we did not identify any specific ethical considerations that warrant discussion. The research does not involve human subjects, sensitive data, or potentially contentious issues that could raise ethical concerns. We do not find any potential risks associated with this study. We have filled out the Responsible NLP research checklist.

References

Mostafa Abdou, Vinit Ravishankar, Artur Kulmizev, and Anders Søgaard. 2022. Word Order Does Matter and Shuffled Language Models Know It. In *Proceedings of the 60th Annual Meeting of the Association for Computational Linguistics (Volume 1: Long Papers)*, pages 6907–6919.

Aryaman Arora, Clara Meister, and Ryan Cotterell. 2022. Estimating the Entropy of Linguistic Distributions. In *Proceedings of the 60th Annual Meeting of the Association for Computational Linguistics (Volume 2: Short Papers)*, pages 175–195, Dublin, Ireland. Association for Computational Linguistics.

Pauline De Baets, Lore Vandevoorde, and Gert De Sutter. 2020. On the usefulness of comparable and parallel corpora for contrastive linguistics. Testing the semantic stability hypothesis. In Renata Enghels, Bart Defrancq, and Marlies Jansegers, editors, *Empirical and Methodological Challenges*, pages 85–126. De Gruyter Mouton, Berlin, Boston.

Christian Bentz, Dimitrios Alikaniotis, Michael Cysouw, and Ramon Ferrer-i Cancho. 2017. The Entropy of Words—Learnability and Expressivity across More than 1000 Languages. *Entropy*, 19(6).

Christian Bentz, Ximena Gutierrez-Vasques, Olga Sozinova, and Tanja Samardžić. 2022. Complexity tradeoffs and equi-complexity in natural languages: a meta-analysis. *Linguistics Vanguard*.

David Crystal. 2010. *The Cambridge encyclopedia of language*. Cambridge University Press Cambridge.

Ramon Ferrer-i Cancho and Fermín Moscoso del Prado Martín. 2011. Information content versus word length in random typing. *Journal of Statistical Mechanics: Theory and Experiment*, 2011(12):L12002.

Philip Gage. 1994. A new algorithm for data compression. *The C Users Journal*, 12(2):23–38.

Edward Gibson, Richard Futrell, Steven P. Piantadosi, Isabelle Dautriche, Kyle Mahowald, Leon Bergen, and Roger Levy. 2019. How efficiency shapes human language. *Trends in Cognitive Sciences*, 23(5):389–407.

Ximena Gutierrez-Vasques, Christian Bentz, Olga Sozinova, and Tanja Samardzic. 2021. From characters to words: the turning point of BPE merges. In *Proceedings of the 16th Conference of the European Chapter of the Association for Computational Linguistics: Main Volume*, pages 3454–3468, Online. Association for Computational Linguistics.

Martin Haspelmath. 2023. Defining the word. *Word*, 69(3):283–297.

T. Florian Jaeger. 2010. Redundancy and reduction: speakers manage syntactic information density. *Cognitive psychology*, 61(1):23–62. Place: Netherlands.

Amanda Kann. 2024. Massively multilingual token-based typology using the parallel Bible corpus. In *Proceedings of the 2024 Joint International Conference on Computational Linguistics, Language Resources and Evaluation (LREC-COLING 2024)*, pages 11070–11079, Torino, Italia. ELRA and ICCL.

Ioannis Kontoyiannis, Paul Algoet, Yuri Suhov, and Abraham Wyner. 1998. Nonparametric Entropy Estimation for Stationary Processesand Random Fields, with Applications to English Text. *Information Theory, IEEE Transactions on*, 44:1319 – 1327.

Alexander Koplenig, Peter Meyer, Sascha Wolfer, and Carolin Müller-Spitzer. 2017. The statistical tradeoff between word order and word structure – Large-scale evidence for the principle of least effort. *PLOS ONE*, 12(3):1–25. Publisher: Public Library of Science.

Natalia Levshina and Steven Moran. 2021. Efficiency in human languages: Corpus evidence for universal principles. *Linguistics Vanguard*, 7(s3):20200081.

Thomas Mayer and Michael Cysouw. 2014. Creating a massively parallel bible corpus. In *Proceedings of the Ninth International Conference on Language Resources and Evaluation (LREC'14)*, Reykjavik, Iceland. European Language Resources Association (ELRA).

George Miller. 1955. Note on the bias of information estimates. *Information theory in psychology: Problems and methods*.

Marcelo A. Montemurro and Damián H. Zanette. 2011. Universal Entropy of Word Ordering Across Linguistic Families. *PLOS ONE*, 6(5):1–9. Publisher: Public Library of Science.

Steven Moran, Christian Bentz, Ximena Gutierrez-Vasques, Olga Pelloni, and Tanja Samardzic. 2022. TeDDi sample: Text data diversity sample for language comparison and multilingual NLP. In *Proceedings of the Thirteenth Language Resources and Evaluation Conference*, pages 1150–1158, Marseille, France. European Language Resources Association.

Thomas Schürmann and Peter Grassberger. 1996. Entropy estimation of symbol sequences. *Chaos: An Interdisciplinary Journal of Nonlinear Science*, 6(3):414–427.

C. E. Shannon. 1948. A mathematical theory of communication. *Bell System Technical Journal*, 27(3):379–423.

Koustuv Sinha, Robin Jia, Dieuwke Hupkes, Joelle Pineau, Adina Williams, and Douwe Kiela. 2021. Masked Language Modeling and the Distributional Hypothesis: Order Word Matters Pre-training for Little. In *Proceedings of the 2021 Conference on Empirical Methods in Natural Language Processing*, pages 2888–2913, Online and Punta Cana, Dominican Republic. Association for Computational Linguistics.

Adam JR Tallman and Sandra Auderset. 2023. Measuring and assessing indeterminacy and variation in the morphology-syntax distinction. *Linguistic Typology*, 27(1):113–156.

The Unicode Consortium. 2022. The Unicode Standard. Technical report, Unicode, Inc. Chapter 3: Conformance.

Aaron D Wyner and Jacob Ziv. 1989. Some asymptotic properties of the entropy of a stationary ergodic data source with applications to data compression. *IEEE Transactions on Information Theory*, 35(6):1250–1258. Publisher: IEEE.

Author Index

Association for Computational Linguistics
209 N. Eighth Street
Stroudsburg, Pennsylvania 18360

ISBN 979-8-3313-1363-0

CURRAN ASSOCIATES INC.
proceedings.com